GRAPHIS POSTER 96

GRAPHIS POSTER 96

· ·

(OPPOSITE) PHOTOGRAPHER: YASUYUKI AMAZUTSUMI

THE INTERNATIONAL ANNUAL OF POSTER ART

DAS INTERNATIONALE JAHRBUCH DER PLAKATKUNST

LE RÉPERTOIRE INTERNATIONAL DE L'ART DE L'AFFICHE

EDITED BY · HERAUSGEGEBEN VON · EDITÉ PAR:

B. MARTIN PEDERSEN

PUBLISHER AND CREATIVE DIRECTOR: B. MARTIN PEDERSEN

EDITORS: HEINKE JENSSEN, ANNETTE CRANDALL

ASSISTANT EDITOR: JÖRG REIMANN

ART DIRECTORS: B. MARTIN PEDERSEN, RANDELL PEARSON

GRAPHIS U.S., INC. NEW YORK, GRAPHIS PRESS CORP. ZÜRICH (SWITZERLAND)

CONTENTS · INHALT · SOMMAIRE

REMARKS

WE EXTEND OUR HEARTFELT THANKS TO CONTRIBUTORS THROUGHOUT THE WORLD WHO HAVE MADE IT POSSIBLE TO PUBLISH A WIDE AND INTERNATIONAL SPECTRUM OF THE BEST WORK IN THIS FIELD.

ENTRY INSTRUCTIONS FOR NEXT YEAR'S ANNUAL MAY BE REQUESTED AT:
GRAPHIS PRESS
141 LEXINGTON AVENUE·
NEW YORK, NY 10016-8193

ANMERKUNGEN

UNSER DANK GILT DEN EINSENDERN AUS ALLER WELT, DIE ES UNS DURCH IHRE BEI-TRÄGE ERMÖGLICHT HABEN, EIN BREITES, INTERNATIONALES SPEKTRUM DER BESTEN ARBEITEN ZU VERÖFFENTLICHEN.

TEILNAHMEBEDINGUNGEN FÜR DAS NÄCHSTE JAHRBUCH SIND ERHÄLTLICH BEIM:
GRAPHIS VERLAG AG
DUFOURSTRASSE 107
8008 ZÜRICH, SCHWEIZ

REMERCIEMENTS

NOUS REMERCIONS LES PARTICIPANTS DU MONDE ENTIER QUI ONT RENDU POSSIBLE LA PUBLICATION DE CET OUVRAGE OFFRANT UN PANORAMA COMPLET DES MEILLEURS TRA-VAUX RÉALISÉS DANS CE DOMAINE.

LES MODALITÉS D'INSCRIPTION PEUVENT ÊTRE OBTENUES AUPRÈS DE:
EDITIONS GRAPHIS
DUFOURSTRASSE 107
8008 ZÜRICH, SUISSE

(OPPOSITE) ART DIRECTOR/DESIGNER/CLIENT: SHIN MATSUNAGA DESIGN FIRM: SHIN MATSUNAGA DESIGN INC. COUNTRY: JAPAN

GRAPHIS PUBLICATIONS

GRAPHIS, THE INTERNATIONAL BI-MONTHLY JOURNAL OF VISUAL COMMUNICATION
GRAPHIS SHOPPING BAG, AN INTERNATIONAL COLLECTION OF SHOPPING BAG DESIGN
GRAPHIS MUSIC CD, AN INTERNATIONAL COLLECTION OF CD DESIGN
GRAPHIS BOOK DESIGN, AN INTERNATIONAL COLLECTION OF BOOK DESIGN
GRAPHIS DESIGN, THE INTERNATIONAL ANNUAL OF DESIGN AND ILLUSTRATION
GRAPHIS STUDENT DESIGN, THE INTERNATIONAL ANNUAL OF DESIGN AND COMMUNICATION DESIGN BY STUDENTS
GRAPHIS ADVERTISING, THE INTERNATIONAL ANNUAL OF ADVERTISING
GRAPHIS BROCHURES, A COMPILATION OF BROCHURE DESIGN
GRAPHIS PHOTO, THE INTERNATIONAL ANNUAL OF PHOTOGRAPHY
GRAPHIS ALTERNATIVE PHOTOGRAPHY, THE INTERNATIONAL ANNUAL OF ALTERNATIVE PHOTOGRAPHY
GRAPHIS NUDES, A COLLECTION OF CAREFULLY SELECTED SOPHISTICATED IMAGES
GRAPHIS POSTER, THE INTERNATIONAL ANNUAL OF POSTER ART
GRAPHIS PACKAGING, AN INTERNATIONAL COMPILATION OF PACKAGING DESIGN
GRAPHIS LETTERHEAD, AN INTERNATIONAL COMPILATION OF LETTERHEAD DESIGN
GRAPHIS DIAGRAM, THE GRAPHIC VISUALIZATION OF ABSTRACT, TECHNICAL AND STATISTICAL FACTS AND FUNCTIONS
GRAPHIS LOGO, AN INTERNATIONAL COMPILATION OF LOGOS
GRAPHIS EPHEMERA, AN INTERNATIONAL COLLECTION OF PROMOTIONAL ART
GRAPHIS PUBLICATION, AN INTERNATIONAL SURVEY OF THE BEST IN MAGAZINE DESIGN
GRAPHIS ANNUAL REPORTS, AN INTERNATIONAL COMPILATION OF THE BEST DESIGNED ANNUAL REPORTS
GRAPHIS CORPORATE IDENTITY, AN INTERNATIONAL COMPILATION OF THE BEST IN CORPORATE IDENTITY DESIGN
GRAPHIS TYPOGRAPHY, AN INTERNATIONAL COMPILATION OF THE BEST IN TYPOGRAPHIC DESIGN

GRAPHIS PUBLIKATIONEN

GRAPHIS, DIE INTERNATIONALE ZWEIMONATSZEITSCHRIFT DER VISUELLEN KOMMUNIKATION
GRAPHIS SHOPPING BAG, TRAGTASCHEN-DESIGN IM INTERNATIONALEN ÜBERBLICK
GRAPHIS MUSIC CD, CD-DESIGN IM INTERNATIONALEN ÜBERBLICK
GRAPHIS BOOKS, BUCHGESTALTUNG IM INTERNATIONALEN ÜBERBLICK
GRAPHIS DESIGN, DAS INTERNATIONALE JAHRBUCH ÜBER DESIGN UND ILLUSTRATION
GRAPHIS STUDENT DESIGN, DAS INTERNATIONALE JAHRBUCH ÜBER KOMMUNIKATIONSDESIGN VON STUDENTEN
GRAPHIS ADVERTISING, DAS INTERNATIONALE JAHRBUCH DER WERBUNG
GRAPHIS BROCHURES, BROSCHÜRENDESIGN IM INTERNATIONAL ÜBERBLICK
GRAPHIS PHOTO, DAS INTERNATIONALE JAHRBUCH DER PHOTOGRAPHIE
GRAPHIS ALTERNATIVE PHOTOGRAPHY, DAS INTERNATIONALE JAHRBUCH ÜBER ALTERNATIVE PHOTOGRAPHIE
GRAPHIS NUDES, EINE SAMMLUNG SORGFÄLTIG AUSGEWÄHLTER AKTPHOTOGRAPHIE
GRAPHIS POSTER, DAS INTERNATIONALE JAHRBUCH DER PLAKATKUNST
GRAPHIS PACKAGING, EIN INTERNATIONALER ÜBERBLICK ÜBER DIE PACKUNGSGESTALTUNG
GRAPHIS LETTERHEAD, EIN INTERNATIONALER ÜBERBLICK ÜBER BRIEFPAPIERGESTALTUNG
GRAPHIS DIAGRAM, DIE GRAPHISCHE DARSTELLUNG ABSTRAKTER TECHNISCHER UND STATISTISCHER DATEN UND FAKTEN
GRAPHIS LOGO, EINE INTERNATIONALE AUSWAHL VON FIRMEN-LOGOS
GRAPHIS EPHEMERA, EINE INTERNATIONALE SAMMLUNG GRAPHISCHER DOKUMENTE DES TÄGLICHEN LEBENS
GRAPHIS MAGAZINDESIGN, EINE INTERNATIONALE ZUSAMMENSTELLUNG DES BESTEN ZEITSCHRIFTEN-DESIGNS
GRAPHIS ANNUAL REPORTS, EIN INTERNATIONALER ÜBERBLICK ÜBER DIE GESTALTUNG VON JAHRESBERICHTEN
GRAPHIS CORPORATE IDENTITY, EINE INTERNATIONALE AUSWAHL DES BESTEN CORPORATE IDENTITY DESIGNS
GRAPHIS TYPOGRAPHY, EINE INTERNATIONALE ZUSAMMENSTELLUNG DES BESTEN TYPOGRAPHIE DESIGN

PUBLICATIONS GRAPHIS

GRAPHIS, LA REVUE BIMESTRIELLE INTERNATIONALE DE LA COMMUNICATION VISUELLE
GRAPHIS SHOPPING BAG, UNE COMPILATION INTERNATIONALE SUR LE DESIGN DES SACS À COMMISSIONS
GRAPHIS MUSIC CD, UNE COMPILATION INTERNATIONALE SUR LE DESIGN DES CD
GRAPHIS BOOKS, UNE COMPILATION INTERNATIONALE SUR LE DESIGN DES LIVRES
GRAPHIS DESIGN, LE RÉPERTOIRE INTERNATIONAL DE LA COMMUNICATION VISUELLE
GRAPHIS STUDENT DESIGN, UN RÉPERTOIRE INTERNATIONAL DE PROJTS D'EXPRESSION VISUELLE D'ÉDUTIANTS
GRAPHIS ADVERTISING, LE RÉPERTOIRE INTERNATIONAL DE LA PUBLICITÉ
GRAPHIS BROCHURES, UNE COMPILATION INTERNATIONALE SUR LE DESIGN DES BROCHURES
GRAPHIS PHOTO, LE RÉPERTOIRE INTERNATIONAL DE LA PHOTOGRAPHIE
GRAPHIS ALTERNATIVE PHOTOGRAPHY, LE RÉPERTOIRE INTERNATIONAL DE LA PHOTOGRAPHIE ALTERNATIVE
GRAPHIS NUDES, UN FLORILÈGE DE LA PHOTOGRAPHIE DE NUS
GRAPHIS POSTER, LE RÉPERTOIRE INTERNATIONAL DE L'AFFICHE
GRAPHIS PACKAGING, LE RÉPERTOIRE INTERNATIONAL DE LA CRÉATION D'EMBALLAGES
GRAPHIS LETTERHEAD, LE RÉPERTOIRE INTERNATIONAL DU DESIGN DE PAPIER À LETTRES
GRAPHIS DIAGRAM; LE RÉPERTOIRE GRAPHIQUE DE FAITS ET DONNÉES ABSTRAITS, TECHNIQUES ET STATISTIQUES
GRAPHIS LOGO, LE RÉPERTOIRE INTERNATIONAL DU LOGO
GRAPHIS EPHEMERA, LE GRAPHISME – UN ÉTAT D'ESPRIT AU QUOTIDIEN
GRAPHIS PUBLICATION, LE RÉPERTOIRE INTERNATIONAL DU DESIGN DE PÉRIODIQUES
GRAPHIS ANNUAL REPORTS, PANORAMA INTERNATIONAL DU MEILLEUR DESIGN DE RAPPORTS ANNUELS D'ENTREPRISES
GRAPHIS CORPORATE IDENTITY, PANORAMA INTERNATIONAL DU MEILLEUR DESIGN D'IDENTITÉ CORPORATE
GRAPHIS TYPOGRAPHY, LE RÉPERTOIRE INTERNATIONAL DU MEILLEUR DESIGN DE TYPOGRAPHIE

PUBLICATION NO. 263 (ISBN 1-888001-00-3)
© COPYRIGHT UNDER UNIVERSAL COPYRIGHT CONVENTION
COPYRIGHT © 1996 BY GRAPHIS U.S., NEW YORK, GRAPHIS PRESS CORP., ZURICH, SWITZERLAND
JACKET AND BOOK DESIGN COPYRIGHT © 1996 BY PEDERSEN DESIGN
141 LEXINGTON AVENUE, NEW YORK, N.Y. 10016 USA

PRINTED IN HONG KONG BY PARAMOUNT PRINTING COMPANY LIMITED

COMMENTARIES

KOMMENTARE

COMMENTAIRES

Warszawa
1975

Teatr
Narodów

ENTRÉE

→

Henryk Tomaszewski

In 1983, Poland was under martial law. The Communists, fearing an uprising led by Lech Walesa and his Solidarity movement, outlawed the victory sign—the "V" hand symbol for the revolution. During the night, a theater poster appeared on the streets of Warsaw. The central image was the victory sign made by two toes. The designer was not a young rebel, nor a would-be politician. He was 69-year-old Henryk Tomaszewski, largely considered the father of the Polish poster school. □ To talk of modern poster design without paying homage to Henryk Tomaszewski is unthinkable. Not only has he survived the atrocities of Hitler, Nazi occupation, and Stalinism, but as a designer, he has thrived. "Politics," he says, "is like the weather. You have to live with it." Recent retrospectives in Amersterdam, Berlin, and Tokyo attest to his continued popularity; at the prestigious Warsaw Poster Biennale he is the only designer to have ever won two gold medals (1970 and 1988) as well as both a gold and silver medal simultaneously (1988). His studio was the training ground for generations of students, including an impressive roster of those who have gone on to achieve international distinction. In the U.S., however, his work is largely unknown or has been ignored completely (witness his omission from the Museum of Modern Art's 1988 exhibit, "The Modern Poster"). □ Tomaszewski (tom-a-SHEV-ski) was born in 1914. Against his parents' wishes he enrolled in the Warsaw Academy of Art to study painting and drawing. Inspired by German caricature from *Simplicissimus* magazine and by the work of George Grosz and John Heartfield, Tomaszewski created a name for himself as a satirical artist. After graduating in 1939, he won first prize in the interior design competition at the New York World's Fair. □ Yet in September of that year, German troops invaded Poland. During the occupation, Tomaszewski stayed in Warsaw eking out a living, and continuing to draw and paint. With liberation in 1944 came Josef Stalin and communism. □ Communist authorities needed an outlet for their political credo and believed artists could be used to that end. Posters would no longer promote capitalist consumer goods, but rather sell the spirit of communism. With a poor radio network and TV unheard of, the street poster was an inexpensive and effective tool for propaganda. □ In 1947 Tomaszewski and a small band of young artists were invited to design film posters for the state-run film distribution agency Centrala Wynajmu Filmow or CWF. Pre-war film posters resembled today's banal portraits of matinee idols. The artists accepted the commission with the stipulation that their designs be printed as drawn. Uncensored. □ The situation was stifling. Supplies were scarce. Limitations, however, stimulated invention: Tomaszewski's 1947 posters—particularly his designs for "Odd Man Out" and "Black Narcissus" —stunned the public. Using bold colors and shapes, he integrated letterforms closely into the design, and more importantly, rather than illustrating actual scenes, he suggested the film's mood by applying cinematic techniques, such as montage and dramatic camera-angle perspectives. □ Thus a new type of poster was born -- one in which the designer's own personal interpretation of the film was as important as the director's. This uncompromising artistic control characterizes the Polish poster school, which thrived from 1952 to 1964. By 1949, Tomaszewski had won no less than five medals at the Vienna National Film Poster Exhibition, which strengthened the designer's position at home. Within a few years, Polish posters were known throughout Europe. □ During the 1950s, Tomaszewski began using a painterly style in combination with simple, collaged elements. Then, for a 1959 exhibit of Henry Moore's sculptures, Tomaszewski created a sculpture garden from the letters of the sculpture's name. This design proved a turning point for Tomaszewski's work. Though the painter/cartoonist was still present, the overall feel of the work was spare. □ Tomaszewski's graphic simplification reached a peak with a poster for Shakespeare's Richard II in 1964. In this design the form is simplified to a purple square surrounded by a sea of white, strengthened by a black border. At first it seems mere minimalism, but the image is actually a strong, if abstract depiction of the plays' content—banishment and "the purple testament of bleeding war." Color as expression, not decoration. □ In 1952 a poster department was created at the Warsaw Academy of Art, headed by Tomaszewski. His teaching wasn't based on graphic design formulae; he taught philosophy, often through abstraction. For example, assignments often involved a visual interpretation of aphorisms such as "Always the other," "Life is but a span," "Interpret," or "Yesterday/Today/Tomorrow." He pressed students to invent new images, encouraging them to surprise their viewers (and themselves) in the process. □ When the Warsaw Academy began admitting foreign students in the late 1960s, students flocked from all over Europe to study with Tomaszewski. Among them: Pierre Bernard and Gerard Paris-Clavel, Michel Quarez, Alain LeQuernec, and Thierry Sarfis. Other prominent former students include Karel Misek from Czechoslovakia and Radovan Jenko from Slovenia. □ Now, semi-retired, Tomaszewski lives on the outskirts of Warsawi. At eighty years old, he radiates strength. Seymour Chwast recalls, "He's a big kid. Play is what it's all about for him." Tomaszewski is still playing, still designing. Ivan Chermayeff says: "He is the only artist besides Picasso to retain his childlike sense of creativity throughout his career." His designs are shaped by an analysis of content: "First I think about the question, then the proper answer, then the best form." Though he may spend hours juggling shapes and type, his designs — tiny gems of personal observation, often with stunning, unexpected meaning — seem to have been created in a moment. ■

JAMES VICTORE IS PRINCIPAL OF VICTORE DESIGN WORKS, NEW YORK. HE WON THE GRAND PRIX AT THE 1994 INTERNATIONAL BIENNALE OF GRAPHIC DESIGN BRNO, THE CZECH REPUBLIC, FOR POSTER DESIGN.

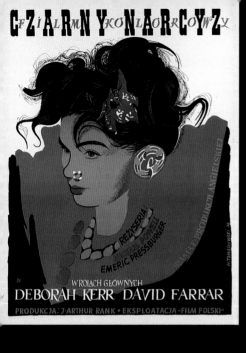

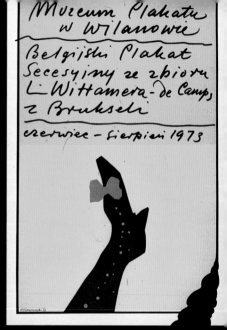

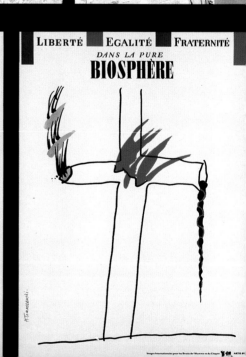

Im Jahre 1983 herrschte in Polen Kriegsrecht. Die Kommunisten, die einen von Lech Walesa und seiner Solidarnosc-Bewegung angeführten Aufstand befürchteten, verboten das Victory-Zeichen, das mit den Fingern geformte V als Symbol der Revolution. Über Nacht tauchte in den grauen Strassen Warschaus ein Theaterplakat auf. Sein Hauptmotiv war ein von zwei Zehen geformtes V. Der Autor dieses Plakates war weder ein junger Rebell noch ein politisch ambitionierter Mann. Es war der 69jährige Henryk Tomaszewski, der allgemein als Vater der polnischen Plakatschule gilt. □ Es ist undenkbar, über moderne Plakatgestaltung zu sprechen, ohne Henryk Tomaszewski zu erwähnen. Er hat die Greueltaten Hitlers, die Nazibesetzung und den Stalinismus überlebt und war dabei als Designer erfolgreich. «Politik ist wie das Wetter», sagt er. «Man muss damit leben.» Die Retrospektiven, die kürzlich in Amsterdam, Berlin und Tokio stattfanden, waren ein riesiger Publikumserfolg. Er hat als einziger Gestalter überhaupt bei der Plakat-Biennale von Warschau zwei Goldmedaillen gewonnen hat (1970 und 1988) bzw. im gleichen Jahr (1988) eine Gold- und eine Silbermedaille. Sein Atelier war Lehrstube für Generationen von Studenten, von denen eine ganze Reihe später selbst international berühmt wurden. In den USA jedoch ist Tomaszewski weitgehend unbekannt. (Er fehlte z.B. bei der Ausstellung «The Modern Poster» im Museum of Modern Art, New York, 1988.) □ Tomaszewski wurde 1914 geboren. Gegen den Wunsch seiner Eltern schrieb er sich an der Warschauer Kunstakademie ein, um Malerei und Zeichnen zu studieren. Inspiriert von den deutschen Karikaturisten im Simplicissimus und der Arbeit von George Grosz und John Heartfield, machte sich Tomaszewski selbst einen Namen als satirischer Künstler. Nach Abschluss der Ausbildung 1939 erhielt er den ersten Preis des Wettbewerbs für Innenarchitektur an der Weltausstellung in New York. □ Am 1. September jenes Jahres jedoch überfielen die deutschen Truppen Polen, und in den folgenden Monaten wurden Millionen von Polen umgebracht; Städte wurden zerstört, und die Wirtschaft und damit auch die Verlage und Graphik-Design kamen zum Erliegen. Tomaszewski blieb während der Besatzungszeit in Warschau und schlug sich irgendwie durch, wobei er weiterhin malte und zeichnete. Mit der Befreiung Polens 1944 kamen Josef Stalin und der Kommunismus. □ Die Kommunisten brauchten ein akzeptables Image für ihr politisches Credo und sie glaubten, die Künstler dafür benutzen zu können. Plakate sollten nicht länger für die Konsumgüter des Kapitalismus werben, sondern für den Geist des Kommunismus. Mit einem schlechten Radionetzwerk und noch ohne Fernsehen war das Strassenplakat ein preiswertes und wirkungsvolles Medium für ihre Propaganda. □ 1947 wurden Tomaszewski und eine kleine Gruppe junger Künstler einladen, Filmplakate für die staatliche Filmverleihgesellschaft Centrala Wynajmu Filmow (CWF) zu entwerfen. Die Filmplakate aus der Zeit vor dem Krieg waren banale Porträts der Filmstars. Die Künstler akzeptieren unter der Bedingung, dass ihre Entwürfe unverändert gedruckt werden würden – unzensiert. □ Die

Bedingungen waren schwierig. Das Material war knapp. Die beschränkten Mittel förderten aber den Erfindungsgeist. Tomaszewskis Filmplakate von 1947 – besonders die für «Odd Man Out» und «Black Narcissus» verblüfften das Publikum. Er benutzte kräftige Farben und Formen und integrierte die Buchstabenformen in das Bild. Noch wichtiger war aber, dass er nicht Szenen illustrierte, sondern mit Hilfe von Montagen und dramatischen Blickpunkten, also den Mitteln des Films, die Stimmung des Films einfing. □ So wurde ein neuer Plakattyp geboren, basierend auf den persönlichen Interpretationen der Filme durch den Plakatkünstler, wobei ihre Vision genau so wichtig war wie die des Regisseurs. Diese kompromisslose Haltung ist typisch für die polnische Plakatschule, die ihren Höhepunkt zwischen 1952 und 1964 erlebte. Im Jahre 1949 hatte Tomaszewski, der damals gerade 35 Jahre alt war, nicht weniger als 5 Medaillen der nationalen Filmplakatausstellung in Wien erhalten. Innerhalb weniger Jahre erwarben sich die polnischen Plakate in ganz Europa einen Ruf. □ In den 50er Jahren verband Tomaszewski seinen malerischen Stil mit einfachen Collage-Elementen. Für die Ausstellung von Henry Moores Skulpturen im Jahre 1959 schuf Tomaszewski einen Skulptur-Garten aus den Buchstaben des Namens des Bildhauers. Diese Arbeit bedeutet für Tomaszewski einen Wendepunkt. Obgleich der Maler/Karikaturist immer noch präsent war, wirkten seine Arbeiten knapp. □ Tomaszewskis graphische Vereinfachung erreichte mit dem Plakat für Krol Ryszard Drugi (Richard II von Shakespeare) 1964 den Höhepunkt. In diesem Plakat ist die Form auf ein einfaches purpurnes Quadrat reduziert, umgeben von einer weissen Fläche, das Ganze wirkungsvoll unterstützt von einer schwarzen Umrandung. Zuerst erscheint dies als Minimalismus, aber das Bild ist tatsächlich eine starke, wenn auch abstrakte Darstellung des Inhalts – Verbannung und das «purpurne Zeugnis eines blutigen Krieges». Hier wird Farbe als Ausdrucksmittel, nicht als Dekoration benutzt. □ 1952 wurde an der Warschauer Kunstakademie ein Studiengang für Plakatgestaltung eingeführt, unter der Leitung von Tomaszewski. Er lehrte seine Studenten nicht das graphische Handwerk, er lehrte Philosophie, oft auf der Basis von Abstraktion. Zum Beispiel bekamen die Studenten die Aufgabe, Aphorismen oder Poesie visuell zu interpretieren: «Immer die anderen», «Das Leben ist nichts als ein kurzer Zeitabschnitt», «Interpretieren» oder «Gestern, heute/morgen». Er ermutigte seine Studenten, neue Bilder zu erfinden, den Betrachter (wie sich selbst) zu überraschen. □ Als die Warschauer Akademie in den späten sechziger Jahren auch ausländische Studenten zuliess, strömten sie aus ganz Europa herbei, um bei Tomaszewski zu studieren. Aus Frankreich kamen u.a. Pierre Bernard und Gérard Paris-Clavel (beide Mitglieder der ehemaligen Grapus-Gruppe) sowie Michel Quarez, Alain LeQuernec und Thierry Sarfis. Zu den prominenten Designern aus anderen Regionen gehören Karel Misek aus der tschechischen Republik und Radovan Jenko aus Slowenien. □ Heute lebt Tomaszewski – halb im Ruhestand – am Rande Warschaus. ■

J A M E S   V I C T O R E   IST LEITER VON VICTORE DESIGN WORKS IN NEW YORK. ER WURDE BEI DER INTERNATIONALEN GRAPHIK-BIENNALE 1994 IN BRNO, TSCHECHISCHE REPUBLIK, MIT DEM GRAND PRIX FÜR PLAKATGESTALTUNG AUSGEZEICHNET.

Au printemps 1983, la Pologne est toujours en état de guerre, déclaré depuis deux ans. Craignant une insurrection populaire fomentée par Lech Walesa et son organisation Solidarnosc («Solidarité»), le gouvernement communiste interdit le signe de la victoire: poing levé, index et majeur érigés en forme de «V». L'emblème de la révolution. Une nuit, une affiche de théâtre pour le moins étrange apparaît dans les rues grises de Varsovie. Son thème? Le signe de la victoire, formé par deux orteils. Son auteur n'est ni un jeune révolutionnaire ni l'apparatchik d'un quelconque parti politique. Ce n'est autre que Henryk Tomaszewski, grand affichiste polonais, alors âgé de 69 ans. □ Il serait inconcevable de parler de la création contemporaine d'affiches sans rendre hommage à cet homme hors du commun, que l'on peut considérer comme le père de l'Ecole polonaise en la matière. Guidé par une philosophie qui tient en une phrase: «La politique, c'est comme le temps, il faut faire avec.», Henryk Tomaszewski a survécu aux atrocités de l'hitlérisme, à l'occupation nazie et au stalinisme tout en s'imposant dans son art. Son atelier a formé plusieurs générations d'étudiants, parmi lesquels nombre de fameux affichistes. Pourtant, ce maître incontesté de l'affiche reste méconnu aux Etats-Unis. □ Tomaszewski, né en 1914, semble n'avoir jamais douté de sa vocation. Passant outre aux réticences de ses parents, il s'inscrit à l'Académie des beaux-arts de Varsovie pour y étudier la peinture et le dessin. Il puise alors son inspiration dans les caricatures du magazine Simplicissimus et les dessins satiriques de George Grosz et de John Heartfield, et se fait un nom comme caricaturiste. En 1939, ses études à peine achevées, il remporte le premier prix du concours d'architecture intérieure à l'Exposition universelle de New York. □ Le 1er septembre de la même année, les troupes allemandes envahissent la Pologne et soumettent la nation à un système d'oppression et de destruction sans précédent. Détruit, pillé, saccagé, le pays se retrouve exsangue. Victimes d'une économie paralysée, les maisons d'édition et l'art graphique connaissent une période de vaches maigres. A Varsovie pendant l'occupation, Tomaszewski continue à peindre et à dessiner en survivant tant bien que mal. 1944, l'année de la libération, marque un nouveau tournant dans l'histoire de la Pologne: un gouvernement procommuniste est mis en place sous la férule de sa puissante voisine, la grande sœur russe. □ Le parti communiste avait besoin d'une image séduisante; l'art allait donc servir sa cause! Ainsi les affiches ne feraient-elles plus l'article des produits de consommation de l'économie capitaliste, mais celui de l'«esprit» du communisme. Dans un pays au réseau radiophonique hésitant, à mille lieues des dernières prouesses cathodiques, l'affiche constituait un instrument de propagande à la fois efficace et peu onéreux. □ En 1947, la société de production cinématographique d'état, la Centrala Wynajmu Filmow, confia la réalisation d'une de ses affiches à Henryk Tomaszewski et à un petit groupe de jeunes artistes. D'une banalité attristante, les affiches d'avant-guerre produites jusqu'alors se limitaient à reproduire le portrait de la vedette du film. Les artistes acceptèrent d'honorer le contrat, mais à la condition expresse que leurs créations soient imprimées telles quelles, sans être soumises à aucune forme de censure. □ La situation ne cessait de se dégrader. Le pays manquait de tout. Mais les difficultés ont le mérite de stimuler l'ingéniosité: les affiches réalisées par Tomaszewski en 1947 stupéfièrent le public. En jouant avec les formes et des couleurs intenses, l'affichiste intégra la typographie à l'image. Pourtant, la grande nouveauté était ailleurs: l'affiche n'illustrait pas une scène du film. Tomaszewski s'était attaché à en suggérer l'atmosphère, en recourant à des techniques cinématographiques – montages ou angles spéciaux permettant de créer des effets dramatiques. □ Un nouveau genre d'affiches était donc né, qui donnait autant de poids à l'interprétation personnelle de l'artiste qu'à celle du réalisateur. Cette conception intransigeante de l'art caractérise l'Ecole polonaise de l'affiche qui connaît son apogée entre 1952 et 1964. En 1949, Tomaszewski, âgé de 35 ans, a déjà remporté cinq médailles dans le cadre de l'Exposition nationale de Vienne consacrée aux affiches de cinéma; ces distinctions prestigieuses lui permettent d'asseoir sa réputation dans son pays. En l'espace de quelques années, les affiches polonaises s'imposent dans toute l'Europe. Dans les années cinquante, Tomaszewski enrichit son style pictural de collages sobres. En 1959, il crée pour l'exposition d'Henry Moore un jardin de sculptures avec les lettres du nom de l'artiste. Cette affiche marque un tournant décisif dans son art. Si le peintre et le caricaturiste sont toujours présents, son œuvre se fait de plus en plus dépouillée. □ Cet épurement graphique atteindra sa quintessence en 1964 avec l'affiche de Richard II. L'expression artistique se résume ici à un carré pourpre sur fond blanc. Le contraste, tranchant, est encore accentué par des contours noirs. Ce qui pourrait de prime abord être perçu comme un minimalisme outrancier est en fait une interprétation abstraite, mais magistrale, de l'œuvre shakespearienne: le bannissement et le «témoignage pourpre d'une guerre sanglante». Dépassant sa fonction purement décorative, la couleur devient moyen d'expression. □ En 1952, l'Académie des beaux-arts de Varsovie consacre l'art de l'affiche en lui attirant une chaire. Le professeur n'est autre que Tomaszewski. Le maître ne se préoccupe pas des techniques de l'art graphique: son enseignement, essentiellement basé sur l'abstraction, est philosophique. Les sujets assignés consistent souvent en une interprétation visuelle d'aphorismes tels que «Les autres», «Toute vie est, par essence, éphémère», «interpréter» ou «hier, aujourd'hui et demain». Il encourage ses élèves à oser l'inédit pour surprendre, étonner les autres autant que soi-même. □ Lorsque, vers la fin des années soixante, l'Académie de Varsovie ouvre ses portes aux étudiants étrangers. Français, tchèques ou slovaques, plusieurs affichistes de talent passeront par l'Ecole de Varsovie. Pierre Bernard, Gérard Paris-Clavel, Michel Quarez, Alain LeQuernec, Thierry Sarfis, Karel Misek ou encore Radovan Jenko viendront en Pologne pour suivre l'enseignement du maître. □ Presque à la retraite, Tomaszewski vit aujourd'hui dans la banlieue de Varsovie. ■

JAMES VICTORE EST DIRECTEUR DE VICTORE DESIGN WORKS, NEW YORK. SES TRAVAUX ONT ÉTÉ RÉCOMPENSÉS EN 1994 PAR LE GRAND PRIX DE LA CRÉATION D'AFFICHES DE LA BIENNALE INTERNATIONALE DES ARTS GRAPHIQUES DE BRNO.

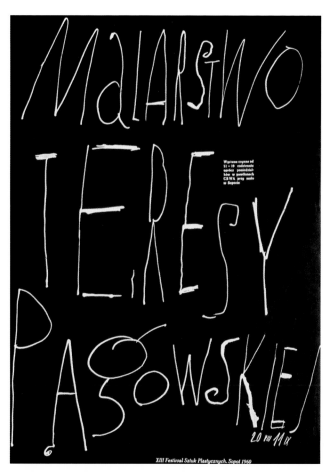

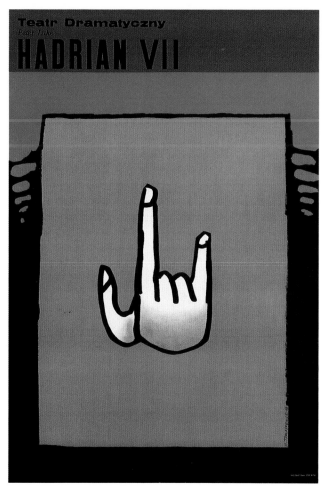

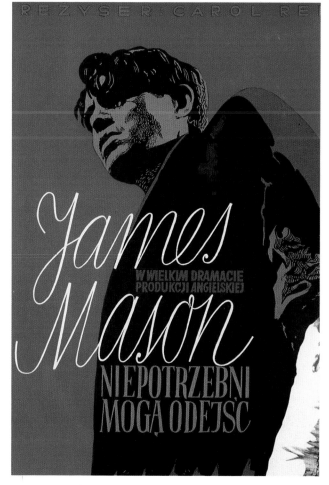

EDVARD MVNCH

XV. VYSTAVA SP.
MANES VPRAZE
KINSKÉHO ZAHRADA
5. VNOR. 12 BREZEN 1905
VSTVP. 1 K. OD 9 DO 5 HOD

LE
CAFE MARTIN

EUG. MARTIN 31, RUE JOUBERT PARIS

CRÉATION LES BELLES AFFICHES . Création 1929

E. NORLIND

BALTISCHE
AUSSTELLUNG
SCHWEDEN MALMÖ 1914

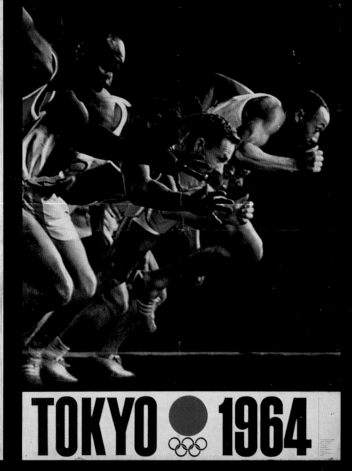

TOKYO ● 1964

The Arts and Crafts of Hamburg: A Poster Collection

The impact of posters was revealed to the good people of Hamburg in 1893, when their museum director Justus Brinckmann afforded them a view of the treasures he had just acquired at that year's World's Fair in Chicago. The mega publicity artworks—enormous color lithographs and woodcuts showing scenes of a circus and New York musicals—were acclaimed by Brinckmann as "the most amazing posters to come from the Promised Land of Advertising." □ To this day Hamburg's poster collectors remain enthusiastically international. The city's Arts and Crafts Museum, originally founded by Brinckmann in 1877 exclusively for the applied arts, keeps in touch with commercial artists throughout the world with an eye toward expanding its poster collection. Only recently the museum (located a mere two minutes away from the main train station) attracted attention with poster shows featuring work by Danish and Hungarian artists. □ For six years Dr. Jürgen Döring has been in charge of the museum's graphic arts collection. Hanging over his desk, a poster by the Japanese artist Makoto Saito underscores Döring's conviction that a whole new dimension in poster design has been achieved by Saito, amongst others. Saito's posters in particular are so outstanding that in spite of small print runs they have been successful worldwide—creating a sensation wherever shown, winning prizes in many countries, and receiving generous media exposure everywhere. "At present, the Japanese are the world's leading poster artists," says Döring. Poster work has been revitalized not only in Asia but in the United States and Europe as well, and Döring is convinced that modern computer technology is doing much to enrich this art. □ The continuity of the museum's outreach to commercial artists and designers in all countries has enabled it to build up one of the world's largest poster collections. Absolutely everything is collected in order to attain the most varied holdings possible. Roughly speaking, the museum archives now boast over 100,000 specimens. Of course quantity as such is not important. "We are interested in the quality of a poster," Döring says, going on to express his worries about running out of room. " We are jammed with works from the basement to the attic." □ That the museum is bursting at the seams is Brinckmann's fault. As early as in 1877 Brinckmann was already convinced of the importance of posters designed for purposes of commercial promotion; during his many travels he was to purchase publicity images in London, Paris, Rome, Vienna, and Brussels and have them shipped to Hamburg. The museum's holdings include all seven original Beggarstaffs posters, an extensive body of works by poster

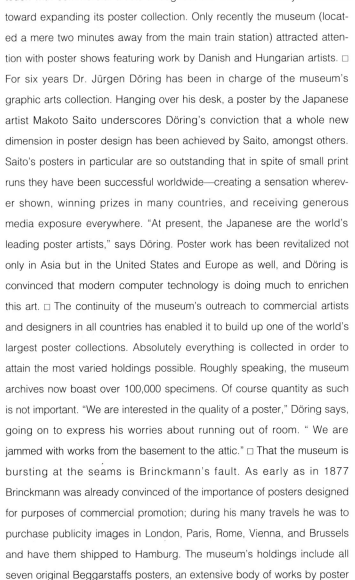

JÜRGEN DÖRING

designers such as Mucha, Hohlwein, Bernhard, and Cassandre, as well as posters by painters such as Kirchner, Pechstein, Heckel, Kokoschka, and Schiele. □ Brinckmann died in 1915 and his immediate successor lacked a flair for commercial art. This left a "great gap that remains to be filled," Döring says. The museum began collecting seriously again only after World War II, and a wide range of significant posters from Germany's economic boom years were purchased then. □ The works in the Hamburg poster collection are lavishly illustrated in *Plakatkunst von Toulouse-Lautrec bis Benetton* (*Poster Art from Toulouse-Lautrec to Benetton*), which was published in 1994 by Edition Braus. Not only do the color plates feature works by famous painters and designers from 'Jugendstil' to Postmoderism, from Bauhaus to Pop Art, but by commercial artists promoting Libby's, Sunlight, Maggi, and Lucky Strike. A provocative introductory quote by the poster artist Jean Carlu stipulates: "Anything goes to get a point across in posters: sentiment, pain, eroticism, illusion, pressure, cynicism ... anything except modest reserve. Posters are to the fine arts as free-style wrestling ... is to good manners." □ But with or without manners, for Döring good posters are just as valuable as outstanding fine art prints. In cases where large editions have been issued, often only one or two examples in good shape remain. For the museum's poster collection curator, the good posters are those that are particularly clever, that provide food for thought and have an unexpected twist. To Döring's taste, works by the commercial artists Holger Matthies and Uwe Loesch, amongst others, convey unusual ideas. "However," he adds, "there are a good number of commercial artists throughout the world coming up with new ways of livening up the field of poster art. I find that cigarette advertising, for instance, since banned from television, has produced posters that are extraordinarily creative. Another noteworthy example is the Nike campaign that uses the faces of successful athletes." □ It makes no difference who designed a poster, be it an ad agency, an individual artist, or a design team, Döring says. To him it all boils down to whether or not a poster is good, and it is this outlook that will no doubt guide him in mounting next spring's major exhibition at Hamburg's Arts and Crafts Museum. Provocatively titled "Heads, Bodies, Aids and Environment—Graphic Design in the Nineties," the show represents a challenge to Döring. As such, it promises to be a landmark event. □ *The Arts and Crafts Museum of Hamburg is open from 10:00 am to 6:00 pm daily except Thursdays, when it is open from 10:00 am to 9:00 pm. The museum is closed on Mondays.* ■

Wie ungeheuer wirksam Plakate sein können, erfuhr Hamburg im Jahre 1893. An der Weltausstellung in Chicago hatte Museumsdirektor Justus Brinckmann Werbetafeln erworben, die fast sechs Meter lang und drei Meter breit waren. «Es sind die erstaunlichsten Plakate aus dem

MARTIN HELMUT LIVES AND WORKS AS A FREELANCE JOURNALIST IN HAMBURG, GERMANY. HIS BY-LINED ARTICLES ON CULTURAL AND POLITICAL AFFAIRS APPEAR REGULARLY IN SEVERAL OF THE LARGER GERMAN DAILIES AND WEEKLIES.

gelobten Land der Reklame», pries Brinckmann die gigantischen Werbe-Kunstwerke, als er sie in Hamburg vorstellte. Die Farblithographien und Holzschnitte zeigten Ausschnitte aus Theatervorführungen in New York und warben für einen Zirkus. Seine Liebe zum Plakat hatte Brinckmann schon ein Jahr zuvor unter Beweis gestellt, als er 1892 für Hamburg eine internationale Plakatausstellung organisierte. ☐ International sind die Plakatsammler von Hamburg geblieben. Das Museum für Kunst und Gewerbe, von Brinckmann 1877 als reines Gewerbemuseum gegründet, pflegt seine Verbindungen zu Gebrauchsgraphikern in aller Welt und ist darauf bedacht, die Plakatsammlung ständig zu erweitern und zu vervollständigen. In jüngster Zeit machte das Museum (zwei Minuten vom Hauptbahnhof entfernt) mit zwei Ausstellungen – Plakate aus Dänemark und Ungarn – von sich reden. ☐ Seit sechs Jahren liegt die Verantwortung für die graphische Sammlung bei Dr. Jürgen Döring. Über seinem Schreibtisch hängt ein Plakat von Makoto Saito. Für Döring einer der Graphiker, die eine neue Dimension in der Plakatkunst erreicht haben. Die Plakate des Japaners sind so gut, dass sie trotz kleiner Auflagen weltweite Werbewirksamkeit haben, weil sie Aufsehen erregen, in vielen Ländern Preise gewinnen und dadurch überall in den Medien gezeigt werden. «Japan ist zur Zeit das führende Land in der Plakatkunst», meint der Kustos der

Museums-Sammlung. Aber nicht nur in Asien, überall ist das Plakat zu neuem Leben erwacht. Und die moderne Computertechnik, davon ist Döring überzeugt, macht diese Kunst noch interessanter und facettenreicher. ☐ Durch die Kontinuität im Umgang mit Graphikern und Plakatgestaltern in allen Kontinenten ist das Museum in den Besitz einer der grössten Plakatsammlungen der Welt gelangt. Gesammelt wird alles. Die Dokumentation soll möglichst umfangreich sein. Vielleicht sind es etwas über 100 000 Werke, die jetzt in den Schubladen lagern. Aber die Zahl ist nicht wichtig. «Uns kommt es auf die Qualität der Plakate an», sagt Döring. Eine seiner Sorgen ist der Platzmangel. «Wir sind vollgestopft vom Keller bis zum Dachboden.» ☐ Die «Schuld» daran, dass das Hamburger Museum aus allen Nähten platzt, trägt Justus Brinckmann. Er hatte schon 1877 die Bedeutung der damals noch jungen Plakatkunst für das Gewerbe erkannt. Auf seinen Reisen kaufte er Werbetafeln in London, Paris, Rom, Wien und Brüssel und schaffte sie nach Hamburg. Das Museum besitzt u.a. alle sieben Beggarstaffs im Original, umfangreiche Werksammlungen der reinen Plakatmaler wie Mucha, Hohlwein, Bernhard und Cassandre, aber auch Plakate bedeutender Künstler wie Kirchner, Pechstein, Heckel, Kokoschka und Schiele. ☐ Brinckmann starb 1915. Sein direkter Nachfolger hatte kein Gespür für die Gebrauchsgraphik. «Die zwanziger Jahre – da klafft bei

uns eine grosse Lücke, die es zu schliessen gilt», sagt Döring. Intensiv gesammelt wurde in Hamburg erst wieder nach dem Zweiten Weltkrieg. Die wichtigen Plakate der deutschen Wirtschaftswunderzeit sind in Hamburg in grosser Auswahl vorhanden. □ Der Farbbildband «Plakat-kunst von Toulouse-Lautrec bis Benetton», 1994 in der Edition Braus erschienen, informiert umfangreich über die in der Hamburger Samm-lung vertretenen Künstler und Werke. Bekannte Maler und Designer vom Jugendstil bis zur Postmoderne, vom Bauhaus bis zur Pop-art sind darin genauso vertreten wie kommerzielle Plakate, die für Libby's und Sunlicht, für Maggi oder Lucky Strike werben. Vorangestellt ist dem Buch das provokante Zitat von dem Plakatkünstler Jean Carlu: «Alle Mittel sind dem Plakat recht, um sein Ziel zu erreichen: Gefühl, Schmerz, Erotik, Täuschung, Erpressung, Zynismus..., alles, ausser schamhafter Zurückhaltung. Zu den schönen Künsten steht das Plakat etwa im Verhältnis, wie das Freistilringen zu guten Manieren.» □ Auch wenn sie keine Manieren haben, für Jürgen Döring sind gute Plakate ebenso wertvoll wie seltene Drucke bildender Künstler. Von den gros-sen Auflagen bleiben oft nur ein oder zwei Exemplare unversehrt. Gute Plakate, das sind für den Kustos Plakate mit pfiffigen Inhalten. Sie

müssen zum Nachdenken anregen und Überraschendes bieten. Unge-wöhnliche Ideen attestiert der Hamburger Experte u.a. den deutschen Graphik-Designern Holger Matthies und Uwe Loesch. Döring: «Aber es gibt viele Graphiker in aller Welt, die immer wieder neue Wege finden, um die Plakatkunst zu beleben. Beeindruckend finde ich zum Beispiel die Zigarettenwerbung, die, seitdem sie aus dem Fernsehen verbannt ist, mit unbeheurer Kreativität in den Plakatmarkt zurückgekehrt ist. Bemerkenswert ist auch die Nike-Werbung mit den ausdrucksstarken Gesichtern erfolgreicher Sportler.» □ Für Döring gibt es keinen Quali-tätsunterschied zwischen den Plakaten von Werbeagenturen und einzelnen Plakatkünstlern bzw. Design-Studios –...«es gibt gute und schlechte Arbeiten auf beiden Seiten.» Diese Überzeugung steht auch hinter der grossen Ausstellung, die im Frühjahr im Hamburger Museum für Kunst und Gewerbe stattfinden wird. Das Thema: «Köpfe, Körper, Aids und Umwelt – Graphik-Design der 90er Jahre.» Keine einfache Thematik, aber für Jürgen Döring eine Herausforderung. Man darf schon jetzt auf die Ausstellung gespannt sein. □ *Das Hamburger Museum für Kunst und Gewerbe ist täglich von 10.00–18.00 Uhr und donnerstags bis 21.00 Uhr geöffnet. Montag geschlossen.* ∎

MARTIN HELMUT LEBT UND ARBEITET ALS FREIER JOURNALIST IN HAMBURG. SEINE BEITRÄGE ÜBER KULTUR, POLITK UND ZEITGESCHEHEN ERSCHEINEN REGELMÄSSIG IN VERSCHIEDENEN ÜBERREGIONALEN TAGES- UND WOCHENZEITUNGEN.

Hambourg a découvert en 1893 l'incroyable puissance évocatrice des affiches. Lors de l'exposition mondiale de Chicago, le directeur du musée de l'époque, Justus Brinckmann, avait acheté des panneaux-réclame de presque six mètres de long sur trois mètres de large. «Ce sont les affiches les plus étonnantes du fameux pays des réclames», s'exclama Brinckmann lorsqu'il présenta ces œuvres d'art gigantesques à Hambourg. Les chromolithographies et les gravures sur bois illustraient des extraits de pièces de théâtre jouées à New York et faisaient de la publicité pour un cirque. Brinckmann avait déjà prouvé son amour des affiches l'année précédente, en organisant en 1882 une exposition internationale d'affiches à Hambourg. □ L'affichothèque de Hambourg est restée résolument internationale. Le Museum für Kunst und Gewerbe (Musée des Arts décoratifs), fondé en 1877 par Brinckmann qui le destinait d'abord exclusivement aux arts et métiers, est en contact permanent avec des affichistes du monde entier et s'efforce d'enrichir et de compléter sans cesse sa collection. Le musée s'est récemment distingué par deux expositions très remarquées, consacrées à des affiches du Danemark et de Hongrie. □ Jürgen Döring est responsable de la collection graphique depuis six ans. Au-dessus de son bureau, une affiche de Makoto Saito: «L'un des graphistes qui a atteint une nouvelle dimension de cette forme d'expression», explique-t-il. Les affiches du Japonais sont d'une qualité telle que leur impact publicitaire est mondial, malgré des tirages limités, parce qu'elles sont saisissantes, sensationnelles et s'attirent des prix dans de nombreux pays qui leur assurent une place dans tous les médias. Selon le conservateur de la collection, le Japon produit, à l'heure actuelle, les affiches les plus intéressantes. Cet art a pourtant connu une renaissance non seulement en Asie, mais dans le monde entier. Et Döring est convaincu que la technique informatique moderne le rend encore plus captivant et diversifié. □ Grâce aux contacts permanents entretenus avec des graphistes et des affichistes du monde entier, le musée possède aujourd'hui l'une des plus importantes collections d'affiches. Afin que la documentation soit aussi large que possible, le musée s'intéresse à tous les courants. C'est ainsi qu'il possède plus de 100 000 œuvres. Mais le nombre n'a pas d'importance. «Nous ne nous attachons qu'à la qualité des œuvres», précise Döring. Le manque de place est l'un de ses principaux soucis. «De la cave au grenier, le musée est archicomble.» □ Cette richesse est attribuable aux efforts et à la clairvoyance de Brinckmann. En effet, il sut reconnaître en 1877 déjà l'influence que les affiches ne manqueraient pas d'exercer sur les arts et métiers. À l'occasion de ses voyages, il acheta des panneaux-réclame à Londres, Paris, Rome, Vienne et Bruxelles pour les ramener à Hambourg. Le musée possède notamment les originaux des sept créations des

Beggarstaff Brothers, une importante collection d'œuvres de célèbres affichistes tels que Mucha, Hohlwein, Bernhard et Cassandre, mais aussi des affiches de grands artistes comme Kirchner, Pechstein, Heckel, Kokoschka et Schiele. □ Brinckmann est décédé en 1915. Son successeur direct ne s'intéressa pas au graphisme commercial. «Les années vingt – la grande lacune que nous devrons combler», explique Döring. Ce n'est qu'a la fin de la Deuxième Guerre mondiale que la collection du musée continua de s'enrichir de façon intense. C'est pourquoi il possède actuellement d'importantes productions réprésentatives de l'ère du «miracle économique allemand». □ Les artistes et œuvres représentés dans la collection de Hambourg occupent une grande place dans l'ouvrage illustré en couleur «Plakatkunst von Toulouse-Lautrec bis Benetton», paru en 1994 aux éditions Braus. On y trouve aussi bien des peintres et affichistes connus de l'Art nouveau jusqu'aux post-modernes, du Bauhaus au pop art, que des affiches commerciales vantant des produits tels que Libby's et Sunlight, Maggi ou Lucky Strike. Une exergue inspirée du Français Jean Carlu explique en substance que l'affiche ne recule devant aucun moyen pour atteindre son but: sentiment, douleur, érotisme, illusion, chantage, cynisme... tout, sauf une certaine retenue pudique. Selon lui, l'affiche est aux beaux-arts à peu près ce que la lutte libre est aux bonnes manières. □ Jürgen Döring considère que les affiches de qualité sont aussi précieuses que n'importe quelle œuvre d'art. En général, il ne reste guère qu'un à deux exemplaires intacts des grands tirages. Pour le conservateur, une bonne affiche est une affiche au contenu astucieux. Elle doit susciter la réflexion et surprendre. L'expert de Hambourg cite notamment les idées insolites des graphistes allemands Holger Matthies et Uwe Loesch. Döring: «Mais il existe beaucoup de graphistes dans le monde qui trouvent sans cesse de nouvelles voies pour donner un nouveau souffle à la conception d'affiches. Je trouve notamment très impressionnant l'exemple de la publicité pour des cigarettes, qui, depuis qu'elle est interdite à la télévision, a retrouvé un incroyable dynamisme. La publicité Nike, avec les visages expressifs de grands sportifs, est elle aussi remarquable.» □ Pour Jürgen Döring, il n'y a pas de différence qualitative entre les affiches des agences de publicité et celles des différents affichistes ou ateliers de création – ...«il y a du bon et du mauvais des deux côtés». Cette conviction a également inspiré la grande exposition du Museum für Kunst und Gewerbe de Hambourg qui aura lieu ce printemps. Intitulée: «Têtes, corps, sida et environnement – design graphique des années 90», elle aborde des thèmes qui, selon le conservateur, sont autant de défis à relever. On peut d'ores et déjà attendre cette exposition avec impatience. □ *Heures d'ouverture : mardi à vendredi de 10.00 à 18.00 h, jeudi à 21.00 h. Fermé les lundis.* ■

MARTIN HELMUT, JOURNALISTE INDÉPENDANT, VIT ET TRAVAILLE À HAMBOURG. SES ARTICLES CULTURELS, POLITIQUES ET SUR L'ACTUALITÉ EN GÉNÉRAL SONT RÉGULIÈREMENT PUBLIÉS DANS DE GRANDS QUOTIDIENS ET HEBDOMADAIRES INTERRÉGIONAUX.

GRAPHIS

POSTER

NINETY-SIX

■ 1 DESIGNER: DIETER MARX CLIENT: EDITION LIDIARTE COUNTRY: GERMANY ■ 1 ONE EXAMPLE OF THE ARCHITECTURAL POSTERS PUBLISHED BY LIDIARTE: "IL EST LIBRE" A DRAWING BY FRENCH ARCHITECT JEAN-JACQUES LEQUEU (1757–1826). ● 1 DIE ILLUSTRATION DIESES VON LIDIARTE HERAUSGEGEBENEN ARCHITEKTURPLAKATES IST EINE FEDERZEICHNUNG DES FRANZÖSISCHEN ARCHITEKTEN JEAN-JACQUES LEQUEU (1757–1826) MIT DEM TITEL «IL EST LIBRE». ▲ 1 INTITULÉE «IL EST LIBRE», CETTE ESTAMPE RÉALISÉE À LA PLUME ET AU LAVIS PAR L'ARCHITECTE JEAN-JACQUES LEQUEU (1757–1826)

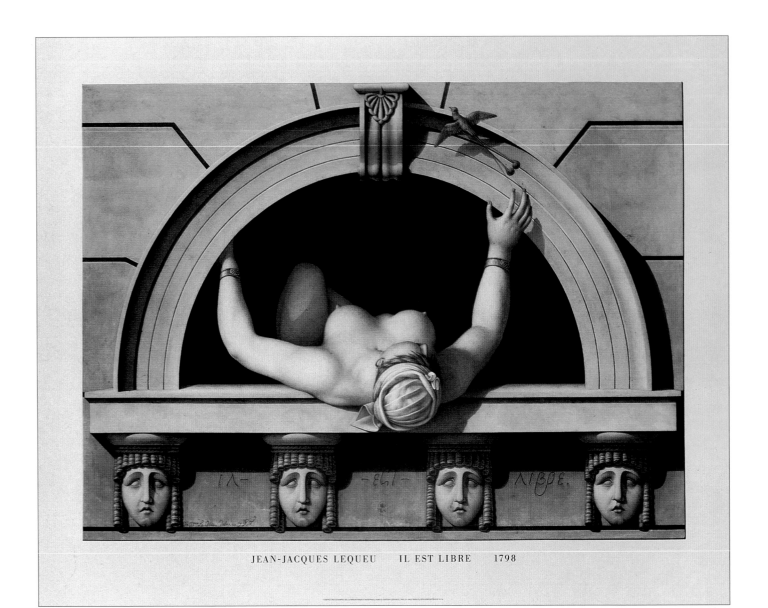

JEAN-JACQUES LEQUEU   IL EST LIBRE   1798

ILLUSTRE UNE AFFICHE PUBLIÉE PAR LIDIARTE SUR LE THÈME DE L'ARCHITECTURE. □ 2, 3 ART DIRECTOR: RICHARD M. BARON DESIGNER: RICHARD M. BARON PHOTOGRAPHERS: GUY SPANGENBERG (2), BRIAN BLADES (3) COUNTRY: USA ■ 2, 3 PART OF THE ROAD & TRACK "ENTHUSIAST" SERIES OF POSTERS ON HIGH-PERFORMANCE, EXOTIC CARS FROM AROUND THE WORLD. ● 2, 3 BEISPIELE AUS EINER FÜR AUTOLIEBHABER BESTIMMTEN PLAKATREIHE ÜBER SPEZIELLE AUTOS AUS ALLER WELT. ▲ 2, 3 AFFICHES D'UNE SÉRIE DÉDIÉE AUX PLUS BELLES VOITURES DU MONDE ET RÉSERVÉE AUX AFICIONADOS.

Lamborghini DIABLO

VIPER

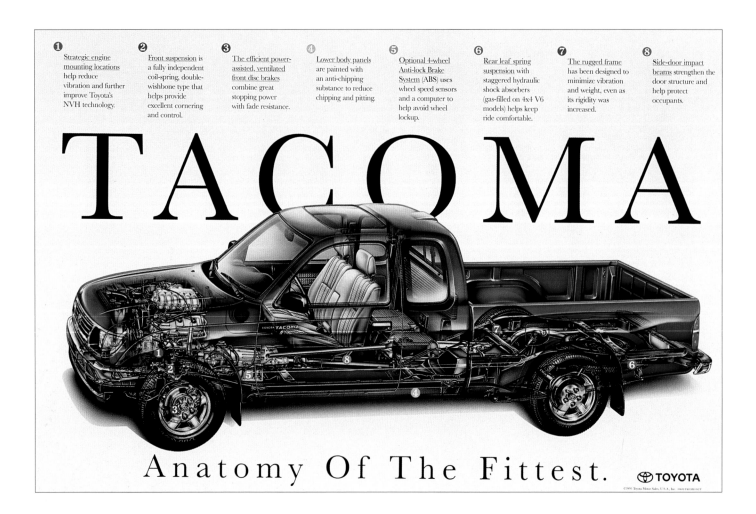

① **Strategic engine mounting locations** help reduce vibration and further improve Toyota's NVH technology.

② **Front suspension is a fully independent coil-spring, double-wishbone type** that helps provide excellent cornering and control.

③ **The efficient power-assisted, ventilated front disc brakes** combine great stopping power with fade resistance.

④ **Lower body panels** are painted with an anti-chipping substance to reduce chipping and pitting.

⑤ **Optional 4-wheel Anti-lock Brake System (ABS)** uses wheel speed sensors and a computer to help avoid wheel lockup.

⑥ **Rear leaf spring suspension** with staggered hydraulic shock absorbers (gas-filled on 4x4 V6 models) helps keep ride comfortable.

⑦ **The rugged frame** has been designed to minimize vibration and weight, even as its rigidity was increased.

⑧ **Side-door impact beams** strengthen the door structure and help protect occupants.

TACOMA

Anatomy Of The Fittest.

TOYOTA

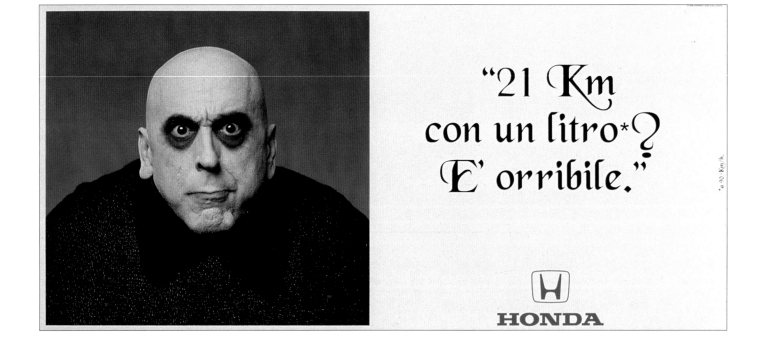

"21 Km con un litro*? E' orribile."

*a 80 Km/h.

HONDA

■ 1 ART DIRECTOR: RON WOLIN ILLUSTRATOR: KEVIN HULSEY ADVERTISING AGENCY: SAATCHI & SAATCHI DFS/PACIFIC CLIENT: TOYOTA MOTOR SALES, U.S.A., INC. COUNTRY: USA ■ 1 A CUTAWAY ILLUSTRATION OF THE TOYOTA "TACOMA" HIGHLIGHTS SOME OF THE VEHICLE'S FEATURES, WHILE THE POSTER'S SUB-HEADLINE IS DERIVED FROM THE NATIONAL ADVERTISING SLOGAN: "THE ARRIVAL OF THE FITTEST." ● 1 «ANATOMIE DES GESUNDESTEN» – WIE BEI EINEM MENSCHLICHEN SKELETT WIRD HIER DAS INNENLEBEN DES TOYOTA TACOMA ERKLÄRT. ▲ 1 «L'ANATOMIE DE LA PLUS SAINE». TEL LE SQUELETTE D'UN CORPS HUMAIN, LA STRUCTURE, «L'ANATOMIE» DE LA TOYOTA TACOMA EST MISE À NU. □ 2 ART DIRECTORS: E. FOSSATI, A. SEGHIZZI PHOTOGRAPHER: VIC HUBER COPYWRITERS: U. TESTONI, F. VALENTINI ADVERTISING AGENCY: PUBBLI-MARKET IDEA2/ALLIANCE CLIENT: HONDA AUTO ITALY CO. COUNTRY: ITALY ■ 2 "LESS THAN 1 QUART FOR 21 KILOMETERS. IT'S HORRIBLE." ● 2 «21 KILOMETER MIT 1 LITER. DAS IST GRAUENVOLL.» ▲ 2 «21 KILOMÈTRES, 1 LITRE! C'EST DIABO-LIQUE!» □ 3 ART DIRECTORS: DENNIS MERRITT, KARIN ARNOLD DESIGNERS: DENNIS MERRITT, KARIN ARNOLD PHOTOGRAPHER: RODNEY RASCONA ADVERTISING AGENCY: SHR PERCEPTUAL MANAGEMENT CLIENT: VOLKSWAGEN OF AMERICA COUNTRY: USA ■ 3 AN EFFORT TO REINFORCE THE IMAGE OF VOLKSWAGEN AS SIMPLE, HONEST, AND RELIABLE, BASED ON ITS REPUTATION OF

SOLID GERMAN ENGINEERING. ● 3 EIN VERSUCH, AUF DER BASIS DES GUTEN RUFS DEUTSCHER TECHNIK DAS IMAGE VON VOLKSWAGEN ALS EINFACHES, EHRLICHES UND ZUVERLÄSSIGES AUTO ZU STÄRKEN. ▲ 3 PUBLICITÉ VOLKSWAGEN S'APPUYANT SUR LA RÉPUTATION DE LA MARQUE ET LA FIABILITÉ DE LA TECHNIQUE ALLEMANDE. □ (FOLLOWING SPREAD) 1–4 ART DIRECTOR: MARK POSNETT DESIGNER: ROBYN BAJKAI PHOTOGRAPHERS: DANIEL DE SOUZA (1), STOCK (2), CLEM SPALDING (3), KEVIN RUDHAM (4) ADVERTISING AGENCY: PENTAGRAPH CLIENT: MERCEDES-BENZ COUNTRY: SOUTH AFRICA ■ (FOLLOWING SPREAD) 1–4 THESE COMPUTER-GENERATED POSTERS FOR THE NEW SMALL MERCEDES-BENZ ARE AIMED AT A YOUNG MARKET. THEY EXPLORE THE EMOTION OF DRIVING WITH MINIMAL EMPHASIS ON THE VEHICLE. ● (NÄCHSTE DOPPEL-SEITE) 1–4 DIESE MIT HILFE DES COMPUTERS HERGESTELLTE PLAKATREIHE («FREUDE», «LEIDENSCHAFT», «STÄRKE», «PERFEKTION») FÜR DEN NEUEN KLEINEN MERCEDES RICHTET SICH AN EIN JUNGES PUBLIKUM. ES GEHT UM DAS FAHRGEFÜHL, DAS AUTO SELBST WURDE BEWUSST IN DEN HINTERGRUND GERÜCKT. ▲ (DOUBLE PAGE SUIVANTE) 1–4 «PLAISIR», «PASSION», «PUISSANCE», «PERFECTION»: SÉRIE D'AFFICHES RÉALISÉES SUR ORDINATEUR POUR LA NOUVELLE MERCEDES COMPACTE, DESTINÉE À UN PUBLIC CIBLE JEUNE. GROS PLAN SUR LE PLAISIR AU VOLANT, LE VÉHICULE JOUE LES SECONDS ROLES.

MERCEDES-BENZ C-CLASS

joy

MERCEDES-BENZ C-CLASS

passion

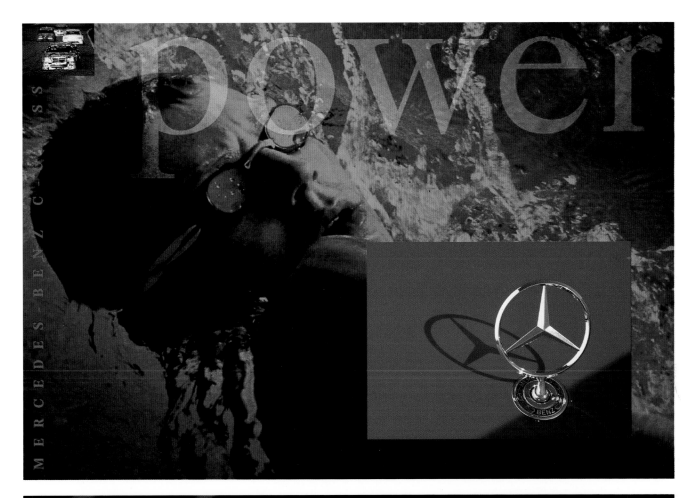

1 ART DIRECTORS/DESIGNERS: STEVE TOLLESON, JENNIFER STERLING PHOTOGRAPHER: JOHN CASADO DESIGN FIRM: TOLLESON DESIGN CLIENT: FOX RIVER PAPER COMPANY COUNTRY: USA ■1 A DESIGNER "CALL FOR ENTRIES" TO SHOWCASE A PAPER LINE CALLED CONFETTI SUGGESTS ELEVATING "BIT" PARTS TO THE LEADING ROLE. ●1 EINE AN GRAPHIKER GERICHTETE EINLADUNG, EINE PAPIERSORTE MIT DEM NAMEN CONFETTI ZU BEWERBEN, INDEM SIE DEM NAMEN ENTSPRECHEND KLEINEN FETZEN DIE HAUPTROLLE ÜBERLASSEN. ▲1 AFFICHE D'UN CONCOURS DE GRAPHISME INVITANT À PROMOUVOIR

UNE GAMME DE PAPIERS INTITULÉE «CONFETTI». IL S'AGISSAIT DE FAIRE RÉFÉRENCE AU NOM EN DONNANT LA VEDETTE AUX PETITES RONDELLES DE PAPIER. □ 2 ART DIRECTOR: ROGER COOK DESIGNER: ROGER COOK PHOTOGRAPHER: ROGER COOK ADVERTISING AGENCY: COOK AND SHANOSKY ASSOCIATES, INC. CLIENT: NJ COMMUNICATIONS ADVERTISING AND MARKETING ASSOCIATION COUNTRY: USA ■ 2 COVER OF THE "CALL FOR ENTRIES" FOR THE 1994–1995 ASTRA ADDY AWARDS. ● 2 EINLADUNG FÜR DIE ASTRA ADDY AWARDS 1994–1995. ▲ 2 INVITATION À PARTICIPER AUX ASTRA ADDY AWARDS 1994–1995.

The 3rd Living Art Competition
第3回リビングアート・コンペティション

"... to foster understanding ..."

The Daimler-Benz Award of Excellence is an annual program sponsored by Daimler-Benz and the Goethe-Institut to foster understanding between the young people of North America and Germany. The theme of the competition for the 1994-95 award is "Berlin - A Young Future".

It is in this spirit that the world renowned artists Christo and Jeanne-Claude Christo have kindly given permission for the use of "Wrapped Reichstag", a depiction of the actual wrapping of the new seat of the German government in Berlin.
The event will take place in the Summer of 1995.

(AR I OO)

10TH annual

r1
a 0

(AR I OO)

AWARD SHOW 1995 CALL FOR ENTRIES

DEADLINE FOR ENTRIES:
APRIL 20, 1995

10TH annual

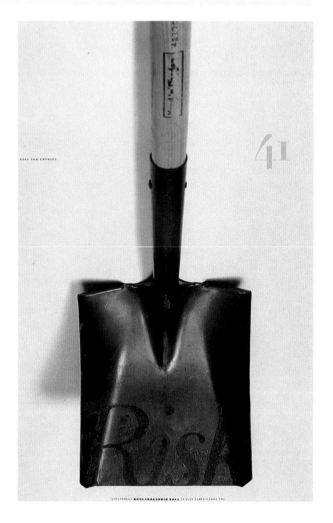

1 ART DIRECTOR: MASSAKI HIROMURA DESIGNERS: MASSAKI HIROMURA, TAKAFUMI KUSAG COPYWRITER: REIKO OKABE DESIGN FIRM: URBAN COMMUNICATIONS, INC. CLIENT: TOKYO GAS CO., LTD. COUNTRY: JAPAN ■1 ANNOUNCEMENT OF A COMPETITION. ●1 ANKÜNDIGUNG EINES WETTBEWERBS FÜR ZEITGENÖSSISCHE KUNST. ▲1 AFFICHE POUR UN CONCOURS D'ART CONTEMPORAIN. □ 2 ART DIRECTOR/DESIGNER: KEN RESEN PHOTOGRAPHER: WOLFGANG VOLZ ILLUSTRATOR: CHRISTO & JEANNE-CLAUDE CHRISTO ADVERTISING AGENCY: PAGE, ARBITRIO & RESEN CLIENT: DAIMLER-BENZ NORTH AMERICA CORPORATION COUNTRY: USA ■2 A POSTER DESIGNED TO INFORM STUDENTS IN THE US OF A PROGRAM OF TRAVEL AND STUDY IN GERMANY SPONSORED BY DAIMLER-BENZ AND THE GOETHE INSTITUTE. ● 2 DAS PLAKAT RICHTET SICH AN STUDENTEN IN DEN USA, DIE ÜBER EIN VON DAIMLER-BENZ UND DEM GOETHE INSTITUT GEFÖRDERTES REISE- UND STUDIENPROGRAMM IN DEUTSCHLAND INFORMIERT WERDEN. ▲ 2 DESTINÉE À DES ÉTUDIANTS AMÉRICAINS, CETTE AFFICHE LES INFORMAIT D'UN VOYAGE D'ÉTUDES EN ALLEMAGNE PARRAINÉ PAR DAIMLER-BENZ ET L'INSTITUT GOETHE. □ 3 ART DIRECTORS/DESIGNERS: STEVEN TOLLESON, JENNIFER STERLING PHOTOGRAPHER: JOHN CASSADO ADVERTISING AGENCY: TOLLESON DESIGN CLIENT: BLACK BOOK MARKETING GROUP COUNTRY: USA ■3 THE "CALL FOR ENTRIES" POSTER PICKS UP ON THE RUNNING NARRATIVE AND PHOTO ESSAY DIVIDING THE 1994 AR100 BOOK INTO CATEGORIES—SPOTLIGHTING BOTH THOSE REPORTS PRODUCED IN BANNER

YEARS AND THOSE IN WHICH THE RESULTS WERE DISAPPOINTING. ● 3 MOTIV DIESER EINLADUNG FÜR EINEN GRAPHISCHEN JAHRESBERICHT-WETTBEWERB SIND TEXT UND BILDER, DIE DAS BUCH AR 100 1994 IN KATEGORIEN UNTERTEILEN – JAHRESBERICHTE AUS ERFOLGREICHEN UND AUS ENTTÄUSCHENDEN GESCHÄFTSJAHREN. ▲ 3 AFFICHE D'UN CONCOURS AXÉ SUR LA CONCEPTION GRAPHIQUE DE RAPPORTS ANNUELS. TEXTES ET IMAGES FONT RÉFÉRENCE AUX CATÉGORIES DE L'ÉDITION AR100 1994. □ 4 ART DIRECTOR/DESIGNER: STEPHEN DOYLE ADVERTISING AGENCY: DRENTTEL DOYLE PARTNERS CLIENT: TYPE DIRECTORS CLUB COUNTRY: USA ■4 CREATED AS A "CALL FOR ENTRIES" FOR THE TYPE DIRECTORS CLUB, THE POSTER ATTEMPTS TO CONVINCE ARTISTS TO TAKE A RISK AND SUBMIT THEIR WORK. ● 4 EINE EINLADUNG ZUR TEILNAHME AM WETTBEWERB DES TYPE DIRECTORS CLUB. ▲ 4 AFFICHE D'UN CONCOURS ORGANISÉ PAR LE TYPE DIRECTORS CLUB. ■ 5 ART DIRECTOR/DESIGNER: SAVAS CEKIC DESIGN FIRM: VALÖR TASARIM LTD. STI. CLIENT: PLASTIK SANATLAR DERNEGI COUNTRY: TURKEY ■ 5 "YOUNG ACTIVITY: FRONTIERS AND BEYOND"—A COMPETITION AND EXHIBITION ORGANIZED BY THE PLASTIC ARTS ASSOCIATION FOR SCULPTURE, FINE ART, INSTALLATIONS, AND PERFORMANCES BY YOUNG TURKISH ARTISTS. ● 5 JUNGE, GRENZÜBERSCHREITENDE KUNST WAR DAS THEMA EINES WETTBEWERBS UND EINER AUSSTELLUNG MIT SKULPTUREN, BILDERN, INSTALLATIONEN UND PERFORMANCES. ▲ 5 «AU-DELÀ DES LIMITES DE L'ART», TEL ÉTAIT LE THÈME D'UN CONCOURS ET D'UNE EXPOSITION D'ARTS PLASTIQUES À ISTANBUL OU DE JEUNES ARTISTES TURCS PRÉSENTÈRENT LEURS TRAVAUX.

1 ART DIRECTOR/DESIGNER/ILLUSTRATOR: BRYAN L. PETERSON ADVERTISING AGENCY: PETERSON & COMPANY CLIENT: SMU FRIENDS OF THE LIBRARIES COUNTRY: USA ■ 1 IN AN EFFORT TO INCREASE PARTICIPATION IN SMU'S ANNUAL BOOK COLLECTING CONTEST, THIS POSTER ENCOURAGES STUDENTS TO GATHER THEIR COLLECTIONS AND RACE TO ENTER. ● 1 HIER GEHT ES UM EINEN WETTBEWERB FÜR BUCHSAMMLER: STUDENTEN SIND AUFGERUFEN, IHRE SAMMLUNGEN DER JURY VORZULEGEN. ▲ 1 AFFICHE D'UN CONCOURS ANNUEL DES COLLECTIONNEURS DE LIVRES. IL S'AGISSAIT DE RELEVER LE TAUX DE PARTICIPATION EN INVITANT LES ÉTUDIANTS À PRÉSENTER LEUR COLLECTION. □ 2, 3 ART DIRECTOR/DESIGNER: JEAN-PIERRE DATTNER PHOTOGRAPHER: LEN SIRMAN DESIGN FIRM: DATTNER PUBLICITÉ CLIENT: SLASH SA COUNTRY: SWITZERLAND ■ 2, 3 POSTERS FOR AN "APPLE CENTER" FOCUSING ON THE STRONG POINTS OF THE MACINTOSH (POWER PC

AND MULTIMEDIA). A PORTRAIT OF AMERICAN FILM COMIC HAROLD LLOYD WAS USED THROUGHOUT THE CAMPAIGN. ● 2, 3 DIESE PLAKATE FÜR EIN «APPLE ZENTRUM» STÜTZTEN SICH AUF DIE STARKEN SEITEN DES MACINTOSH (POWER PC UND MULTIMEDIA). DER ROTE FADEN DER KAMPAGNE IST DAS PORTRÄT DES AMERIKANISCHEN FILMKOMIKERS HAROLD LLOYD. ▲ 2, 3 AFFICHES POUR UN CENTRE APPLE AXÉES SUR LES POINTS FORTS DE MACINTOSH (POWER PC ET MULTIMÉDIA) AVEC COMME FIL ROUGE POUR TOUTE LA CAMPAGNE LE PORTRAIT DU COMIQUE AMÉRICAIN HAROLD LLOYD. □ 4, 5 PHOTOGRAPHER: ANTONIUS ABLINGER CLIENT: PIXNER COMPUTERS COUNTRY: AUSTRIA ■ 4, 5 COMPUTER-GENERATED POSTERS ANNOUNCING AN EXHIBITION. ● 4, 5 COMPUTER-GENERIERTE PLAKATE FÜR EINE AUSSTELLUNG DIGITALER PHOTOGRAPHIE, VERANSTALTET VON EINER COMPUTERFIRMA. ▲ 4, 5 AFFICHES RÉALISÉES SUR ORDINATEUR POUR UNE EXPOSITION D'IMAGES DIGITALISÉES.

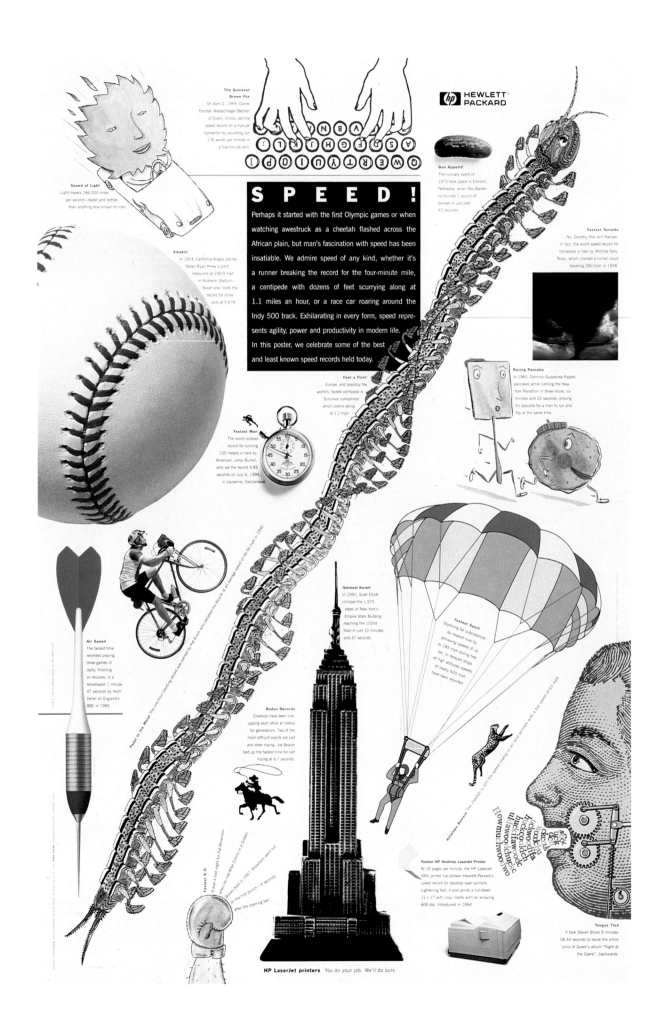

SPEED!

Perhaps it started with the first Olympic games or when watching awestruck as a cheetah flashed across the African plain, but man's fascination with speed has been insatiable. We admire speed of any kind, whether it's a runner breaking the record for the four-minute mile, a centipede with dozens of feet scurrying along at 1.1 miles an hour, or a race car roaring around the Indy 500 track. Exhilarating in every form, speed represents agility, power and productivity in modern life. In this poster, we celebrate some of the best and least known speed records held today.

HP LaserJet printers You do your job. We'll do ours.

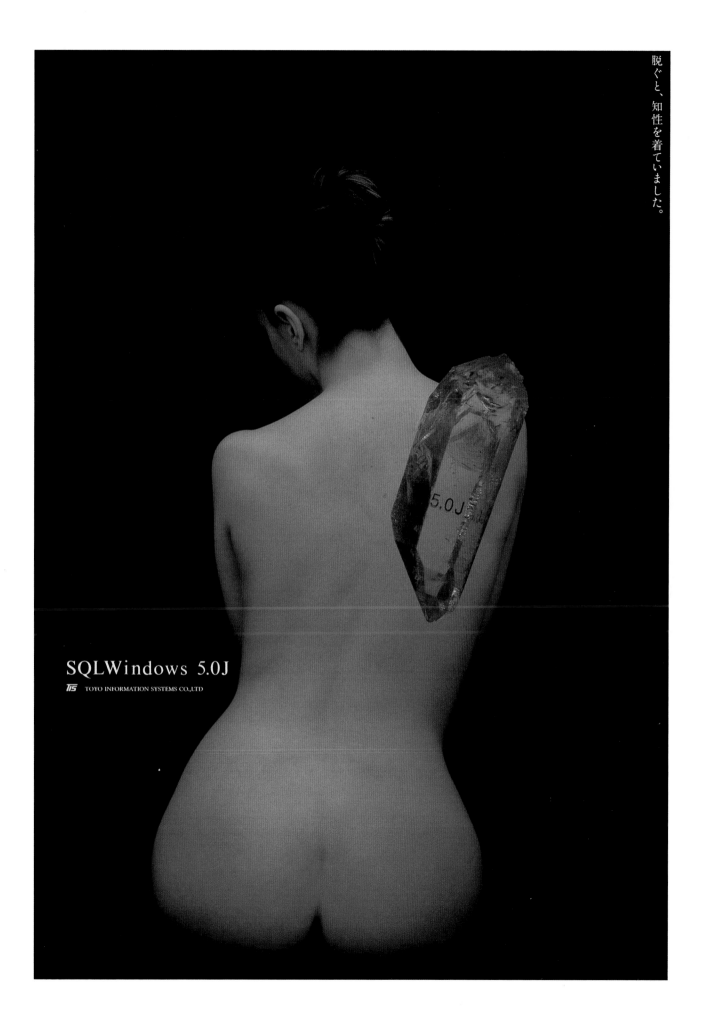

脱ぐと、知性を着ていました。

SQLWindows 5.0J

TIS TOYO INFORMATION SYSTEMS CO.,LTD

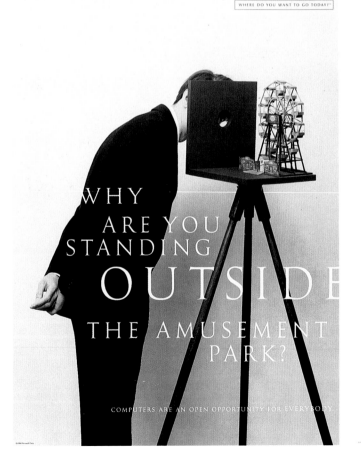

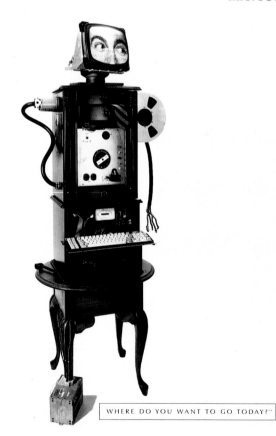

(PRECEDING SPREAD LEFT) 1 Art Director: KIT HINRICHS Designer: LISA MILLER Photographers: JOHN LUND, BOB ESPARZA, TOM TRACY Illustrators: DAVE STEVENSON, JOHN CRAIG, JEFFERY WEST, REGAN DUNNICK, JESSIE HARTLAND, JACK UNRUH Advertising Agency: PENTAGRAM DESIGN Client: FLOATHE-JOHNSON ADVERTISING AGENCY Country: USA ■1 PENTAGRAM DESIGNED THE "SPEED" POSTER FOR HEWLETT-PACKARD AS A DIRECT-MAIL PIECE TO INTRODUCE THE NEW FASTEST HP DESKTOP LASERJET PRINTER. ●(VORANGEHENDE DOPPELSEITE LINKS) 1 DIESES PLAKAT WURDE ALS DIRECT MAIL KONZIPIERT. ES DIENT DER EINFÜHRUNG DES 'SCHNELLSTEN' HP DESTOP LASERJET PRINTER. ▲(DOUBLE PAGE PRÉCÉDENTE À GAUCHE) 1 AFFICHE DE PUBLICITÉ DIRECTE, RÉALISÉE POUR LE LANCEMENT D'UNE NOUVELLE IMPRIMANTE DESKTOP LASERJET DE HEWLETT-PACKARD, LA PLUS RAPIDE DE SA CATÉGORIE. □(PRECEDING SPREAD RIGHT) 2 Art Director: NAONOBU NAKAMURA Designer: TSUTAMU NAKAJIMA Photographer: JUROH HAYASHI Copywriter: MASUMI KATAYORI Design Firm: MAGNA INC. Client: TOYO INFORMATION SYSTEM Country: JAPAN ■2 A WOMAN'S NATURAL BEAUTY AND THE MYSTERIOUS BRILLIANCE OF A ROUGH CRYSTAL SERVE HERE AS SYMBOLS FOR THE PERFECTION OF A NEWLY DEVELOPED COMPUTER OPERATING SYSTEM. ●(VORANGEHENDE DOPPELSEITE RECHTS) 2 DIE NATÜRLICHE SCHÖNHEIT DER FRAU UND DIE GEHEIMNISVOLLE KLARHEIT EINES ROHEN KRISTALLS DIENEN HIER ALS SYNONYM FÜR DIE PERFEKTION EINES NEUEN COMPUTER-BETRIEBSSYSTEMS. ▲(DOUBLE PAGE PRÉCÉDENTE À DROITE) 2 LA BEAUTÉ NATURELLE DE LA FEMME ET LA PURETÉ DU CRISTAL BRUT ÉVOQUENT LA PERFEC-TION D'UN NOUVEAU SYSTÈME INFORMATIQUE JAPONAIS. □(THIS SPREAD) 1, 2 Art Director/Designer: YUSAKU KAMEKURA

Design Firm: KAMEKURA DESIGN OFFICE Client: IBM JAPAN, LTD. Country: JAPAN ■1, 2 HIGH SPEED AT LOW COST IS THE MES-SAGE OF THESE POSTERS FOR IBM-PCS. ●1, 2 HOHE GESCHWINDIGKEIT, NIEDRIGE KOSTEN – WERBUNG FÜR PCS VON IBM. ▲1, 2 VITESSE GRAND V À PETITS PRIX – PUBLICITÉ POUR DES ORDINATEURS IBM. □3–5 Art Director: JOHN C. JAY Designer: STEVEN SANDSTROM Photographer: GEOF KERN Advertising Agency: SANDSTROM DESIGN Client: MICROSOFT Country: USA ■ 3–5 POSTERS CREATED FOR AN IN-STORE DISPLAY, AS PART OF A WIDESPREAD IMAGE/BRAND CAMPAIGN FOR THE SOFTWARE GIANT MICROSOFT. ●3–5 FÜR DEN LADENAUSHANG BESTIMMTE PLAKATE ALS TEIL EINER GROSSANGELEGTEN IMAGE- UND MARKENKAMPAGNE FÜR DEN SOFTWARE-RIESEN MICROSOFT. ▲3–5 AFFICHES DE P.L.V. RÉALISÉES DANS LE CADRE D'UNE VASTE CAMPAGNE PUBLICITAIRE DU GÉANT DE L'INFORMATIQUE MICROSOFT. □6 Creative Director: JOHN C. JAY Art Director: BILL THORBURN Designer: ALEX TYLEVICH Photographers: VARIOUS Design Firm: THORBURN DESIGN Advertising Agency: WIEDEN & KENNEDY Client: MICROSOFT Country: USA ■6 ORIGINALLY INTENDED TO BE SEEN IN PLACES ONE LEAST WANTS TO BE—NEAR TRAFFIC JAMS, COMMUTER CONGESTION—THIS POSTER STRESSES THE UNLIMITED POSSIBILITIES OF MICROSOFT SOFTWARE. ●6 DIESES PLAKAT UNTERSTREICHT DIE UNBEGRENZTEN MÖGLICHKEITEN DER MICROSOFT SOFTWARE. URSPRÜNGLICH SOLLTE ES VOR ALLEM AN NOTORISCHEN VERKEHRSSTAUPUNKTEN AUSGEHÄNGT WERDEN, UM PENDLER ZU ÜBERZEUGEN, DASS SIE SICH DIES ERSPAREN KÖNNTEN. ▲6 CONÇUE À L'ORIGINE POUR LES CARREFOURS PÉRIPHÉRIQUES, CETTE AFFICHE PRÉSENTE LES POSSIBILITÉS ILLIMITÉES DES LOGICIELS MICROSOFT, PAR EXEMPLE S'ÉVITER LES TRACAS D'UN EMBOUTEILLAGE.

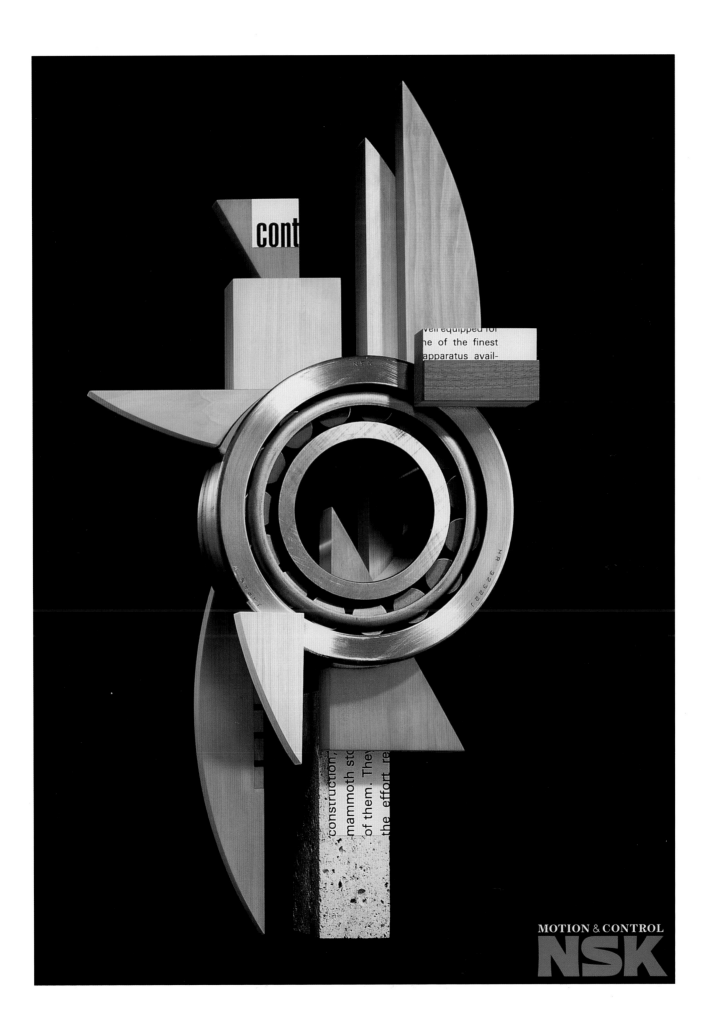

(PRECEDING SPREAD) **1, 2** ART DIRECTOR: SHINICHI SHINOHARA DESIGNER: TAKEHIKO AKIYAMA PHOTOGRAPHER: SHIGERU TANAKA DESIGN FIRM: FUJI AD. SYSTEMS CORP. CLIENT: NSK LTD. COUNTRY: JAPAN ■**1, 2** IMAGE POSTERS FOR NSK LTD, FEATURING THE COMPANY'S BEARINGS AND BALL SCREWS. ● (VORANGEHENDE DOPPELSEITE) **1, 2** DYNAMISCHE, SCHÖNE BILDER, IN DENEN VOR ALLEM DIE PRODUKTE DER FIRMA – Z.B. KUGELLAGER – VERWENDET WERDEN. IMAGE-PLAKATE FÜR NSK. ▲ (DOUBLE PAGE PRÉCÉDENTE) **1, 2** DYNAMIQUES, SUPERBES, CES IMAGES DE ROULEMENTS À BILLES NSK CHOISIES PAR LA SOCIÉTÉ JAPONAISE POUR SA PUBLICITÉ DE MARQUE. □ (THIS SPREAD) **1** DESIGNER: MICHAEL DABBS PHOTOGRAPHER: CHUCK CARLTON ADVERTISING AGENCY: FGI ADVERTISING & DESIGN CLIENT: REICHHOLD COUNTRY: USA ■**1** THE FIRST COMPONENT OF AN INTERNATIONAL EMPLOYEE COMMUNICATIONS PROGRAM FOR REICHHOLD CHEMICALS, THIS POSTER ANNOUNCES THE RESTRUCTURING OF THE COMPANY THROUGH SIX CORPORATE INITIATIVES. ●**1** ALS ERSTE STUFE EINES KOMMUNIKATIONSPROGRAMMS DER CHEMIEFIRMA REICHHOLD INFORMIERT DAS PLAKAT ÜBER DIE UMSTRUKTURIERUNG DES UNTERNEHMENS DURCH SECHS MASS-

NAHMEN. ▲**1** ELÉMENT D'UNE STRATÉGIE DE COMMUNICATION DE LA SOCIÉTÉ AMÉRICAINE REICHHOLD CHEMICALS, CETTE AFFICHE ANNONCE LA RESTRUCTURATION DE L'ENTREPRISE SELON UN PROGRAMME ARTICULÉ AUTOUR DE SIX MESURES. □**2** ART DIRECTOR/DESIGNER: FRIEDER GRINDLER CLIENT: WAGNER SIEBDRUCK GMBH COUNTRY: GERMANY ■**2** POSTER FOR A SILK-SCREEN PRINTER. ●**2** PLAKAT FÜR EINE SIEBDRUCKEREI. ▲**2** AFFICHE POUR UNE IMPRIMERIE SPÉCIALISÉE DANS LA SÉRIGRAPHIE. □**3** ART DIRECTOR/DESIGNER: RICK BAPTIST ILLUSTRATOR: RON FINGER ADVERTISING AGENCY: FGI ADVERTISING & DESIGN CLIENT: EDWARD VALVES COUNTRY: USA ■**3** TARGETED TO SPECIFIERS AT ELECTRIC UTILITY POWER PLANTS WORLDWIDE, THIS IS THE SECOND POSTER IN A SERIES DESIGNED TO HIGHLIGHT NEW PRODUCT INNOVATIONS FROM EDWARD VALVES. ●**3** DAS AN EXPERTEN VON ELEKTRIZITÄTSWERKEN IN ALLER WELT GERICHTETE PLAKAT IST DAS ZWEITE EINER REIHE, IN DER NEUE PRODUKTE VON EDWARD VALVES VORGESTELLT WERDEN. ▲**3** AFFICHE DESTINÉE AUX EXPERTS DE CENTRALES ÉLECTRIQUES, RÉALISÉE DANS LE CADRE D'UNE CAMPAGNE INTERNATIONALE CONSACRÉE AUX DERNIÈRES INNOVATIONS EDWARD VALVES.

1 ART DIRECTOR: JOSÉ SERRANO DESIGNER: JOSÉ SERRANO ILLUSTRATOR: NANCY STAHL ADVERTISING AGENCY: MIRES DESIGN INC. CLIENT: DELEO CLAY TILE CO. COUNTRY: USA ■ **1** ATTACHED TO SHIPPING PALETTES, THE POSTER EMPHASIZES THE CONCEPT OF QUALITY CRAFTSMANSHIP. ● **1** FÜR TRANSPORT-PALETTEN EINES FLIESENHERSTELLERS BESTIMMT, UNTERSTREICHT DAS PLAKAT DIE HOHE QUALITÄT DER PRODUKTE. ▲ **1** CONÇUE POUR LES PALETTES D'UN FABRICANT DE CARRELAGE, L'AFFICHE VANTE LA QUALITÉ SUPÉRIEURE DES PRODUITS. □ **2–5** ART DIRECTOR: JAMES POTOCKI DESIGNER: JAMES POTOCKI ILLUSTRATOR: JAMES POTOCKI ADVERTISING AGENCY: JAMES POTOCKI COMMUNICATIONS CLIENT: VISIBILITY INC.

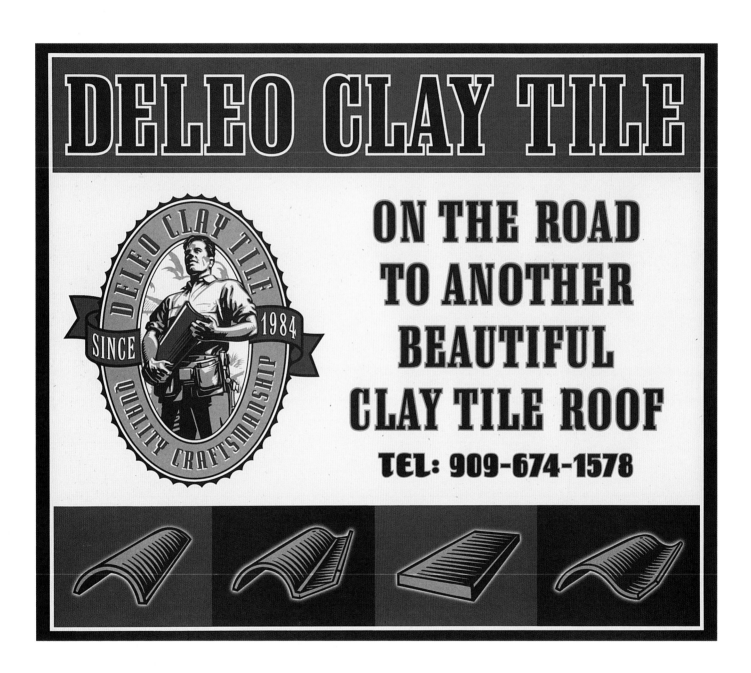

COUNTRY: USA ■ **2–5** DESIGNED FOR VISIBILITY INC., A COMPANY THAT DEVELOPS, MARKETS, AND SUPPORTS SOFTWARE FOR MANUFACTURERS OF MAKE-TO-ORDER, ENGINEER-TO-ORDER, AND ASSEMBLE-TO-ORDER PRODUCTS AND PROCESSES, THIS SERIES OF POSTERS IS CENTERED AROUND THE THEME OF EARLY MANUFACTURING. ● **2–5** THEMA DIESER PLAKATREIHE FÜR VISIBILITY INC. SIND DIE FRÜHEN JAHRE DES INDUSTRIEZEITALTERS. DIE FIRMA ENTWICKELT UND VERMARKTET SOFTWARE FÜR HERSTELLER VON NICHT GENORMTEN PRODUKTEN IN SPEZIALANFERTIGUNG. ▲ **2–5** LES DÉBUTS DE L'ÈRE INDUSTRIELLE, TEL ÉTAIT LE THÈME DE CETTE SÉRIE D'AFFICHES VISIBILITY INC., FIRME AMÉRICAINE SPÉCIALISÉE DANS LE DÉVELOPPEMENT ET LA COMMERCIALISATION DE LOGICIELS DESTINÉS À LA FABRICATION DE PRODUITS HORS NORMES.

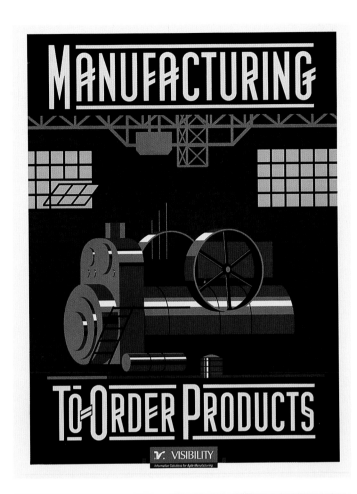

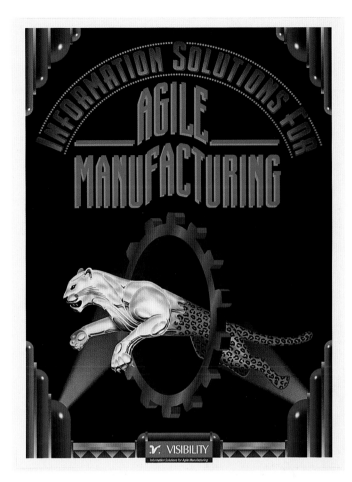

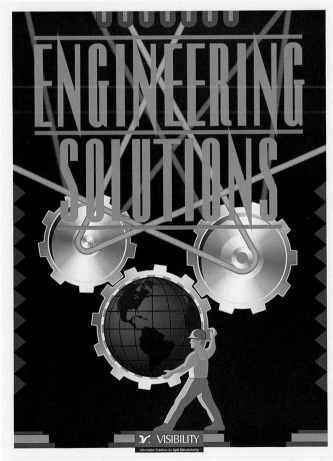

1–3 ART DIRECTOR/DESIGNER: STEVE WEDEEN PHOTOGRAPHERS: MICHAEL BARLEY, DAVE NUFER, DAN SIDOR ADVERTISING AGENCY: VAUGHN WEDEEN CREATIVE CLIENT: JONES INTERCABLE COUNTRY: USA ■ 1–3 AS PART OF AN IMAGE-REPOSITIONING CAMPAIGN FOR A CABLE TELEVISION OPERATOR, THESE POSTERS WERE INSTALLED IN STORE LOBBIES TO REINFORCE NEWSPAPER, TELEVISON, AND COLLATERAL ADVERTISING. VISUAL SYMBOLS AND WHITE SPACE DIFFERENTIATE JONES FROM THE USUAL "49 CHANNELS FOR $19.95" APPROACH. ● 1–3 DIESE PLAKATE GEHÖREN ZU EINER NEUEN IMAGE-KAMPAGNE EINES KABELSENDER-ANBIETERS. SIE WURDEN ZUSÄTZLICH ZUR PRINT- UND TV-WERBUNG IN GESCHÄFTEN AUFGEHÄNGT. ▲ 1–3 DESTINÉES À CONTRIBUER AU REPOSITIONNEMENT D'UN OPÉRATEUR DE RÉSEAUX TV CÂBLÉS, CES AFFICHES DE MAGASIN S'INSCRIVAIENT DANS LE CADRE D'UNE VASTE CAMPAGNE MULTIMÉDIA. □ 4–6 ART DIRECTOR/DESIGNER: ALAN COLVIN ILLUSTRATORS: ANTHONY RUSSO (4), JOHN KERSEY (5), GEORGE ABE (6) DESIGN FIRM: DUFFY DESIGN CLIENT: AMERITECH

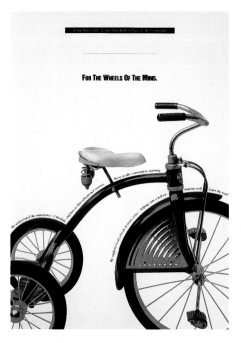  

COUNTRY: USA ■ 4–6 THESE POSTERS WERE DESIGNED AS PART OF AN INTERNAL COMPANY PROGRAM TO ENCOURAGE BETTER COMMUNICATION. ● 4–6 DIESE PLAKATE GEHÖREN ZU EINEM INTERNEN FIRMENPROGRAMM, DAS BESSERE KOMMUNIKATION FÖRDERN SOLL. ▲ 4–6 AFFICHES RÉALISÉES POUR UNE STRATÉGIE D'ENTREPRISE INTERNE VISANT À STIMULER LA COMMUNICATION AU SEIN DE LA COMPAGNIE. □ 7 DESIGNER: HEINZ SCHAAF PHOTOGRAPHER/COPYWRITER/DESIGN FIRM: STUDIO HEINZ SCHAAF CLIENT: METALLURGICA GESELLSCHAFT FÜR HÜTTENWERKSTECHNIK COUNTRY: GERMANY ■ 7 "STAY COOL, YOUR STEEL IS CLEAN." THE POSTER WAS USED AS A DIRECT-MAIL INSTRUMENT INFORMING STEEL COMPANIES ABOUT A SPECIAL AGENT USED TO PRODUCE VERY THIN, HIGH QUALITY STEEL. ● 7 ALS DIREKTVERWERBUNG AN STAHLFABRIKEN VERSANDTES PLAKAT, DAS ÜBER EINEN SPEZIELLEN ZUSATZ INFORMIERT, DER DIE HERSTELLUNG VON SEHR DÜNNEM, HOCHWERTIGEM STAHLBLECH ERLAUBT. ▲ 7 ENVOYÉE EN PUBLIPOSTAGE À DES ACIÉRIES, CETTE AFFICHE VANTE LES MÉRITES D'UN COMPOSANT SPÉCIAL PERMETTANT LA PRODUCTION D'UN ACIER TRÈS FIN DE QUALITÉ SUPÉRIEURE.

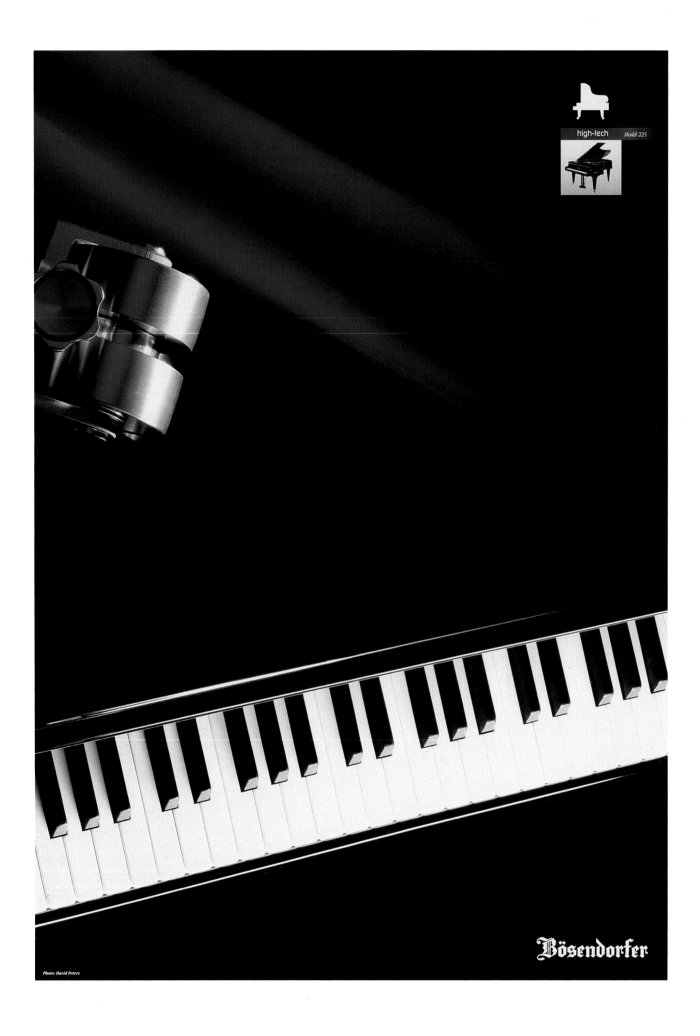

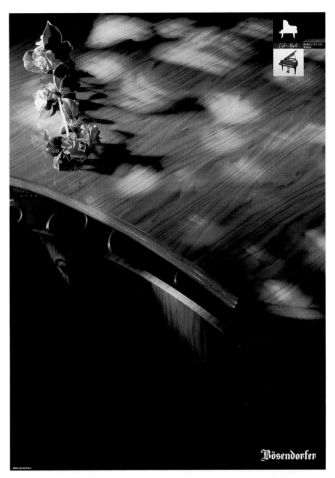

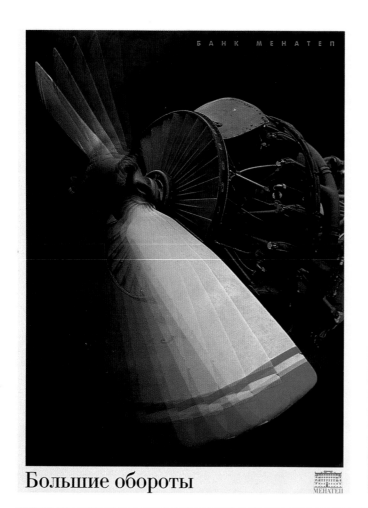

Большие обороты

Большие обороты

(PRECEDING SPREAD) 1–5 ART DIRECTOR/DESIGNER: RICHARD MACH PHOTOGRAPHER: DAVID PETERS DESIGN FIRM: ATELIER MACH-ART CLIENT: BÖSENDORFER KLAVIERFABRIK AG COUNTRY: AUSTRIA ■ 1–5 A SERIES OF POSTERS FOR THE ONLY PIANO MAKER IN AUSTRIA, DESIGNED FOR DISTRIBUTORS, FAIRS AND PUBLIC GIVEAWAY. THE ACCESSORIES AND OBJECTS SERVE TO EMPHASIZE THE SPECIAL CHARACTER OF THE DIFFERENT MODELS. ● (VORANGEHENDE DOPPELSEITE) 1–5 EINE SERIE VON PLAKATEN FÜR DEN EINZIGEN KLAVIER- UND FLÜGELHERSTELLER IN ÖSTERREICH. DIE PLAKATE GINGEN AN DIE HÄNDLER, WURDEN BEI MESSEN VER-WENDET UND DIENTEN ALS GIVE-AWAY. DIE ACCESSOIRES UND OBJEKTE UNTERSTREICHEN DEN CHARAKTER DER VERSCHIEDENEN MODELLE. ▲ (DOUBLE PAGE PRÉCÉDENTE) 1–5 AFFICHES POUR LES PIANOS BÖSENDORFER, SEUL FABRICANT AUTRICHIEN DE PIANOS DROITS ET DE PIANOS À QUEUE. ELLES ONT ÉTÉ ENVOYÉES AUX MAGASINS SPÉCIALISÉS, UTILISÉES LORS DE SALONS PROFESSIONNELS OU REMISES EN GUISE DE CADEAU. LES ACCESSOIRES ET LES OBJETS SOULIGNENT LE CARACTÈRE PARTICULI-ER DE CHAQUE INSTRUMENT. □ (THIS SPREAD) 1, 2 ART DIRECTOR: ARSENY MESHERYAKOV DESIGNER: DMITRY CHERNOGAEV PHOTOGRAPHER: DENIS KOZYREV DESIGN FIRM: AGEY TOMESH CLIENT: MENATEP BANK COUNTRY: RUSSIA ■ 1, 2 POWER AND MOVEMENT IS THE THEME OF THESE POSTERS FOR A RUSSIAN BANK. ● 1, 2 STÄRKE UND BEWEGUNG SIND DAS THEMA DIESER BEIDEN PLAKATE FÜR EINE RUSSISCHE BANK. ▲ 1, 2 PUISSANCE ET MOUVEMENT SONT LES THÈMES DE CES DEUX AFFICHES D'UNE BANQUE RUSSE. ■ 3 ART DIRECTOR/DESIGNER: SHANNON ARMSTRONG PHOTOGRAPHER: LARRY LADIG ADVERTISING AGENCY: QUINLAN ADVERTISING CLIENT: TWIN DISC, INCORPORATED COUNTRY: USA ■ 3 TARGETED TO NAVAL ARCHITECTS, BOAT BUILDERS AND DEAL-

ERS, THIS POSTER WAS DESIGNED TO ENCOURAGE THE USE OF AN ADVANCED SURFACE-PIERCING PROPULSION SYSTEM. ● 3 AN BOOTSWERFTEN UND -BAUER GERICHTETES PLAKAT, DAS FÜR HOCHENTWICKELTE ANTRIEBSSYSTEME WIRBT. ▲ 3 DESTINÉE AUX CONSTRUCTEURS NAVALS, CETTE AFFICHE VANTE LES QUALITÉS D'UN PROPULSEUR HAUTEMENT SOPHISTIQUÉ. ■ 4 ART DIRECTORS: ZEMPAKU SUZUKI, JUN UENO DESIGNERS: ZEMPAKU SUZUKI, MASAHIRO NAITOH ILLUSTRATOR: SEIJI SAITOH COPYWRITER: MARIKO HAYASHI DESIGN FIRMS: DENTSU INC., B-BI STUDIO INC. CLIENT: THE TOYO TRUST & BANKING CO., LTD. COUNTRY: JAPAN ■ 4 THE TOYO TRUST & BANKING CO. HAS ADOPTED MUTTLEY (KNOWN AS KENKEN IN JAPAN) FROM THE POPULAR US TELEVI-SION CARTOON SERIES *WACKY RACES* AS ITS MASCOT. THE POSTER ANNOUNCES THE NEW KENKEN ACCOUNT BOOKS AND BANK CARDS. ● 4 DIE TOYO TRUST & BANKING CO. BENUTZT MUTTLEY (IN JAPAN ALS KENKEN BEKANNT) AUS DER POPULÄREN US ZEICHENTRICKSERIE *WACKY RACES* ALS MASKOTTCHEN. MIT DIESEM PLAKAT INFORMIERT DIE BANK ÜBER NEUE «KENKEN-KONTOBÜCHER UND -BANKKARTEN» (DIE IN JAPAN EIN GROSSER ERFOLG WURDEN). DURCH DEN KONTRAST ZWISCHEN KENKEN UND DEM ART DECO HINTERGRUND SOLL EINERSEITS DIE PROFESSIONALITÄT, ANDERERSEITS DIE FREUNDLICHE ATMOSPHÄRE DER BANK ZUM AUSDRUCK KOMMEN. ▲ 4 REBAPTISÉ KENKEN POUR LE PUBLIC JAPONAIS, MUTTLEY, LE PERSONNAGE DU DESSIN ANIMÉ AMÉRICAIN *WACKY RACES*, EST DEVENU LA MASCOTTE DE LA TOYO TRUST & BANKING CO. CETTE AFFICHE SERVIT AU LANCEMENT DES NOUVEAUX LIVRETS ET CARTES BANCAIRES «KENKEN» QUI REMPORTÈRENT UN ÉNORME SUCCÈS AU JAPON. KENKEN CRÉE UN CLIMAT DE SYMPATHIE, LE FOND ARTS DÉCO ÉVOQUE LE PROFESSIONNALISME DE LA BANQUE.

1 DESIGNER: MARIA WHITE PHOTOGRAPHER: EARL RIPLING CLIENT: ORIGINS COUNTRY: USA ■1 ADVERTISING POSTER FOR ORIGINS COSMETICS. ●1 WERBEPLAKAT FÜR ORIGINS-KOSMETIKA. ▲1 PUBLICITÉ POUR LES COSMÉTIQUES ORIGINS. □2 ART DIRECTOR: JERRY SULLIVAN ILLUSTRATOR: BILL MAYER DESIGN FIRM/CLIENT: SULLIVAN HAAS COYLE COUNTRY: USA ■2 A SELF-PROMOTION PIECE FOR THE ATLANTA-BASED ADVERTISING AGENCY SULLIVAN HAAS COYLE. ●2 EIGENWERBUNG DER WERBEAGENTUR SULLIVAN HAAS COYLE AUS ATLANTA. ▲2 PUBLICITÉ AUTOPROMOTIONNELLE DE L'AGENCE SULLIVAN HAAS COYLE, ÉTABLIE À ATLANTA.

IF YOU HAVE A MARKETING PROBLEM STARING YOU IN THE FACE, CALL US.

Metal Freaks "Toughness" 1993
Sculpture by Shin Matsunaga
This sculpture is made possible by
special collaboration with
Takahara Works Co. Ltd.

Ink screen printing by
Fujihoodera and other Printing Co. Ltd.

M E T A L   F R E A K S

A **WIFE** AND husband

DESIGN PARTNERSHIP

KRISTIN AND Lanny

481 GLENN ROAD

STATE COLLEGE PA 16803

CALL 814-238-7484

FAX 814-863-8664

SOMMESE
DESIGN

(PRECEDING SPREAD LEFT) 1 ART DIRECTOR/DESIGNER: SHIN MATSUNAGA DESIGN FIRM: SHIN MATSUNAGA DESIGN INC. COUNTRY: JAPAN ■ 1 "OUROBOROS," A SNAKE EATING ITS OWN TAIL IS THE SYMBOL OF ETERNAL LIFE AND THE UNITY OF THE UNIVERSE. THIS POSTER IS PART OF A SERIES OF WORKS (PAPER FREAKS) CREATED FOR THE DESIGNER'S ONE-MAN EXHIBITION. ● (VOR-ANGEHENDE DOPPELSEITE LINKS) 1 «OUROBOROS», EINE SCHLANGE, DIE SICH SELBST IN DEN SCHWANZ BEISST. ES IST DAS SYMBOL EWIGEN LEBENS UND DER EINHEIT DES UNIVERSUMS. DAS PLAKAT GEHÖRT ZU EINER REIHE VON ARBEITEN (PAPER FREAKS) FÜR EINE AUSSTELLUNG DES DESIGNERS. DER BEGRIFF 'FREAKS' STEHT FÜR EIGENWILLIGE KREATIVE AUSDRUCKSFORMEN. ▲ (DOUBLE PAGE PRÉCÉDENTE À GAUCHE) 1 «OUROBOROS», LE SERPENT QUI MORD SA QUEUE. IL SYMBO-LISE LA VIE ÉTERNELLE ET L'UNITÉ DE L'UNIVERS. EXTRAITE D'UNE SÉRIE DE TRAVAUX INTITULÉE «PAPER FREAKS» CETTE AFFICHE A ÉTÉ RÉALISÉE POUR UNE EXPOSITION DU DESIGNER. LE TERME «FREAKS» SYMBOLISE UNE FORME D'EXPRESSION CRÉATIVE OU LA FANTAISIE NE CONNAÎT PAS DE LIMITES. □ (PRECEDING SPREAD RIGHT) 2 ART DIRECTOR/DESIGNER/CLIENT: SHIN MATSUNAGA DESIGN FIRM: SHIN MATSUNAGA DESIGN INC. COUNTRY: JAPAN ■ 2 THIS POSTER DEPICTS ONE OF THE BRONZE SCULP-TURES IN SHIN MATSUNAGA'S ONE-MAN EXHIBITION. ● (VORANGEHENDE DOPPELSEITE RECHTS) 2 DIESES PLAKAT ZEIGT EINE DER BRONZESKULPTUREN DES KÜNSTLERS AUS EINER AUSSTELLUNG. ▲ (DOUBLE PAGE PRÉCÉDENTE À 2 AFFICHE RÉALISÉE POUR UNE EXPOSITION ET PRÉSENTANT UN BRONZE DU SCULPTEUR. □ (OPPOSITE) 1 ART DIRECTORS: LANNY SOMMESE, KRISTIN

SOMMESE DESIGNER: KRISTIN SOMMESE ILLUSTRATOR: LANNY SOMMESE DESIGN FIRM/CLIENT: SOMMESE DESIGN COUNTRY: USA ■ (OPPOSITE) 1 THIS SELF-PROMOTION POSTER BY THE HUSBAND-AND-WIFE TEAM OF SOMMESE DESIGN, USES TONGUE-IN-CHEEK IMAGERY TO EXPLORE THE SERIOUS ISSUE OF SEXUAL HARRASSMENT. ● (GEGENÜBER) 1 KRISTIN UND LANNY SOMMESE BENUTZEN IRONISCHE BILDER FÜR EIN ERNSTES THEMA: SEXUELLE BELÄSTIGUNG. ▲ (CI-CONTRE) 1 PUBLICITÉ AUTOPROMOTIONNELLE DE L'AGENCE AMÉRICAINE SOMMESE DESIGN. LES AUTEURS ONT CHOISI DE RECOURIR À DES IMAGES IRONIQUES POUR TRAITER D'UN THEME SÉRIEUX: LE HARCELEMENT SEXUEL. □ (THIS PAGE) 2 ART DIRECTOR: LOWELL L. WILLIAMS DESIGNER: BILL CARSON PHOTOGRAPHER: DAVID GRIMES DESIGN FIRM/CLIENT: PENTAGRAM DESIGN COUNTRY: USA ■ 2 THE CLOCK POSTER SERVED AS AN OPENING ANNOUNCEMENT FOR THE PENTAGRAM AUSTIN OFFICE. THE BLACK-AND-WHITE CLOCKS WERE CHOSEN TO REPRESENT THE EXISTING PENTAGRAM OFFICES, WHILE THE AUSTIN CLOCK SYMBOLIZES THE HERITAGE AND NOSTALGIA OF TEXAS. ● (DIESE SEITE) 2 ANKÜNDIGUNG DER ERÖFFNUNG DER PENTAGRAM-DESIGN-STUDIOS IN AUSTIN. DIE SCHWARZ-WEISSEN UHREN SYMBOLISIEREN DIE SCHON EXISTIERENDEN PENTAGRAM-BÜROS, WÄHREND DIE AUSTIN-UHR SICH AUF DAS TEXANISCHE ERBE BEZIEHT. ▲ (CI-DESSUS) 2 AFFICHE ANNONÇANT L'OUVERTURE D'UNE NOUVELLE AGENCE DE DESIGN PENTAGRAM À AUSTIN. LES PENDULES NOIR ET BLANC FONT RÉFÉRENCE AUX AGENCES DÉJÀ EXISTANTES DU GROUPE, TANDIS QUE L'HORLOGE AUSTIN SYMBOLISE L'APPORT DE L'HÉRITAGE TEXAN.

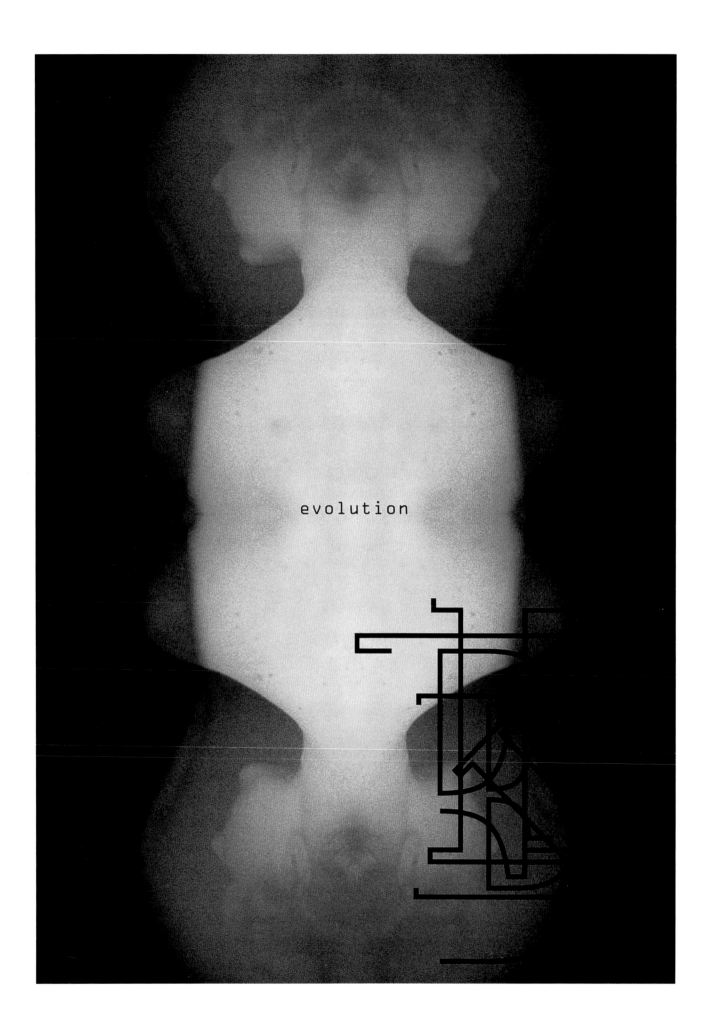

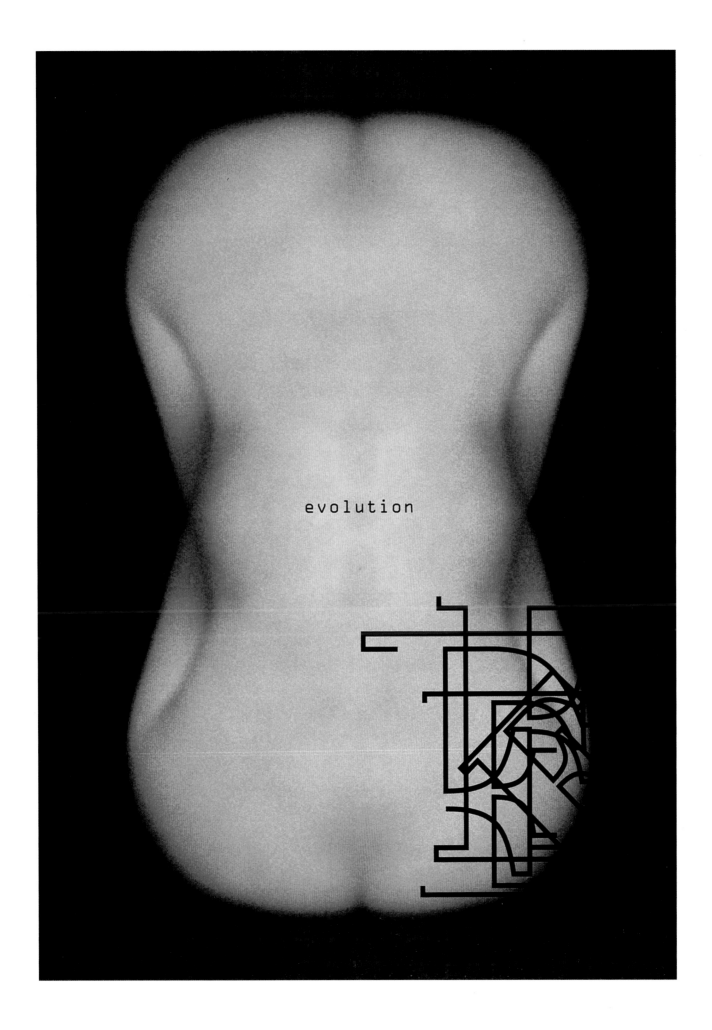

evolution

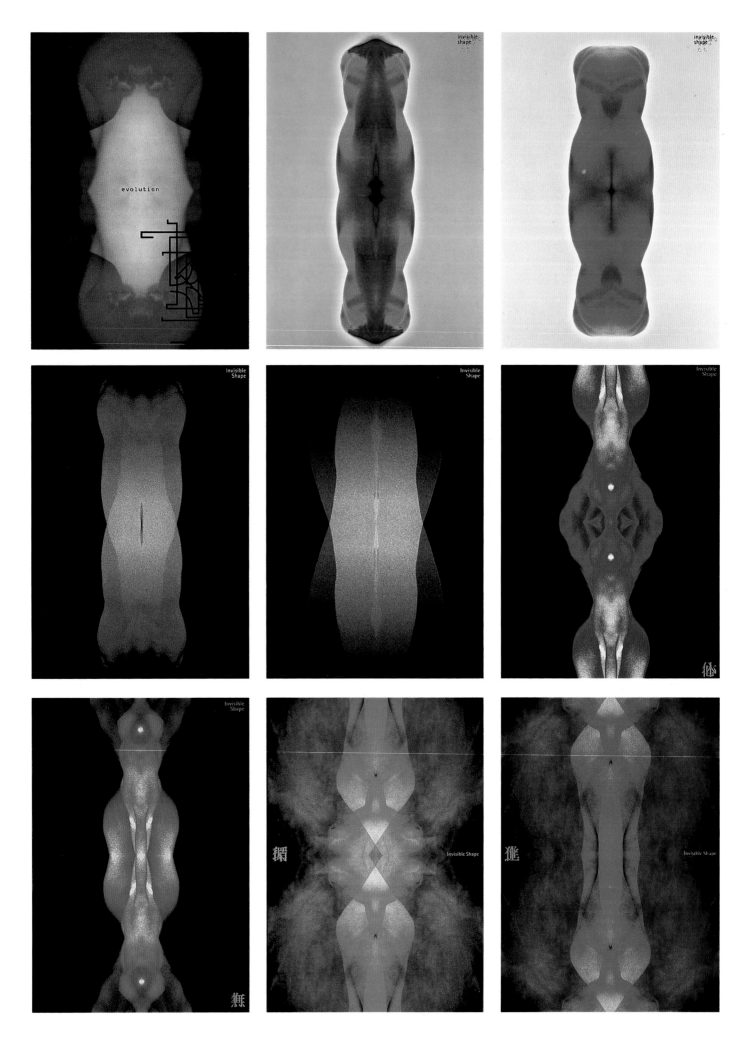

Named one of the top U.S. Companies to work for in *The 100 Best Companies to Work for in America*, Herman Miller has been a design leader for decades. (But is it fun to work there?) Under the leadership of creative director Stephen Frykholm (He's a real gas!), the team at Herman Miller has helped the company win awards like the AIGA Design Leadership and Fortune & American Center for Design Beacon Award. The NY Art Director's Club, CA, Graphis, ID, and AIGA Communication Graphics have also recognized Herman Miller's graphic design. (Some of these awards are really cool.) Herman Miller offers an attractive beginning designer's salary (n̶o̶t̶ but enough to pay the rent). Interested candi̶d̶a̶t̶e̶s̶ BFA or MFA degree (and a lively imaginat̶i̶o̶n̶ by sending a maximum of twenty slides of ̶w̶o̶r̶k̶ ̶a̶n̶d̶ a resume by June, 1994. Please include ed̶u̶c̶a̶t̶i̶o̶n̶ ̶a̶n̶d̶ work experience references. (Don't worry, young designers getting the job before you didn't have much either.) Send resumes to: Herman Miller Inc., Staffing department 0162, PO Box 302, Zeeland, Michigan 49464-0302. (Don't try to buck the system by sending your stuff directly to Steve. He'll lose it.) Include a self-addressed, stamped envelope for return of slides; please do not send actual portfolios. Selected candidates will be contacted by August, 1994 to arrange interviews. (We'll buy lunch and give you the real low-down.)

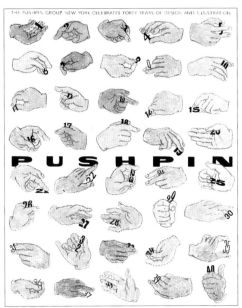

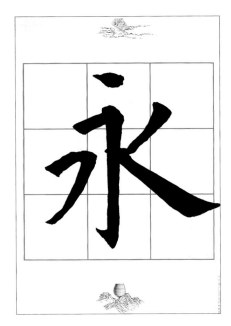

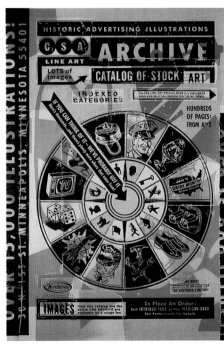

1 ART DIRECTOR/DESIGNER: LESLIE CHAN WING KEI DESIGN FIRM: LESLIE CHAN DESIGN CO., LTD. CLIENT: TAIWAN IMAGE POSTER DESIGN ASSOCIATION COUNTRY: TAIWAN ■ 1 A SELF-PROMOTION FOR THE DESIGNER. ● 1 EIGENWERBUNG DES DESIGNERS. ▲ 1 PUBLICITÉ AUTOPROMOTIONNELLE D'UN GRAPHISTE TAIWANAIS. □ 2 ART DIRECTOR/DESIGNER: SEYMOUR CHWAST ILLUSTRATOR: SEYMOUR CHWAST DESIGN FIRM/CLIENT: THE PUSHPIN GROUP COUNTRY: USA ■ 2 POSTER ANNOUNCING THE 40TH ANNIVERSARY OF THE PUSHPIN GROUP. ● 2 PLAKAT ANLÄSSLICH DES 40JÄHRIGEN BESTEHENS DER PUSHPIN-GRUPPE. ▲ 2 AFFICHE RÉALISÉE À L'OCCASION DU 40ᴱ ANNIVERSAIRE DU GROUPE PUSHPIN. □ 3 ART DIRECTOR/DESIGNER: WILLIAM SLOAN ILLUSTRATOR: WILLIAM SLOAN DESIGN FIRM/CLIENT: THREE COUNTRY: USA ■ 3 A PROMOTIONAL POSTER FOR THE GRAPHIC DESIGN FIRM THREE EMPHASIZES BEGINNINGS AND OPPORTUNITY. ● 3 ANFÄNGE UND CHANCEN SIND DAS THEMA DIESES PLAKATES FÜR DAS DESIGN-STUDIO THREE. ▲ 3 «DÉBUTS ET OPPORTUNITÉS», TEL ÉTAIT LE THEME DE CETTE AFFICHE AUTOPROMOTIONNELLE RÉALISÉE PAR L'AGENCE DE GRAPHISME AMÉRICAINE THREE. □ 4 DESIGNER: KIRK RICHARD SMITH PHOTOGRAPHER: WILL SHIVELY ILLUSTRATOR: KIRK RICHARD SMITH DESIGN FIRM/CLIENT: FIREHOUSE 101 ART + DESIGN COUNTRY: USA ■ 4 TARGETING RECORD AND BOOK COMPANIES, THIS SELF-PROMOTIONAL POSTER FOR FIREHOUSE 101 ART + DESIGN STRESSES THE EMOTIVE QUALITIES OF COMMUNICATION. ● 4 DIESES AN SCHALLPLATTEN- UND BUCHVERLAGE GERICHTETE PLAKAT EINES DESIGN-STUDIOS UNTERSTREICHT DIE EMOTIONALEN ASPEKTE DER KOMMUNIKATION. ▲ 4 DESTINÉE AUX MAISONS DE DISQUES ET D'ÉDITION, CETTE AFFICHE RÉALISÉE PAR L'AGENCE DE DESIGN FIREHOUSE 101 ART + DESIGN MET EN EXERGUE LES ASPECTS ÉMOTIONNELS DE LA COMMUNICATION. □ 5 ART DIRECTOR/DESIGNER/CLIENT: KEVIN MITCHELL COUNTRY: USA ■ 5 A SELF-PROMOTIONAL POSTER FOR GRAPHIC DESIGNER KEVIN MITCHELL. ● 5 EIGENWERBUNG EINES GRAPHIK DESIGNERS. ▲ 4 AUTOPROMOTION DU GRAPHISTE KEVIN MITCHELL. □ 6 ART DIRECTOR: CHARLES S. ANDERSON DESIGNERS: CHARLES S. ANDERSON, TODD PIPER-HAUSWIRTH, JOEL TEMPLIN, PAUL HOWALT DESIGN FIRM: CHARLES S. ANDERSON DESIGN CO. CLIENT: CSA ARCHIVE COUNTRY: USA ■ 6 THE COVER OF THE

CSA ARCHIVE BOOK, MADE INTO A POSTER. ● 6 UMSCHLAG DES ARCHIVKATALOGS VON CHARLES S. ANDERSON DESIGN IN PLAKATFORMAT. ▲ 6 REPRODUCTION DE LA COUVERTURE D'UN CATALOGUE DE L'AGENCE DE DESIGN AMÉRICAINE CSA ARCHIVE. □ 7 CREATIVE DIRECTOR: MICHAEL FOUNTAIN ART DIRECTOR/DESIGNER: JANET FRIED PHOTOGRAPHER: WALTER COLLEY COPYWRITER: MARILYN LEWIS DESIGN FIRM/CLIENT: ICE INC. COUNTRY: USA ■ 7 AS PART OF A MAILING TO PROSPECTIVE AND

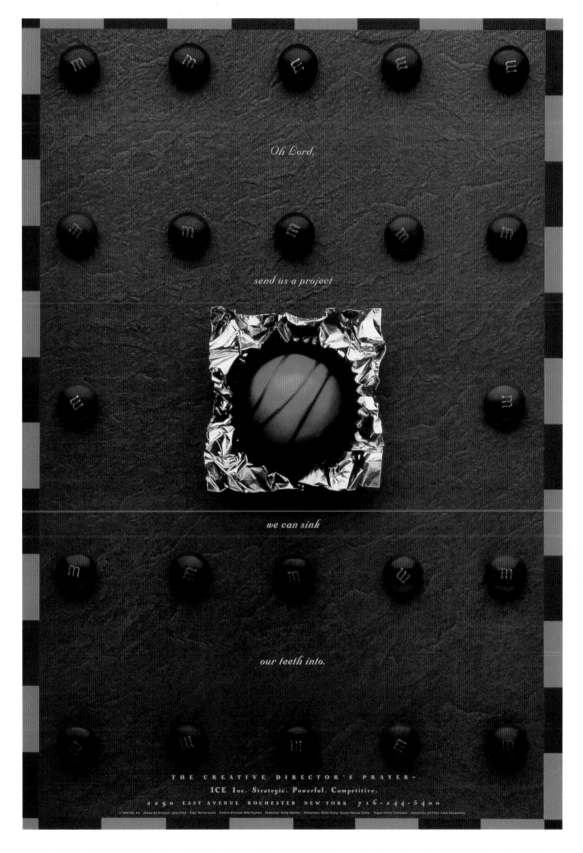

EXISTING CLIENTS, THIS POSTER ATTEMPTS TO DRAMATIZE THE DIFFERENCE BETWEEN ICE'S CREATIVE WORK AND THAT OF ITS COMPETITORS. ● 7 VORHANDENE UND POTENTIELLE KUNDEN SOLLEN HIERMIT VON DER EINMALIGKEIT DER KREATIVEN ARBEIT VON ICE ÜBERZEUGT WERDEN. ▲ 7 RÉALISÉE DANS LE CADRE D'UNE PUBLICITÉ DIRECTE, L'AFFICHE SOULIGNE LA SUPÉRIORITÉ DU TRAVAIL CRÉATIF DE L'AGENCE ICE FACE À CELUI DE LA CONCURRENCE.

1, 2 DESIGNER/CLIENT: HITOMI SAGO COUNTRY: JAPAN ■ 1, 2 THIS THREE-DIMENSIONAL INTERPRETATION OF "LETTERS" AND "WORDS" WAS THE WINNER OF THE TYPE DIRECTORS CLUB IN JAPAN 94-95 CONTEST. IT IS THE DESIGNER'S REACTION TO DIGITIZED LETTERING: SHE CUT OUT EACH LETTER AND ARRANGED THEM BEFORE THEY WERE SHOT FROM VARIOUS ANGLES. ● 1, 2 DIESE DREIDIMENSIONALE INTERPRETATION DER BEGRIFFE «BUCHSTABEN» UND «WORTE» GING IM WETTBEWERB DES TOKYO TYPE DIRECTORS CLUB 94–95 ALS GEWINNER HERVOR. DIE DESIGNERIN REAGIERT AUF DIE DIGITALE REVOLUTION: SIE SCHNITT DIE VON IHR ENTWORFENEN BUCHSTABEN AUS PAPIER UND ARRANGIERTE SIE, BEVOR

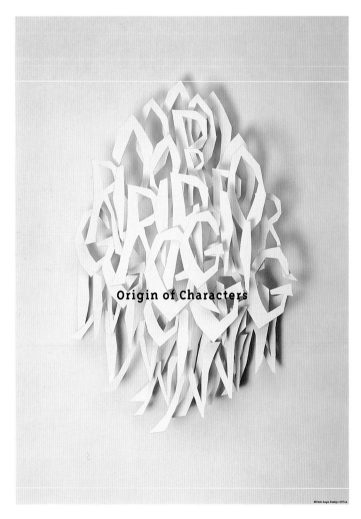

Origin of Characters

Chaos of Characters

SIE MIT UNTERSCHIEDLICHEM LICHT UND AUS VERSCHIEDENEN BLICKWINKELN PHOTOGRAPHIERT WURDEN. ▲ 1, 2 CETTE INTERPRÉTATION TRIDIMENSIONNELLE DES TERMES «LETTRES» ET «MOTS» A REMPORTÉ LE PREMIER PRIX CONCOURS DU TOKYO TYPE DIRECTORS CLUB 94–95. ELLE TRADUIT LA RÉACTION DU DESIGNER À LA RÉVOLUTION DIGITALE: ELLE A DÉCOUPÉ CHAQUE LETTRE QU'ELLE A CRÉÉ DANS DU PAPIER, PUIS LES A AGENCÉES AVANT DE LES PHOTOGRAPHIER SOUS DES ANGLES ET DES ÉCLAIRAGES DIFFÉRENTS. □ 3–6 ART DIRECTOR/DESIGNER: TAKU SATOH PHOTOGRAPHER: MEGUMU WADA CLIENT: TAKU SATOH DESIGN OFFICE INC. COUNTRY: JAPAN ■ 3–6 SELF-PROMOTIONAL POSTERS FOR A DESIGN STUDIO. ● 3–6 EIGENWERBUNG EINES DESIGN-STUDIOS. ▲ 3–6 PUBLICITÉ AUTOPROMOTIONNELLE D'UNE AGENCE DE DESIGN.

REBUILD / TAKU SATOH DESIGN OFFICE INC.
1993 TAKARA SUPER CANCHU-HI

REBUILD / TAKU SATOH DESIGN OFFICE INC.
1993 LOTTE GUM MINE LINE

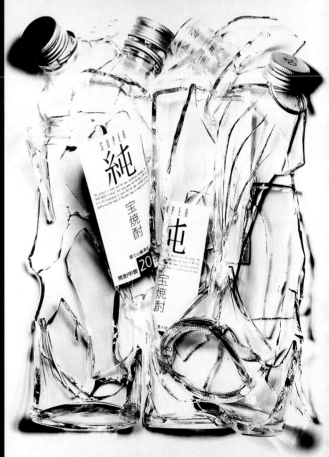

REBUILD / TAKU SATOH DESIGN OFFICE INC.

REBUILD / TAKU SATOH DESIGN OFFICE INC.
1993 TAKARA SUPER JUN

Levi's are strong.

ART DIRECTOR/DESIGNER: STEVEN SANDSTROM PHOTOGRAPHER: STEVE BONINI (1) DESIGN FIRM: SANDSTROM DESIGN ADVERTISING AGENCY: FOOTE CONE & BELDING CLIENT: LEVI STRAUSS & CO. COUNTRY: USA ■ 1, 2 TRANSIT/IN-STORE POSTERS FOR LEVI'S ORANGE TAB

AND RED TAB JEANS. ● 1, 2 FÜR DEN AUSHANG IN ÖFFENTLICHEN VERKEHRSMITTELN UND LÄDEN BESTIMMTE PLAKATE FÜR
LEVI'S JEANS-LINIEN. ▲ 1, 2 AFFICHES POUR LES JEANS LEVI'S, CONÇUE POUR LES TRANSPORTS EN COMMUN ET LES MAGASINS.

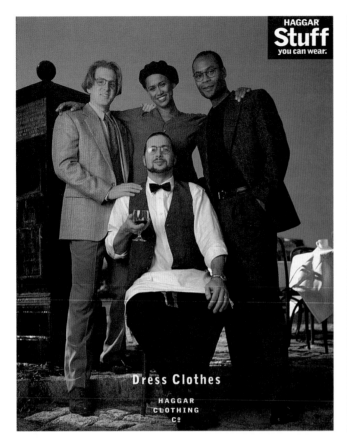

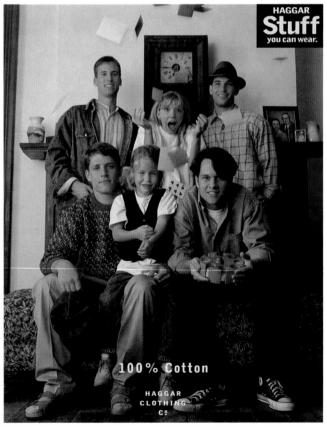

1–5 ART DIRECTORS: PAUL CURTIN, KEITH ANDERSON DESIGNER: KEITH ANDERSON PHOTOGRAPHERS: JIM ERICKSON, JAMES WOJACK, BRUCE DEBOAR ADVERTISING AGENCY: GOODBY SILVERSTEIN + PARTNERS CLIENT: HAGGAR APPAREL CO. COUNTRY: USA ■ 1–5 THESE IN-STORE POSTERS RE-INTRODUCE HAGGAR AS A MORE COMFORTABLE, MORE NATURAL, MORE CASUAL BRAND. ENVIRONMENTAL IMAGES REPRESENT DIFFERENT CLOTHING CATEGORIES, WHILE

PORTRAITS SHOW OFF THE CLOTHES THEMSELVES. ● 1–5 DIESE LADENPLAKATE DIENEN DER NEUPOSITIONIERUNG
DER KLEIDERMARKE HAGGAR, DEREN KOLLEKTIONEN NOCH BEQUEMERE, NATÜRLICHERE UND LÄSSIGERE KLEIDUNG
BIETEN. ▲ 1–5 CES AFFICHES DE P.L.V. DOIVENT REPOSITIONNER LA MARQUE DE VÊTEMENTS HAGGAR ET SA NOU-
VELLE COLLECTION QUI PROMET D'ÊTRE ENCORE PLUS CONFORTABLE, PLUS NATURELLE ET PLUS DÉCONTRACTÉE.

1 ART DIRECTOR: PAUL MATTHAEUS DESIGNER: WILL HYDE PHOTOGRAPHER: WILLIAM HAWKES ILLUSTRATOR: WILL HYDE ADVERTISING
AGENCY: MATTHAEUS HALVERSON CLIENT: VIRTUAL I-O. COUNTRY: USA ■1 THE VIRTUAL I-O POSTER WAS CREATED TO INTRO-
DUCE A NEW CATEGORY OF HEAD-MOUNTED DISPLAYS THAT ARE CAPABLE OF GENERATING HIGH-RESOLUTION 3-D IMAGERY,
ALONG WITH STEREOPHONIC SOUND. ●1 DIESE AM KOPF ZU MONTIERENDEN BILDSCHIRME LASSEN DREIDIMENSIONALE
BILDER IN HOHER AUFLÖSUNG ENTSTEHEN UND BIETEN STEREO-TON. ▲1 AFFICHE RÉALISÉE POUR LE LANCEMENT D'ÉCRANS
HAUTE DÉFINITION DE LA FIRME AMÉRICAINE VIRTUAL I-O À PORTER À MEME LA TETE, PERMETTANT LA VISUALISATION
D'IMAGES TRIDIMENSIONNELLES AVEC UN SON STÉRÉOPHONIQUE. □ 2, 3 ART DIRECTOR/DESIGNER: MAKOTO SAITO
PHOTOGRAPHERS: WALTER CHIN (2), KENJI SASAKI (3) PRODUCER: RUKI MATSUMOTO DESIGN FIRM: MAKOTO SAITO DESIGN

OFFICE INC. CLIENT: ONWARD KASHIYAMA CO., LTD. COUNTRY: JAPAN ■2, 3 POSTERS FOR A JAPANESE FASHION HOUSE.
TRANSPARENCY AND FRESHNESS WAS EXPRESSED BY USING FLUORESCENT INK (2), WHILE THE POSTER FOR THE FALL/WIN-
TER SEASON (3) WITH THE COMBINATION OF TWO PHOTOGRAPHS CONVEYS A FEELING OF THE SEASON AND THE FASHION
THAT GOES WITH IT. ●2, 3 PLAKATE FÜR EIN JAPANISCHES MODEHAUS. TRANSPARENZ UND FRISCHE (2) WURDE DURCH DIE
VERWENDUNG FLUORESZENDIERENDER FARBEN ERREICHT, WÄHREND DAS PLAKAT FÜR DIE HERBST/WINTERSAISON (3)
DURCH DIE KOMBINATION DER BEIDEN PHOTOS DAS MODISCHE KONZEPT UND DIE ENTSPRECHENDE STIMMUNG VERMITTELT.
▲ 2, 3 AFFICHES POUR UN GRAND MAGASIN DE MODE JAPONAIS. L'UTILISATION D'ENCRES FLUORESCENTES A PERMIS
D'OBTENIR L'EFFET DE TRANSPARENCE ET DE FRAICHEUR (2) DE LA PREMIERE AFFICHE. L'ATMOSPHERE RECHERCHÉE POUR
L'AFFICHE DE LA COLLECTION AUTOMNE/HIVER (3) A POUR SA PART ÉTÉ CRÉÉE PAR LA SURIMPRESSION DE DEUX PHOTOS.

You'll never know what you can do until you try. And, you'll never know how far you can go until you get there. What are you waiting for? Get in gear. It's time to shine.

1, 2 ART DIRECTOR/DESIGNER: GREGG MCGOUGH PHOTOGRAPHER: JOHN HUET ADVERTISING AGENCY: SLAUGHTER HANSON ADVERTISING CLIENT: L.A. GEAR COUNTRY: USA ■ 1, 2 EXAMPLES FROM AN ADVERTISING CAMPAIGN FOR L.A. GEAR. ● 1, 2 BEISPIELE AUS EINER ANZEIGENKAMPAGNE FÜR L.A. GEAR. ▲ 1, 2 EXEMPLES D'UNE SÉRIE D'AFFICHES POUR L.A. GEAR.

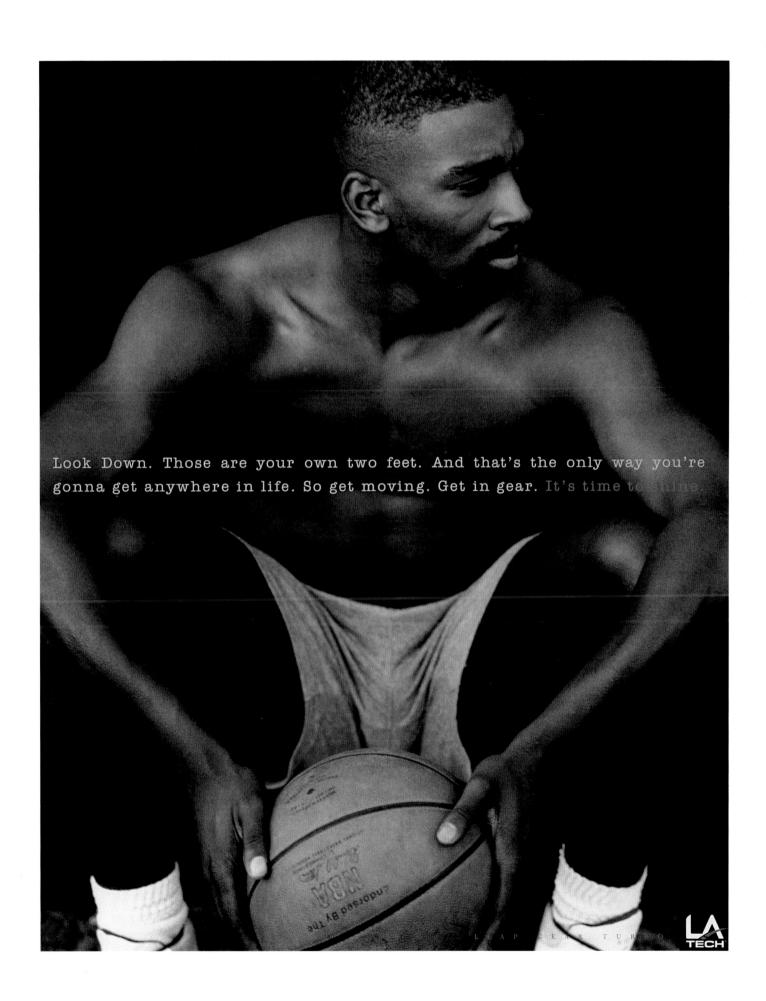

Look Down. Those are your own two feet. And that's the only way you're gonna get anywhere in life. So get moving. Get in gear. It's time to shine.

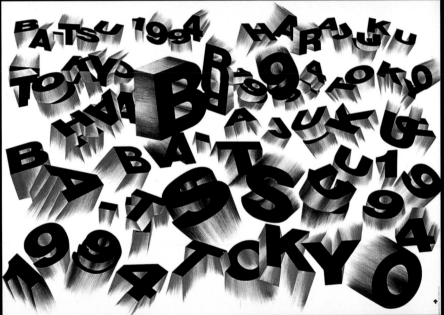

1–3 ART DIRECTOR/DESIGNER/PHOTOGRAPHER: MAKOTO SAITO DESIGN FIRM: MAKOTO SAITO DESIGN OFFICE INC. CLIENT: BA-TSU CO., LTD. COUNTRY: JAPAN ■ 1–3 POSTERS FOR AN APPAREL RETAILER WHO SELLS NATIONWIDE FROM HIS BASE IN THE HARAJUKU DISTRICT OF TOKYO, A POPULAR GATHERING PLACE FOR TEENAGERS. ● 1–3 DIE DREI PLAKATE DIESER SERIE KÖNNEN AUCH EINZELN AUFGEHÄNGT WERDEN. BA-TSU IST EIN MODEHAUS, DAS LANDESWEIT VON SEINER BASIS AUS IM HARAJUKU-DISTRIKT VON TOKIO VERKAUFT. HARAJUKU IST DER BELIEBTESTE TREFFPUNKT DER TEENAGER, UND DIE BILDER SIND AUSDRUCK DIESER JUNGEN LEUTE, IHRER SUCHE UND

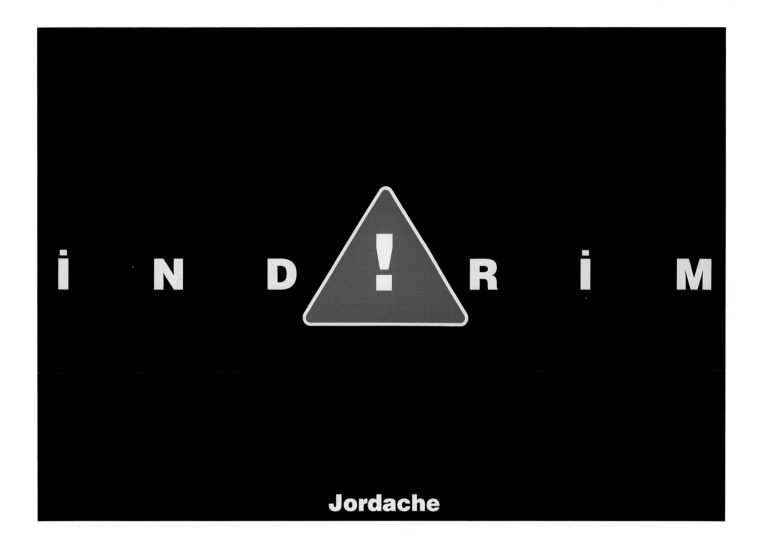

ERWARTUNGEN. ▲ 1–3 MEME PRISES SÉPARÉMENT, LES AFFICHES DE CETTE TRILOGIE GARDENT TOUT LEUR IMPACT. COMMERCIALISÉS DANS TOUT LE PAYS, LES VÊTEMENTS DE LA MARQUE JAPONAISE BA-TSU SONT FABRIQUÉS À TOKYO, DANS LE QUARTIER DE HARAJUKU QUI EST AUSSI LE LIEU DE RENCONTRE PRIVILÉGIÉ DES ADOLESCENTS. A L'IMAGE DE CES JEUNES, LES AFFICHES TRADUISENT LEURS ASPIRATIONS ET LEURS ATTENTES. □ 4 ART DIRECTOR/DESIGNER: SAHIN AYMERGEN COPYWRITER: DENIZ BARLAS DESIGN FIRM: PARS/MCCANN-ERICKSON CLIENT: JORDACHE JEANS COUNTRY: TURKEY ■ 4 ANNOUNCEMENT OF A PRICE REDUCTION AT JORDACHE JEANS. ● 4 »ROTE PREISE« FÜR JORDACHE JEANS. ▲ 4 AFFICHE ANNONÇANT UNE PROMOTION SPÉCIALE SUR LES JEANS JORDACHE.

(THIS SPREAD) 1–4 ART DIRECTOR: NIKKO AMANDONICO DESIGNER: PAUL BARRY (3, 4) PHOTOGRAPHER: MAGNUS REED PHOTODIRECTOR: MAGNUS SKOGSBERG COPYWRITER: TIA BORRI DESIGN FIRM: ENERGY PROJECT CLIENT: BENETTON GROUP COUNTRY: ITALY ■ 1–4 EXAMPLES FROM A SERIES OF POSTERS FOR SISLEY FASHION REFERRING TO PARTICULAR CITIES. HERE: CAPE TOWN AND OSAKA. ● 1–4 BEISPIELE AUS EINER PLAKATSERIE FÜR SISLEY-MODE, DIE SICH AUF BESTIMMTE ORTE BEZIEHT, HIER KAPSTADT UND OSAKA. ▲ 1–4 EXEMPLES D'UNE SÉRIE D'AFFICHES SISLEY CONSACRÉE À DIVERSES VILLES, ICI LE CAP ET OSAKA. 1–4 ART DIRECTOR: NIKKO AMANDONICO DESIGNER: PAUL BARRY (3, 4) PHOTOGRAPHER: MAGNUS REED PHOTODIRECTOR: MAGNUS SKOGSBERG COPYWRITER: TIA BORRI DESIGN FIRM: ENERGY PROJECT CLIENT: BENETTON GROUP COUNTRY: ITALY ■ 1–4 EXAMPLES FROM A SERIES OF POSTERS FOR SISLEY FASHION REFERRING TO PARTICULAR CITIES. HERE: CAPE TOWN AND OSAKA. ● 1–4 BEISPIELE AUS EINER PLAKATSERIE FÜR SISLEY-MODE, DIE SICH AUF BESTIMMTE ORTE BEZIEHT, HIER KAPSTADT UND OSAKA. ▲ 1–4 EXEMPLES D'UNE SÉRIE D'AFFICHES SISLEY CONSACRÉE À DIVERSES VILLES, ICI LE CAP ET OSAKA. ■ (FOLLOWING SPREAD) ● 1 ART DIRECTOR/DESIGNER: KEVIN FLATT ILLUSTRATOR: STEVE JOHNSON, LOU FRANCHER ADVERTISING AGENCY: NIKE DESIGN CLIENT: NIKE, INC. COUNTRY: USA ■ 1 PLAYING ON BOTH THE STEPPING

 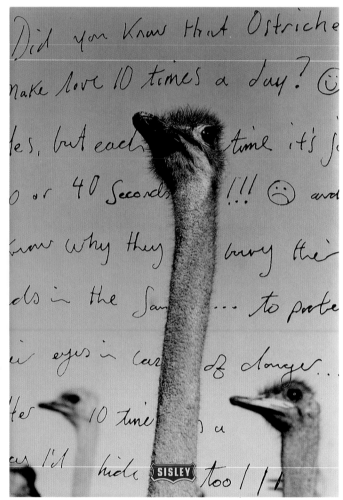

MOTION OF THE POPULAR AEROBIC EXERCISE, AND MARCEL DUCHAMP'S FAMOUS PAINTING "NUDE DESCENDING A STAIR-CASE," THIS POSTER USES A QUOTE FROM HELEN KELLER TO PROVIDE AN INSPIRATIONAL MESSAGE ABOUT INNER DRIVE. ● 1 EINE ANSPIELUNG AUF AEROBIC WIE AUCH AUF MARCEL DUCHAMPS'S BERÜHMTES BILD «AKT, EINE TREPPE HERABSTEIGEND». BEI DIESEM PLAKAT MIT EINEM ZITAT VON HELEN KELLER GEHT ES UM DEN INNEREN ANTRIEB. ▲ 1 INSPIRÉE DE L'AÉROBIC ET DU CÉLÈBRE TABLEAU DE MARCEL DUCHAMP NU DESCENDANT UN ESCALIER, CETTE AFFICHE UTILISE UNE CITATION D'HELEN KELLER POUR ÉVOQUER L'ÉNERGIE VITALE. ■ 2 CREATIVE DIRECTORS: DAN WIEDEN, SUSAN HOFFMAN, JIM RISWOLD, JAMIE BARRETT ART DIRECTOR: JOHN C. JAY DESIGNER: IMIN PAO COPYWRITER: JIMMY SMITH PHOTOGRAPHER: JOHN HUET ADVERTISING AGENCY: WIEDEN & KENNEDY CLIENT: NIKE, INC. COUNTRY: USA ■ 2 THIS CAMPAIGN IS PART OF THE NIKE OVERALL EFFORT ACKNOWLEDGING THE UNIQUE CULTURE OF BASKETBALL IN NEW YORK CITY, WHICH COMBINES AGGRESSIVENESS WITH AGILI-TY AND FLAIR FOR STYLE. ● 2 DIESES PLAKAT GEHÖRT ZU EINER NIKE-KAMPAGNE, DIE DER EINZIGARTIGEN BASKETBALL-KULTUR IN NEW YORK GEWIDMET IST: AGGRESSIVITÄT VERBUNDEN MIT BEWEGLICHKEIT UND STIL. ▲ 2 AFFICHE NIKE DÉDIÉE AU BASKET-BALL «NEW-YORKAIS», VÉRITABLE INSTITUTION ET SUBTIL MÉLANGE D'AGRESSIVITÉ, D'ADRESSE ET D'ÉLÉGANCE.

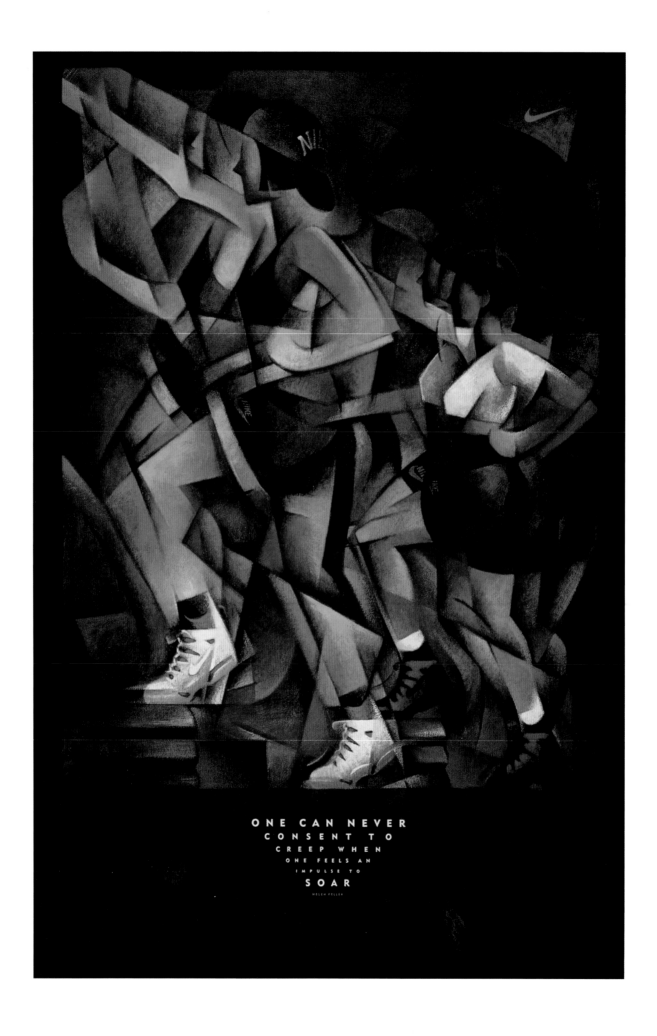

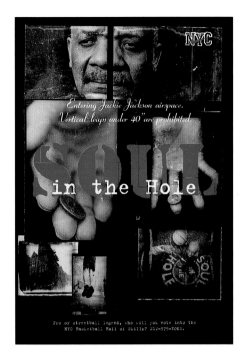

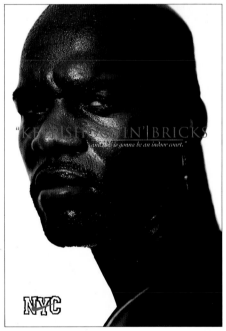

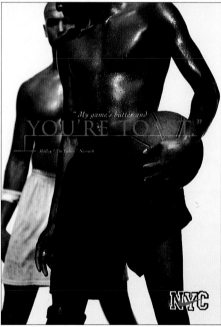

1–3 CREATIVE DIRECTORS: DAN WIEDEN, SUSAN HOFFMAN, JOHN C. JAY ART DIRECTOR: YOUNG KIM PHOTOGRAPHER: EXUM COPYWRITER: JIMMY SMITH ADVERTISING AGENCY: WIEDEN & KENNEDY CLIENT: NIKE, INC. COUNTRY: USA ■ 1–3 THE "COURTS" POSTERS—PART OF THE NIKE NYC CAMPAIGN THAT CELEBRATES BASKETBALL IN NEW YORK CITY—SPECIFICALLY HONOR THE LOCAL NEIGHBORHOOD LEGENDS AND THE PLAYGROUND COURTS WHERE THEY DEMONSTRATE THEIR SKILLS. ● 1–3 DIESE PLAKATE SIND TEIL DER NIKE-KAMPAGNE, DIE DER BASKETBALL-KULTUR IN NEW YORK GEWIDMET IST. HIER GEHT ES UM DIE ZU LEGENDEN GEWORDENEN SPIELER AUS DER NÄCHSTEN NACHBARSCHAFT UND UM DIE SPORTPLÄTZE, AUF DENEN SIE ZU HAUSE SIND. ▲ 1–3 «LES STARS DU BASKET COTÉ COUR». AFFICHES NIKE CONSACRÉES AUX STARS NEW-YORKAISES DU BAS-KET, ÉLEVÉES AU RANG DE LÉGENDE. □ 4–6 CREATIVE DIRECTORS: DAN WIEDEN, SUSAN HOFFMAN, JIM RISWOLD, JAMIE BARRETT ART DIRECTOR: JOHN C. JAY DESIGNER: IMIN PAO COPYWRITER: JIMMY SMITH PHOTOGRAPHER: JOHN HUET ADVERTISING AGENCY: WIEDEN & KENNEDY CLIENT: NIKE, INC. COUNTRY: USA ■ 4–6 THIS CAMPAIGN IS PART OF THE NIKE OVERALL EFFORT ACKNOWLEDGING THE UNIQUE CULTURE OF BASKETBALL IN NEW YORK CITY, WHICH COMBINES AGGRESSIVENESS WITH AGILI-TY AND FLAIR FOR STYLE. ● 4–6 DIESE PLAKATE GEHÖREN ZU EINER NIKE-KAMPAGNE, DIE DER EINZIGARTIGEN BASKETBALL-KULTUR IN NEW YORK GEWIDMET IST: AGGRESSIVITÄT VERBUNDEN MIT BEWEGLICHKEIT UND STIL. ▲ 4–6 AFFICHE NIKE DÉDIÉE AU BASKET-BALL «NEW-YORKAIS», VÉRITABLE INSTITUTION ET SUBTILE MÉLANGE D'AGRESSIVITÉ, D'ADRESSE ET D'ÉLÉGANCE. □ 7 ART DIRECTOR/DESIGNER: GUIDO BROUWERS PHOTOGRAPHER: PETE STONE ADVERTISING AGENCY: NIKE DESIGN CLIENT: NIKE INC. COUNTRY: USA ■ 7 ANFERNEE HARDAWAY, ONE OF THE "NEW SCHOOL" OF NBA SUPER STARS. ● 7 «DIE ZUKUNFT HAT BEGONNEN» – BASKETBALLSPIELER ANFERNEE HARDAWAY WIRBT FÜR NIKE. ▲ 7 ANFERNEE HARDAWAY, JOUEUR DE L'ÉQUIPE DE BASKET-BALL NEW-YORKAISE, POUR UNE PUBLICITÉ NIKE. □ 8 ART DIRECTOR/DESIGNER: MICHAEL TIEDY PHOTOGRAPHER: KAREN MOSKOWITZ ADVERTISING AGENCY: NIKE DESIGN CLIENT: NIKE INC. COUNTRY: USA ■ 8 THE GOAL OF THE

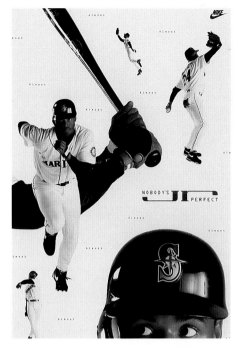

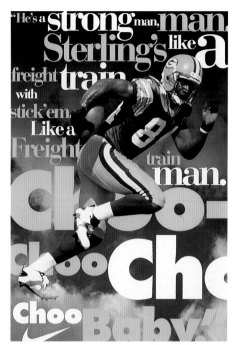

"ALMOST NOBODY IS PERFECT" POSTER WAS TO ILLUSTRATE KEN GRIFFEY'S SUCCESS AS A COMPLETE BASKETBALL PLAYER THROUGH THE USE OF MULTIPLE IMAGES. ● 8 «FAST NIEMAND IST PERFEKT» – HIER GEHT ES UM KEN GRIFFEYS ERFOLG ALS BASKETBALL-SPIELER. ▲ 8 «PERSONNE N'EST PARFAIT OU PRESQUE.» PUBLICITÉ NIKE VANTANT LES EXPLOITS DU BASKET-TEUR KEN GRIFFEY. □ 9 ART DIRECTOR/DESIGNER: RON DUMAS PHOTOGRAPHER: ANDY HAYT ADVERTISING AGENCY: NIKE DESIGN CLIENT: NIKE INC. COUNTRY: USA ■ 9 THE POSTER'S HEADLINE TIES INTO A COMMERCIAL WITH DENNIS HOPPER, AND ITS TYPE WAS EMPHASIZED IN A WAY THAT COMPLEMENTED THE PHOTOGRAPH OF FOOTBALL PLAYER STERLING SHARPE. ● 9 DIE HEADLINE DIESES NIKE-PLAKATES BEZIEHT SICH AUF EINEN TV-SPOT MIT DENNIS HOPPER. GEZEIGT IST DER FOOTBALL STAR STERLING SHARPE. ▲ 9 STERLING SHARPE, STAR DU FOOTBALL AMÉRICAIN, POUR UNE PUBLICITÉ NIKE. L'ACCROCHE, QUI FAIT RÉFÉRENCE À UN SPOT TOURNÉ AVEC UNE AUTRE STAR, RENFORCE ENCORE L'IMPACT DE L'AFFICHE. □ 10 ART DIRECTOR/DESIGNER: KEVIN FLATT PHOTOGRAPHERS: MARK HANAUER, DAVID SUTHERLAND ADVERTISING AGENCY: NIKE DESIGN .010 MICHAEL IRVIN, THE WIDE-RECEIVER FOR THE DALLAS COWBOYS KNOWN FOR HIS ABILITY TO MAKE INCREDIBLE LEAP-ING CATCHES, IS PHOTOGRAPHED AS IF HE WERE A PLANE COMING IN FOR AN END ZONE LANDING WITH BALL IN HAND. ● 10 MICHAEL IRVIN VOM FOOTBALL-TEAM DALLAS COWBOYS IN AKTION. ER IST FÜR SEINE SPRUNGKRAFT BERÜHMT. ▲ 10 AFFICHE NIKE ILLUSTRANT MICHAEL IRVIN «SUSPENDU» EN PLEIN VOL, FOOTBALLEUR DE L'ÉQUIPE DES «DALLAS COWBOYS», CÉLÈBRE POUR SES PLAQUAGES MAGIQUES. □ 11 ART DIRECTOR/DESIGNER: MICHAEL TIEDY PHOTOGRAPHER: STEPHEN WILKES ADVERTISING AGENCY: NIKE DESIGN CLIENT: NIKE INC. COUNTRY: USA ■ 11 THE DESIGN, COPY, AND PHOTOGRAPHY OF THE "BACK TO BASICS" POSTER WAS CREATED TO CONVEY THE MESSAGE THAT ANDRE AGASSI IS BACK FROM INJURY AND CONCENTRATING ON THE STYLE OF PLAY THAT MADE HIM SUCCESSFUL. ● 11 DIE BOTSCHAFT DES 'BACK-TO-BASICS'-PLAKATES IST, DASS ANDRÉ

AGASSI NACH SEINER VERLETZUNG WIEDER DA IST UND SICH AUF DEN STIL BESINNT, DER IHN ZU EINEM DER ERFOLGRE-
ICHSTEN TENNISSPIELER MACHTE. ▲ 11 «BACK TO BASICS». AFFICHE NIKE MONTRANT ANDRÉ AGASSI: REMIS DE SES
BLESSURES, LE FAMEUX TENNISMAN AMÉRICAIN ENTEND RETROUVER LE STYLE QUI LUI A VALU DE S'AFFIRMER COMME
L'UNE DES PREMIERES TETES DE SÉRIE. □ 12 ART DIRECTOR/DESIGNER: KEVIN FLATT PHOTOGRAPHER: TONY DIZINNO
ILLUSTRATOR: MARGO CHASE ADVERTISING AGENCY: NIKE DESIGN CLIENT: NIKE INC. COUNTRY: USA ■ 12 DENNIS RODMAN, THE
"BAD BOY" OF PROFESSIONAL BASKETBALL, IS ALWAYS GRABBING ATTENTION WITH HIS EVER-CHANGING HAIR COLOR,
BODY PIERCING, AND TATOOS. ● 12 DENNIS RODMAN, DER «BAD-BOY» DES PROFI-BASKETBALLS, MACHT MIT STÄNDIG
WECHSELNDER HAARFARBE, PIERCINGS UND TÄTOWIERUNGEN AUF SICH AUFMERKSAM. ▲ 12 DENNIS RODMAN, LE MAUVAIS
GARÇON DU BASKET-BALL PROFESSIONNEL. COIFFURES DÉCAPANTES, PIERCINGS ET TATOUAGES, TOUT EST BON POUR
ATTIRER L'ATTENTION. ■ (THIS SPREAD) 1 ART DIRECTOR: JEFF WEITHMAN DESIGNERS: JEFF WEITHMAN, CRAIG BAREZ
ADVERTISING AGENCY: NIKE DESIGN CLIENT: NIKE INC. COUNTRY: USA ■1 TO CELEBRATE NATIONAL BLACK HISTORY MONTH,
THIS POSTER INTEGRATES THE NAMES OF THOSE WHO LAID THE GROUNDWORK FOR THE CIVIL RIGHTS MOVEMENT, THE SIG-
NIFICANT PROTESTS THAT LED TO THE VOTING RIGHTS ACT, AND THE ACCOMPLISHMENTS OF EARLY CIVIL RIGHTS PIO-
NEERS. ● 1 IM RAHMEN EINES «MONATS DER GESCHICHTE DER SCHWARZEN BEVÖLKERUNG DER USA» ENTSTANDENES

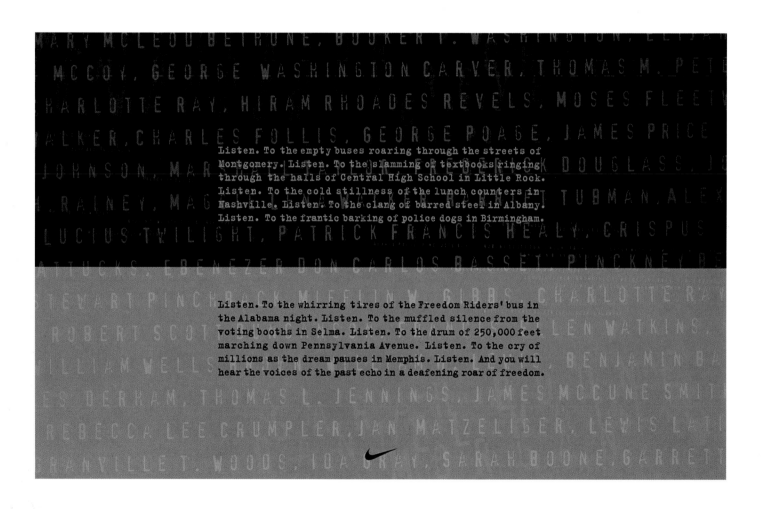

PLAKAT. ES FÜHRT DIE NAMEN ALL JENER AUF, DIE DIE GRUNDLAGEN FÜR DIE BÜRGERRECHTSBEWEGUNGEN UND FÜR
WICHTIGE PROTESTAKTIONEN SCHUFEN, DIE ZUM GESETZLICH VERBRIEFTEN WAHLRECHT FÜHRTEN, UND ES BERICHTET VON
DEN ERFOLGEN DER ERSTEN BÜRGERRECHTLER. ▲1 RÉALISÉE DANS LE CADRE D'UN MOIS CONSACRÉ À L'HISTOIRE DU PEUPLE
NOIR AMÉRICAIN, CETTE AFFICHE ÉNUMERE TOUTES LES PERSONNALITÉS MARQUANTES QUI SE SONT BATTUES POUR LA
RECONNAISSANCE DES DROITS CIVILS DES NOIRS EN AMÉRIQUE. □ 2, 4 CREATIVE DIRECTORS: DAN WIEDEN, SUSAN HOFFMAN
ART DIRECTOR: JOHN C. JAY DESIGNER: IMIN PAO, NICOLE MISITI PHOTOGRAPHER: BRAD HARRIS COPYWRITER: JIMMY SMITH
ADVERTISING AGENCY: WIEDEN & KENNEDY CLIENT: NIKE INC. COUNTRY: USA ■2, 4 THIS WAS THE LAUNCH OF A NIKE EFFORT TO
SALUTE THE UNIQUE CHARACTER OF BASKETBALL IN LOS ANGELES. ● 2, 4 THEMA DIESER NIKE-KAMPAGNE IST DIE
BASKETBALL-KULTUR IN LOS ANGELES. ▲2,4 AFFICHES NIKE CÉLÉBRANT LA «CULTURE» DU BASKET-BALL À LOS ANGELES. □
3 CREATIVE DIRECTORS: DAN WIEDEN, SUSAN HOFFMAN ART DIRECTOR: JOHN C. JAY DESIGNER: IMIN PAO ILLUSTRATOR: JAVIER
MICHAELSKI ADVERTISING AGENCY: WIEDEN & KENNEDY CLIENT: NIKE INC. COUNTRY: USA ■3 THIS CAMPAIGN IS A CONTINUATION
OF THE "NIKE NYC" EFFORT TO HIGHLIGHT THE IMPORTANCE OF BASKETBALL TO THE CITY OF NEW YORK. ● 3 DIESE
KAMPAGNE IST EINE FORTSETZUNG VON NIKES NEW-YORK-CITY-THEMA, DER BEDEUTUNG VON BASKETBALL FÜR DIE STADT. ▲
3 AFFICHE NIKE REPRENANT LE THEME D'UNE PRÉCÉDENTE CAMPAGNE SUR LE CULTE VOUÉ AU BASKET-BALL À NEW YORK.

1, 3 ART DIRECTOR: REINER HEBE COPYWRITER: REINER HEBE PHOTOGRAPHER: LOTHAR BERTRAMS DESIGN FIRM: HEBE WERBUNG & DESIGN CLIENT: KENNY S. GMBH COUNTRY: GERMANY ■ 1, 3 IN-STORE POSTERS FOR A SMALL REGIONAL BRAND OF JEANS. ● 1, 3 LADENPLAKATE FÜR EINEN KLEINEN, REGIONAL BEKANNTEN JEANS-HERSTELLER. ▲ 1, 3 AFFICHE DE MAGASIN POUR UN PETIT FABRICANT DE JEANS RENOMMÉ. □ 2 ART DIRECTOR/COPYWRITER: REINER HEBE PHOTOGRAPHER: CORINNA MÜLLER-VOSS DESIGN FIRM: HEBE WERBUNG & DESIGN CLIENT: SCHUHHAUS WERDICH GMBH & CO. COUNTRY: GERMANY ■ 2 "LOVERS." ROMEO: "HOW MANY PROOFS OF MY LOVE DO I STILL HAVE TO GIVE YOU?" JULIET: "ONE PAIR, MY LOVE, ONLY ONE PAIR." ● 2 BEISPIEL AUS EINER SERIE VON LADENPLAKATEN FÜR EIN SCHUHHAUS. ▲ 2 AFFICHE PUB-LICITAIRE POUR UN MAGASIN DE CHAUSSURES. □ 4, 6 ART DIRECTOR: JOE PARSLEY DESIGNERS: JOE PARSLEY (4, 6), CHRIS MCCULLICK (4) PHOTOGRAPHERS: CHRIS WIMPEY (4), LIBERO DIZINNO (6) ILLUSTRATOR: CHRIS MCCULLICK COPYWRITER: STANLEY HAINSWORTH AGENCY: NIKE DESIGN CLIENT: NIKE INC. COUNTRY: USA ■ 4, 6 OUTDOOR POSTERS ILLUSTRATING THE ACTION AND EXCITEMENT OF MOUNTAIN BIKING AND SNOWBOARDING. ● 4, 6 DIE MIT SNOWBOARDS UND MOUNTAIN BIKES VERBUNDENE SPORTLICHE TÄTIGKEIT UND FREUDE SIND GEGENSTAND DIESER PLAKATE. ▲ 4, 6 CES AFFICHES PRÉSENTENT LES ACTIVITÉS

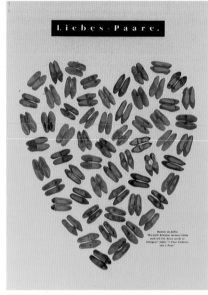

LIÉES AU SNOWBOARD ET AU V.T.T. ET LES PLAISIRS QU'ILS PROCURENT. □ 5 CREATIVE DIRECTOR: MAGGIE GROSS DESIGNER: GARETH DEBENHAM COPYWRITER: ANNE BUHL PHOTOGRAPHY: STOCK ADVERTISING AGENCY: GAP ADVERTISING CLIENT: GAP COUNTRY: USA ■ 5 CREATED TO DESIGNATE THE MEN'S AND WOMEN'S SWIM DEPARTMENTS WITHIN GAP STORES, THIS POSTER WAS INTENDED TO BE TRIMMED DOWN IN ORDER TO ACCOMODATE INDIVIDUAL SPACE REQUIREMENTS. ● 5 DIESES PLAKAT, DAS SICH DEN INDIVIDUELLEN RAUMVERHÄLTNISSEN ANPASSEN LÄSST, IST FÜR DIE KENNZEICHNUNG DER BADEMODEN-ABTEILUNGEN IN DEN GAP-WARENHÄUSERN BESTIMMT. ▲ 5 AFFICHE INDIQUANT LE RAYON MAILLOTS DE BAIN DANS LES GRANDS MAGASINS GAP. LE FORMAT PEUT ETRE ADAPTÉ EN FONCTION DE L'ESPACE DISPONIBLE. □ 7 ART DIRECTOR/DESIGNER/PHOTOGRAPHER: LARRY KUNKEL PUBLISHER: CELESTIAL ARTS COUNTRY: USA ■ 7 COMPRISING MORE THAN 80 SEPARATE PHOTOGRAPHS OF BERRIES AND BERRY VINES, THIS POSTER—CREATED FOR SALE TO THE PUBLIC— WAS DESIGNED TO REVEAL THE DETAILED, DIMENSIONAL BEAUTY OF THE FRUIT. ● 7 DAS AUS ÜBER 80 SEPARATEN AUFNAHMEN VON BEEREN UND TRAUBEN BESTEHENDE PLAKAT IST GANZ DER SCHÖNHEIT DER WEINTRAUBE GEWIDMET UND FÜR DEN VERKAUF BESTIMMT. ▲ 7 «L'ART ET LES FRUITS». PLUS DE 80 IMAGES ONT ÉTÉ NÉCESSAIRES À LA RÉALISATION DE CETTE AFFICHE DESTINÉE À LA VENTE.

ƒ BERRIES

THE BERRIES • TOP LEFT CORNER: Blue Ray & O'Neil blueberries, TO THE RIGHT: Oregon evergreen thornless wild blackberry, Tayberry, Golden raspberries, BELOW: Cape gooseberry, LEFT: Pixwell gooseberries (solo & branchlet), Delight blueberries (rubbed), Marionberry, Orange raspberries, RIGHT: Choctaw blackberries, Red Lake currants, BELOW: Japanese wineberries, Brandywine raspberries, BACK LEFT BELOW TITLE: Randall black currants, RIGHT: Joe Mullo winter red raspberries, Keriberries, "Fraises des bois" (Alpine wild strawberries), BELOW: Pineapple wild strawberries, Elderberries, Lucretia dewberry, LOWER RIGHT CORNER: Brandywine (aerial view), BELOW: Jewel blackcap raspberries, LEFT: Olallieberry, DOWN LEFT: Garden huckleberries, LOWER LEFT: Kiwi & Goldie raspberries, Berkeley blueberries, LOWER LEFT CENTER: Purple Royalty raspberry, TO Mulberries (branch & single) - courtesy Iron Horse Vineyards, OR Boysenberry (thornless), BELOW: Lingonberries, Loganberry, DOWN: Cranberries, THIRD RIGHT: Commander strawberry - courtesy Driscoll's.

GROWN by Joe's 21st Century Berries at Green Valley Specialty Farms, Watsonville • TELEPHONE: 408.848.0146   ART/WORK by Larry Kunkel, San Francisco   PUBLISHED by Celestial Arts, Post Office Box 7327, Berkeley, California 94707 • TELEPHONE: 510.559.1000

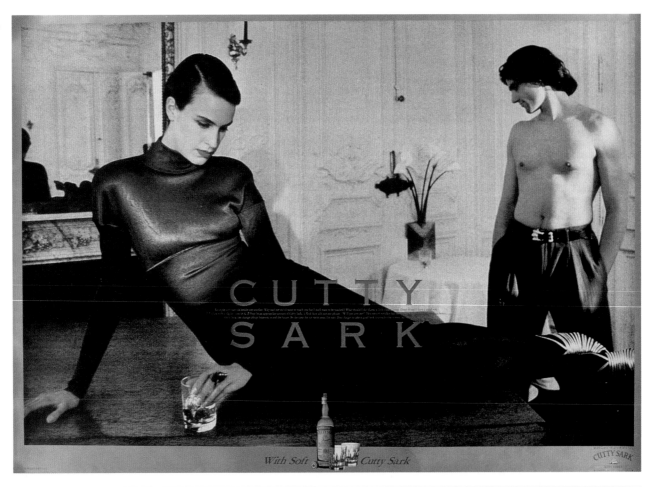

(PRECEDING SPREAD) 1–4 ART DIRECTOR/DESIGNER: TAKASHI KINGA PHOTOGRAPHERS: SHEILA METZNER (1, 3, 4), LOIS GREENFIELD (2) COPYWRITERS: TETUYA SAKOTA (1, 3, 4), HIROSHI AIZAWA (2) DESIGN FIRM: HAKUHODO INC. CLIENT: CUTTY SARK JAPAN COUNTRY: JAPAN ■ 1–4 "IT IS BEST WITH A SMOOTH SCOTCH." A SERIES OF POSTERS FOR CUTTY SARK WHISKY. ● (VORANGEHENDE DOPPELSEITE) 1–4 «ES IST AM SCHÖNSTEN MIT EINEM MILDEN SCOTCH», EINE PLAKATSERIE FÜR WHISKY DER MARKE CUTTY SARK. ▲ (DOUBLE PAGE PRÉCÉDENTE) 1–4 «DOUCEUR ET VOLUPTÉ, LE SCOTCH DES INSTANTS PRIVILÉGIÉS». SÉRIE D'AFFICHES POUR LE WHISKY CUTTY SARK. □ (THIS SPREAD) 1–3 ART DIRECTOR/DESIGNER: STEVEN SANDSTROM PHOTOGRAPHER: PETE STONE DESIGN FIRMS: SANDSTROM DESIGN, ARTSY-FARTSY PRODUCTIONS CLIENT: BURGERVILLE COUNTRY: USA ■ 1 AN IN-STORE POSTER PROMOTING A MEATLESS HAMBURGER. ■ 2 AN IN-STORE POSTER PROMOTING COCA-COLA WITH A CLASSIC COKE GLASS GIFT-WITH-PURCHASE OFFER. ■ 3 AN IN-STORE POSTER TO BE

MOUNTED ON FREEZERS STOCKED WITH POPSICLES. ● 1 «EIGENTLICH SCHMECKT ES MEHR NACH EINEM HAMBURGER ALS NACH EINEM GARTEN.» FÜR DEN INNENAUSHANG BESTIMMTES PLAKAT FÜR FLEISCHLOSE HAMBURGER. ● 2 «NEUE GLÄSER IN WENIGER ALS FÜNF MINUTEN.» LADENPLAKAT FÜR COCA-COLA: BEIM KAUF EINER COCA-COLA ERHÄLT MAN EIN KLASSI- SCHES COCA-COLA-GLAS. ● 3 «WIR BRAUCHEN DIE GEFRIERTRUHEN NICHT FÜR RINDFLEISCH, WIR BENUTZEN SIE FÜR EIS AM STIEL.» DAS PLAKAT WIRD AUF GEFRIERTRUHEN ANGEBRACHT. ▲ 1 «EN FAIT, ÇA A PLUS LE GOÛT D'UN HAMBURGER QUE CELUI D'UN JARDIN POTAGER!» AFFICHE DE PLV POUR UN HAMBURGER VÉGÉTARIEN. ▲ 2 «DE NOUVEAUX VERRES EN MOINS DE CINQ MINUTES.» AFFICHE DE PLV POUR COCA-COLA. A L'ACHAT D'UN COCA-COLA, LE CLIENT REÇOIT UN VERRE COCA-COLA. ▲ 3 «NOUS N'AVONS PAS BESOIN DE CONGÉLATEURS POUR DU BŒUF – ALORS NOUS LES UTILISONS POUR LES POPSICLE.» AFFICHE DE PLV DESTINÉE À ÊTRE PLACÉE SUR LES CONGÉLATEURS REMPLIS DE GLACES POPSICLE.

WE DON'T NEED FREEZERS *for* BEEF- SO WE'RE USING THEM *for* POPSICLES.®

Order any Burgerville Value Meal and Popsicles are on us.

1–4 ART DIRECTORS: ALEXANDER BARTEL, FLORIAN FINK, OLIVER DIEHR, MARKUS LANGE PHOTOGRAPHER: NIKO SCHMID-BURGK
COPYWRITER: BERND FRIEDRICH DESIGN FIRM: HEYE + PARTNER GMBH CLIENT: MCDONALD'S WERBE-GES.M.B.H. COUNTRY: AUSTRIA ■
1–4 "MCWHAT?" "LOOK, JUST LIKE AT HOME." "LET THEM THERE." "WHEN WILL THEY FINALLY HAVE A SPECIAL SENIOR'S PACK?"
A POSTER SERIES FOR MCDONALD'S IN AUSTRIA. ● 1–4 PLAKATREIHE FÜR MCDONALD'S IN ÖSTERREICH. ▲ 1–4 «MAC QUOI?»;
«TU VOIS, C'EST COMME À LA MAISON!»; «LAISSE TOMBER!»; «ET LE MENU GRAND-PÈRE, C'EST POUR QUAND?». SÉRIE
D'AFFICHES POUR MCDONALD'S AUTRICHE. □ 5–7 ART DIRECTOR: DÄNI SULZER DESIGNER: FREDY STEINER PHOTOGRAPHER: NICOLAS
MONKEWITZ COPYWRITER: FRANK BODIN DESIGN FIRM: AEBI, STREBEL AG, WERBEAGENTUR BSW CLIENT: WARTECK BRAUEREI UND

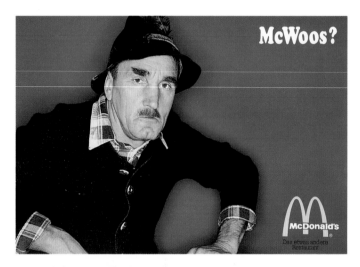

GETRÄNKE AG COUNTRY: SWITZERLAND ■ 5–7 "THE OUTRAGEOUS BEER." THESE POSERS PROMOTE WARTECK AS THE BEER FOR PAS-
SIONATE BEER DRINKERS WHO WOULD LOVE TO TAP THEIR BEER IN ANY PLACE AND AT ANY TIME. ● 5–7 DIE BOTSCHAFT DIESER
PLAKATE: WARTEK IST DAS BIER FÜR BIERLIEBHABER, DIE AM LIEBSTEN IMMER UND ÜBERALL EINES ZAPFEN WÜRDEN. DIE ANWORT
EINES PRIMÄR REGIONALEN UNTERNEHMENS ANGESICHTS DER DRAMATISCHEN VERÄNDERUNGEN IM BIERMARKT DURCH STEIGENDE
IMPORTKONKURRENZ UND PREISVERFALL IST DIE KONZENTRATION AUF DIE EIGENEN STÄRKEN. ▲ 5–7 «UNE WARTECK SINON RIEN!».
WARTECK EST LA BIÈRE DES CONNAISSEURS PRÊTS À DESSERRER LEUR COL D'UN CRAN N'IMPORTE OÙ, N'IMPORTE QUAND POUR UNE
WARTECK AVEC OU SANS FAUX COL. POUR UNE BIÈRE RÉGIONALE DE QUALITÉ SUPÉRIEURE, LE SEUL MOYEN DE LUTTER CONTRE LA
CONCURRENCE DÉLOYALE DES BIÈRES ÉTRANGÈRES IMPORTÉES À BAS PRIX EST DE SE CONCENTRER SUR SES PROPRES FORCES.

DAS UNVERSCHÄMTE BIER.

DAS UNVERSCHÄMTE BIER.

DAS UNVERSCHÄMTE BIER.

1 ART DIRECTOR/DESIGNER: SHIN MATSUNAGA DESIGN FIRM: SHIN MATSUNAGA DESIGN INC. CLIENT: IWASAKI ELECTRIC CO. COUNTRY: JAPAN ■ 1 IMAGE POSTER FOR A LIGHTING MANUFACTURER. THE HEADLINE PROMISES ADVANCED, HIGH QUALITY LIGHTING THAT PROVIDES A GENTLE, COMFORTABLE LIGHT. ● 1 IMAGE-PLAKAT FÜR EINEN BELEUCHTUNGSHERSTELLER. DIE HEADLINE VERSPRICHT ZUKUNFTSORIENTIERTE, HOCHWERTIGE BELEUCHTUNG, DIE DEM MENSCHEN SANFTES, ANGENEHMES LICHT GIBT. ▲ 1 PUBLICITÉ

POUR UN FABRICANT DE LUMINAIRES. LE SLOGAN PROMET UN ÉCLAIRAGE EXCEPTIONNEL, RÉSOLUMENT NOVATEUR, QUI CONFÈRE À L'HABITAT UNE LUMIÈRE DOUCE ET AGRÉABLE. □ 2 ART DIRECTOR: ADELAIDE ACERBI DESIGN FIRM: LAMBDA S.R.L. CLIENT: DRIADE COUNTRY: ITALY ■ 2 A DIRECT-MAIL POSTER FOR DESIGNER FURNITURE. ● 2 VORDERSEITE EINES FÜR DEN DIREKTVERSAND BE-STIMMTEN PLAKATES FÜR DESIGNER-MÖBEL. ▲ 2 RECTO D'UNE AFFICHE DE PUBLIPOSTAGE POUR DES MEUBLES DESIGN.

ERCO

We make light work

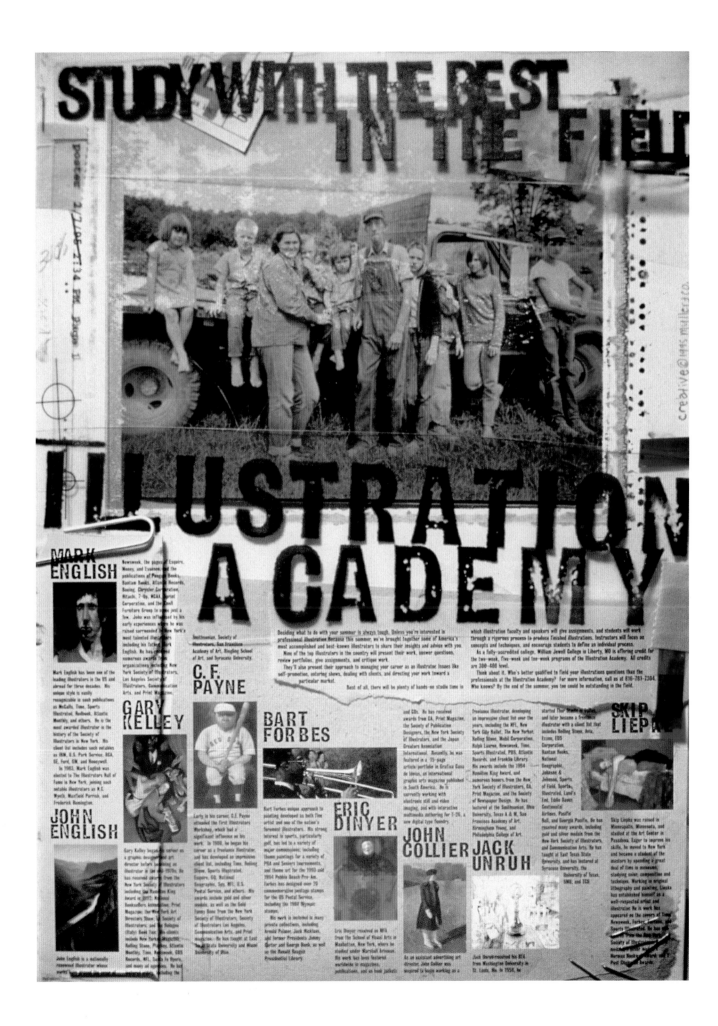

(PRECEDING SPREAD) 1 ART DIRECTORS: KLAUS J. MAACK, EIKO ISHIOKA DESIGNER: EIKO ISHIOKA PHOTOGRAPHER: DAVID SEIDNER CLIENT: ERCO LEUCHTEN COUNTRY: GERMANY ■ 1 THE FIRST OF A SERIES TO BE PUBLISHED ANNUALLY ON THE SUBJECT OF LIGHT BY A LAMP PRODUCER. THE FIRST ARTIST TO DESIGN A POSTER OF THE SERIES IS EIKO ISHIOKA. SHE WILL NAME THE ARTIST TO DESIGN NEXT YEAR'S POSTER. ● 1 DAS ERSTE AUS EINER REIHE VON PLAKATEN ZUM THEMA LICHT VON DER FIRMA ERCO. IM FOLGENDEN JAHR WIRD EIN VON DER DIESJÄHRIGEN GESTALTERIN, EIKO ISHIOKA, BESTIMMTER DESIGNER DAS PLAKAT GESTALTEN. ▲ 1 «ET LA LUMIÈRE EST». PREMIÈRE AFFICHE D'UNE SÉRIE SPÉCIALE CONSACRÉE AU THÈME DE LA LUMIÈRE ET RÉALISÉE PAR EIKO ISHIOKA POUR LES LUMINAIRES ERCO. C'EST À L'ARTISTE MÊME QU'INCOMBERA LE SOIN DE DÉSIGNER SON SUCCESSEUR, CHARGÉ DE RÉALISER LA PROCHAINE AFFICHE ANNUELLE. ☐ 2 ART DIRECTOR: JOHN MULLER, JON SIMONSEN DESIGNER: JON SIMONSEN ILLUSTRATOR: MIKE REGNIER ADVERTISING AGENCY: MULLER + COMPANY CLIENT: JOHN ENGLISH COUNTRY: USA ■ 2 AN ANNOUNCEMENT FOR A SIX-WEEK ILLUSTRATION WORKSHOP TAUGHT BY SOME OF THE PREMIER ILLUSTRATORS IN THE FIELD. ● 2 ANKÜNDIGUNG EINES SECHSWÖCHIGEN ILLUSTRATIONS-WORKSHOPS BEI EINEM ANGESEHENEN ILLUSTRATOR. ▲ 2 AFFICHE ANNONÇANT UN SÉMINAIRE DE SIX SEMAINES, DONNÉ PAR UN ILLUSTRATEUR RENOMMÉ. ☐ (THIS SPREAD) 1 ART DIRECTORS/DESIGNERS: PETER GOOD, JANET CUMMINGS GOOD PHOTOGRAPHER: JIM COON ILLUSTRATOR: PETER GOOD ADVERTISING AGENCY: PETER GOOD GRAPHIC DESIGN CLIENT: UNISOURCE COUNTRY: USA ■ 1 AN ADJUNCT TO A CALENDAR, THIS POSTER PLAYS ON THE THEME OF "CHANCE." ●

(DIESE DOPPELSEITE) 1 «GLÜCK» ALS THEMA EINES PLAKATES, DAS ZU EINEM KALENDER GEHÖRT. ▲ (CETTE DOUBLE PAGE) 1 «LA CHANCE», TEL ÉTAIT LE THÈME DE CETTE AFFICHE JOINTE À UN CALENDRIER. ☐ (THIS SPREAD) 2–5 ART DIRECTORS: JOHN ROBERTSON, JEFF CARROLL ILLUSTRATOR: JEFF CARROLL ADVERTISING AGENCY: ROBERTSON DESIGN CLIENTS: ATHENS PAPER, FRENCH PAPER CO. COUNTRY: USA ■ 2–5 EXAMPLES FROM A SERIES OF POSTERS FOR TWO PAPER MANUFACTURERS. ● (DIESE DOPPELSEITE) 2–5 BEISPIELE AUS EINER PLAKATSERIE FÜR ZWEI PAPIERHERSTELLER. ▲ 2–5 EXEMPLES D'UNE SÉRIE D'AFFICHES POUR FABRICANTS DE PAPIER. ☐ (FOLLOWING SPREAD)1, 2 ART DIRECTOR/DESIGNER: KENYA HARA DESIGN FIRM: NIPPON DESIGN CENTER, INC. CLIENT: TAKEO CO., LTD. COUNTRY: JAPAN ■ 1, 2 PART OF A SERIES ANNOUNCING A PAPER EXHIBITION, THESE POSTERS FOCUS ON A NEW, STONE-LIKE TEXTURE. ● (NÄCHSTE DOPPELSEITE) 1, 2 DIESE SERIE ENTSTAND FÜR EINE PAPIERAUSSTELLUNG, IN DER ES UM EINE NEUE QUALITÄT MIT STEINÄHNLICHER TEXTUR GEHT. DER DESIGNER DACHTE AN GRUNDFORMEN, DIE IM KOLLEKTIVEN GEDÄCHTNIS DES MENSCHEN EXISTIEREN UND SETZTE SIE AUF ZEITGENÖSSISCHE ART UM. ▲ (DOUBLE PAGE SUIVANTE) 1, 2 SÉRIE RÉALISÉE POUR UNE EXPOSITION OÙ FUT PRÉSENTÉE UNE NOUVELLE QUALITÉ DE PAPIER DONT LA STRUCTURE RAPPELLE LA PIERRE. LE DESIGNER S'INSPIRA DE FORMES PRIMAIRES ANCRÉES DANS LA MÉMOIRE COLLECTIVE ET LES TRANSPOSA DANS UN STYLE CONTEMPORAIN.

FRENCH DUR-O-TONE BY ATHENS

VISION

It takes far more than luck to stand the test of time. Athens salutes those who have endured.

FRENCH DUR-O-TONE BY ATHENS

PROFICIENCY

It takes far more than luck to stand the test of time. Athens salutes those who have endured.

FRENCH DUR-O-TONE BY ATHENS

IMAGINATION

It takes far more than luck to stand the test of time. Athens salutes those who have endured.

FRENCH DUR-O-TONE BY ATHENS

PERSEVERANCE

It takes far more than luck to stand the test of time. Athens salutes those who have endured.

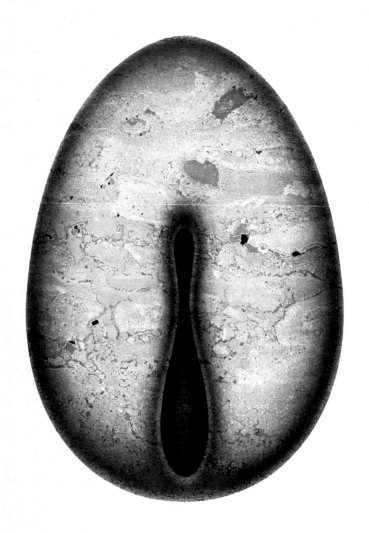

TAKEOPAPERWORLD '94

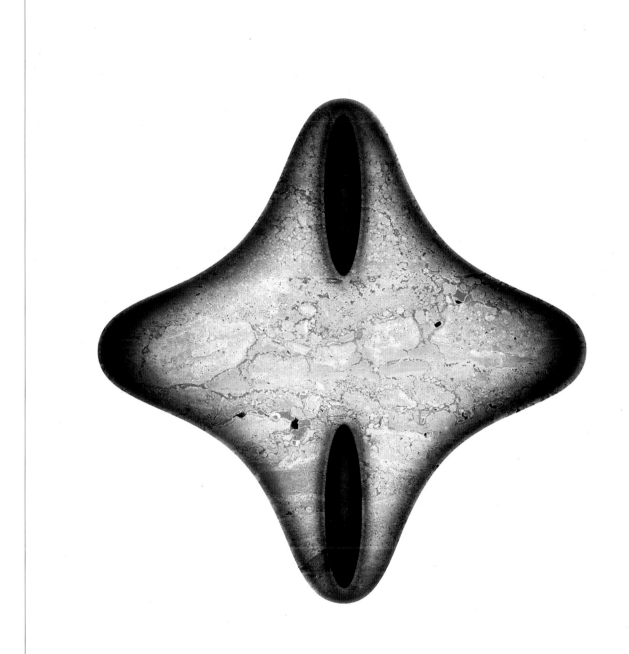

TAKEO PAPER WORLD '94

1, 2 ART DIRECTOR/DESIGNER: FRANK VIVA DESIGN FIRM: VIVA DOLAN COMMUNICATIONS + DESIGN CLIENT: CONQUEROR FINE PAPERS COUNTRY: USA ■ 1 DESIGNED FOR A CHAIN OF RETAIL PAPER STORES IN THE US CALLED THE PAPER ZONE, THIS POSTER ATTEMPTS TO DIFFERENTIATE CONQUEROR FROM ITS COMPETITION BY PLAYING UP THE BRITISH ORIGINS OF THE PAPER. ■ 2 DESIGNED FOR CONQUEROR FINE PAPERS, THIS POSTER HELPED LAUNCH A NEW SWATCHBOOK FEATURING AN UPDATED LINE OF TEXTURES AND COLORS FOR THE NORTH AMERICAN MARKET. ● 1 BESTIMMT FÜR EINE KETTE VON PAPIERLÄDEN IN DEN USA MIT DEM NAMEN PAPER ZONE, SOLL DIESES PLAKAT DURCH BERUFUNG AUF DIE BRITISCHE HERKUNFT DIE QUALITÄTEN DES CONQUEROR-PAPIERS HERVORHEBEN. ● 2 HIER GEHT ES UM DIE LANCIERUNG EINES PAPIERMUSTERBUCHES MIT NEUEN QUALITÄTEN UND FARBEN FÜR DEN AMERIKANISCHEN MARKT. ▲ 1 ADRESSÉE À LA CHAÎNE DE PAPETERIES AMÉRICAINE PAPER ZONE, CETTE AFFICHE PUBLICITAIRE VANTE LES MULTIPLES ATOUTS DU PAPIER CONQUEROR QUI RÉPOND À DES CRITÈRES DE QUALITÉ BRITANNIQUES. ▲ 2 AFFICHE RÉALISÉE POUR LE LANCEMENT D'UN CATALOGUE D'ÉCHANTILLONS PRÉSENTANT LES DERNIÈRES GAMMES DE PAPIER CONQUEROR. □ 3, 4 ART DIRECTOR:

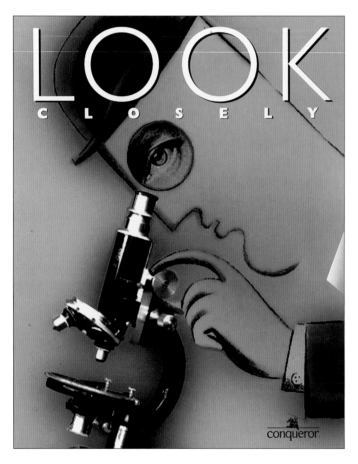

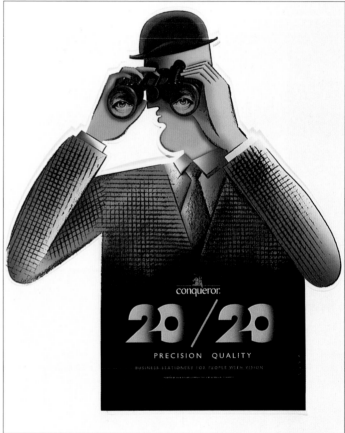

JOHN BATESON DESIGNERS: DEBORAH OSBORNE, ANDREW ROSS, MICHAEL DENNY PHOTOGRAPHER: TIM FLACH DESIGN FIRM: ROUNDEL DESIGN GROUP CLIENT: ZANDERS FEINPAPIERE AG COUNTRY: GERMANY ■ 3, 4 THE KEY MESSAGE OF THESE POSTERS IS THAT THIS PAPER'S COST BENEFITS AND GREEN CREDENTIALS DO NOT COMPROMISE ZANDERS' REPUTATION FOR QUALITY. THE CAMPAIGN HAD TO WORK ACROSS INTERNATIONAL BOUNDARIES. ● 3, 4 DIE BOTSCHAFT DIESER PLAKATE IST, DASS TROTZ DER KOSTENVORTEILE UND GUTEN UMWELTVERTRÄGLICHKEIT DES PAPIERS DIE GEWOHNT HOHE QUALITÄT VON ZANDERS NICHT BEEINTRÄCHTIG WURDE. DIE KAMPAGNE MUSSTE INTERNATIONAL VERSTÄNDLICH SEIN. HIER WIRD DAS EXOTISCHE NEBEN DAS GEWÖHNLICHE GESTELLT. ▲ 3, 4 LE MESSAGE DE CES AFFICHES: UN PRIX AVANTAGEUX ET UNE PRODUCTION RESPECTUEUSE DE L'ENVIRONNEMENT NE COMPROMETTENT NULLEMENT LES CRITÈRES DE QUALITÉ QUI FONT LA RÉPUTATION DES PAPIERS ZANDERS. LA CAMPAGNE DEVAIT AUSSI PRÉSENTER UN CARACTÈRE INTERNATIONAL. LE CONCEPT VISUEL JOUE SUR LE CONTRASTE ENTRE STANDARDS HABITUELS ET EXOTISME, RENFORCÉ PAR UN SLOGAN EXPLICITE: «IL EXISTE PLUSIEURS TYPES DE PAPIER COUCHÉ RECTO VERSO. MAIS UN SEUL DE QUALITÉ ZANDERS MEGA.»

1 ART DIRECTOR: PAUL WHARTON DESIGNER: TOM RIDDLE ILLUSTRATOR: JANET WOOLY ADVERTISING AGENCY: LITTLE & COMPANY CLIENT: CROSS POINTE PAPER CORPORATION COUNTRY: USA ■ 1 PART OF A SERIES TO PROMOTE THE GENESIS PAPER LINE FROM CROSS POINTE. EACH ILLUSTRATOR AND PHOTOGRAPHER WAS ASKED TO VISUALIZE DIFFERENT VARIATIONS ON THE WORD "NATURAL" TO EMPHASIZE THE FIBER-ADDED QUALITY OF THIS RECYCLED PAPER. ● 1 BEISPIEL AUS EINER PLAKATREIHE FÜR DIE PAPIERSORTE GENESIS, EINE QUALITÄT AUS ALTPAPIER, VEREDELT MIT TEXTILFASERN. DIE ILLUSTRATOREN UND PHOTOGRAPHEN HATTEN DIE AUFGABE, DEN BEGRIFF «NATÜRLICH» ZU INTERPRETIEREN. ▲ 1 PUBLICITÉ

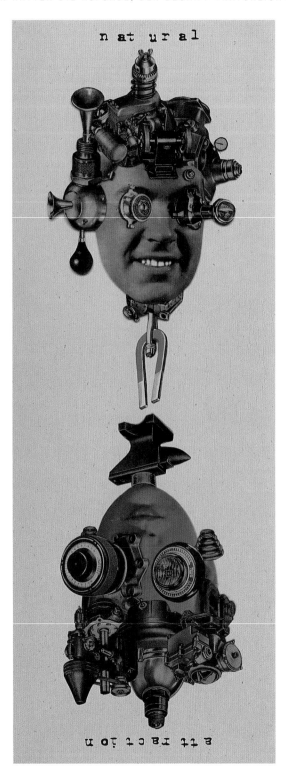

POUR UNE NOUVELLE GAMME DE PAPIER CROSS POINTE. ILLUSTRATEURS ET PHOTOGRAPHES AVAIENT POUR TÂCHE DE DÉCLINER LE CONCEPT «NATUREL» SOUS TOUTES SES FORMES POUR SOULIGNER LA QUALITÉ SUPÉRIEURE DE CE PAPIER RECYCLÉ. □ 2–5 ART DIRECTOR/DESIGNER/ILLUSTRATOR: JOAO MACHADO CLIENT: PAPÉIS CARREIRA COUNTRY: PORTUGAL ■ 2–5 THESE POSTERS FOR A PAPER MANUFACTURER SYMBOLIZE THE SEASONS AND DEMONSTRATE THE SPECIAL PRINTING QUALI- TIES OF A STOCK CALLED INAMAT SILK. ● 2–5 DIESE PLAKATE FÜR EINEN PAPIERHERSTELLER SYMBOLISIEREN DIE VIER JAHRESZEITEN. ES GEHT HIER UM DIE DRUCKQUALITÄT DER PAPIERSORTE INAMAT SILK. ▲ 2–5 CES AFFICHES SYMBOLISENT LES QUATRE SAISONS ET DÉMONTRENT LA QUALITÉ D'IMPRESSION EXCEPTIONNELLE DU PAPIER INAMAT SILK.

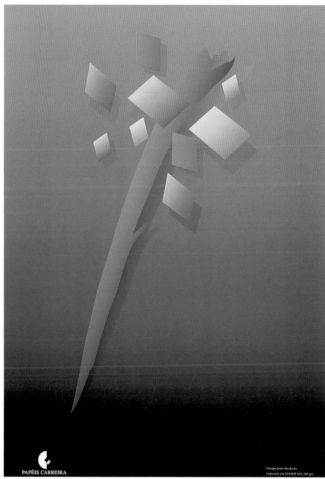

1 ART DIRECTOR/PHOTOGRAPHER: KUNIO KIYOMURA STUDIO: KST CREATIONS INC. COUNTRY: JAPAN ■ **1** A PHOTOGRAPHER'S SELF-PROMOTION INSPIRED BY THE DISTRASTROUS EARTHQUAKE IN JAPAN IN EARLY 1995. THE IMAGE IS MEANT TO EXPRESS THE UNCONTROLLABLE POWER OF NATURE. ● **1** EIGENWERBUNG DES PHOTOGRAPHEN. INSPIRIERT DURCH DAS VERHEERENDE ERDBEBEN IN JAPAN ANFANG 1995, SOLL DIESES BILD DIE UNKONTROLLIERBARE KRAFT DER NATURELEMENTE AUSDRÜCKEN.

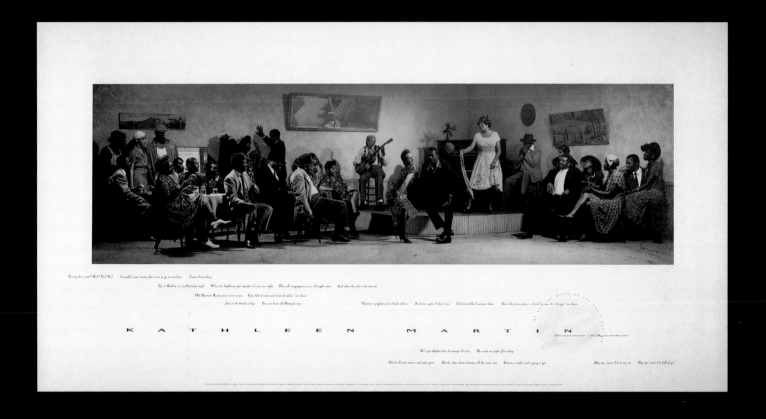

▲ **1** PUBLICITÉ AUTOPROMOTIONNELLE DE L'ARTISTE. INSPIRÉE DES TREMBLEMENTS DE TERRE DÉVASTATEURS QUI ONT SEC-OUÉ LE JAPON DÉBUT 1995. CETTE PHOTO EXPRIME LA FORCE INCONTRÔLABLE DES ÉLÉMENTS NATURELS. ■ **2** ART DIRECTOR: KATHLEEN MARTIN DESIGNERS: JOHN DUDEK, COOMES DUDEK PHOTOGRAPHER: KATHLEEN MARTIN CLIENT: KATHLEEN MARTIN COUNTRY: USA ■ **2** A SELF-PROMOTIONAL POSTER FOR PHOTOGRAPHER KATHLEEN MARTIN. ● **2** EIGENWERBUNG DER PHOTO-GRAPHIN KATHLEEN MARTIN. ▲ **2** PUBLICITÉ AUTOPROMOTIONNELLE DE LA PHOTOGRAPHE AMÉRICAINE KATHLEEN MARTIN.

CHRIS COLLINS 35 WEST 20TH STREET NYC 10011 212·633·1670
REPRESENTED BY JOE DIBARTOLO & LAURA LEMKOWITZ 212·297·0041

1 ART DIRECTOR: CHRIS COLLINS PHOTOGRAPHER: CHRIS COLLINS CLIENT: CHRIS COLLINS STUDIO COUNTRY: USA ■ 1 CALLED "THE LONGEST DOG," THIS SELF-PROMOTION STRESSES THE PHOTOGRAPHER'S EXPERTISE IN ANIMAL PHOTOGRAPHY. ● 1 «DER LÄNGSTE HUND» – DIESER PHOTOGRAPH IST SPEZIALIST FÜR TIERAUFNAHMEN. ▲ 1 «LE CHIEN LE PLUS LONG». IMAGE DESTINÉE À UNE PUBLICITÉ AUTOPROMOTIONNELLE DE L'ARTISTE, SPÉCIALISÉ DANS LA PHOTO ANIMALIÈRE. □ 2–5 ART DIRECTORS: TODD MCLEOD, CHARLES REGISTER LOGO DESIGNER: PATRICK SHORT, BLACKBIRD CREATIVE PHOTOGRAPHERS:

TODD MCLEOD, CHARLES REGISTER CLIENT: THE LIGHTHOUSE PROJECT COUNTRY: USA ■ 2–5 PART OF A SERIES OF LIMITED-EDITION POSTERS DEPICTING NORTH CAROLINA'S HISTORIC LIGHTHOUSES, THESE POSTERS WERE INTENDED FOR BOTH SELF-PROMOTIONAL PURPOSES AND RETAIL SALE. ● 2–5 BEISPIELE AUS EINER PLAKATREIHE IN LIMITIERTER AUFLAGE, DIE DEN HISTORISCHEN LEUCHTTÜRMEN VON NORTH CAROLINA GEWIDMET IST. DIE PLAKATE SIND IM HANDEL ERHÄLTLICH. ▲ 2–5 AFFICHES DÉDIÉES AUX ANCIENS PHARES DE CAROLINE DU NORD. SÉRIE LIMITÉE DESTINÉE À LA VENTE.

CANNONBALL GRAPHICS

408 943 9511

TRADE SHOW GRAPHICS

1 ART DIRECTORS: DAVE PAYNE, DARREN BRILLS DESIGNER: MICHAEL SCHWAB DESIGN ILLUSTRATOR: MICHAEL SCHWAB DESIGN STUDIO: MICHAEL SCHWAB DESIGN CLIENT: CANNONBALL GRAPHICS COUNTRY: USA ■ 1 ONE-COLOR SCREEN PRINTED POSTER TO PROMOTE CANNONBALL GRAPHICS. ● 1 SIEBDRUCKPLAKAT FÜR CANNONBALL GRAPHICS. ▲ 1 AFFICHE POUR LA PROMOTION DE CANNONBALL GRAPHICS, SÉRIGRAPHIE. □ 2 ART DIRECTOR/DESIGNER: MARTA IBARRONDO COPYWRITER: TOM GIVONE AGENCY: MEZZINA/BROWN CLIENT: PRINTBOX APPLIED GRAPHICS COUNTRY: USA ■ 2 A POSTER TO PROMOTE HIGHLY SOPHISTICATED ELECTRONIC RETOUCHING TECHNIQUES. ● 2 WERBUNG FÜR ANSPRUCHSVOLLE ELEKTRONISCHE RETUSCHIERTECHNIKEN. ▲ 2 PUBLICITÉ POUR DES TECHNIQUES DE RETOUCHE ÉLECTRONIQUES HAUT DE GAMME. □ (FOLLOWING SPREAD) 1, 3 ART DIRECTOR/DESIGNER: GIICHI OKAZAKI DESIGN FIRM: MAKOTO SAITO DESIGN OFFICE INC. CLIENT: TANAKA SANGYO CO., LTD. COUNTRY: JAPAN ■ (FOLLOWING SPREAD) 1, 3 VARIATIONS OF A CALENDAR POSTER FOR A PRINTER. ASIDE FROM SHOWING THE DATES OF THE YEAR, THE DESIGNER USED THE CIRCLE, CLOUDS, AND THE JUXTAPOSITION OF RED AND BLUE—SYMBOLIZING MORNING AND EVENING—TO EXPRESS THE PASSING OF TIME. ● (NÄCHSTE DOPPELSEITE) 1, 3 VARIATIONEN EINES KALENDERPLAKATES FÜR EINE DRUCKEREI. STATT SICH AUF DIE DATENANGABE ZU BESCHRÄNKEN, GING ES DEM GESTALTER UM DIE VERGÄNGLICHKEIT DER ZEIT: DER KREIS, DIE WOLKEN UND DIE GEGENÜBERSTELLUNG VON ROT UND BLAU (SYMBOLISCH FÜR DEN MORGEN UND DEN ABEND) SIND AUSDRUCK DIESES GEDANKENS. ZEIT UND RAUM JENSEITS DES LOCHES IM ZENTRUM SIND NICHT VON DIESER WELT. ▲ (DOUBLE PAGE SUIVANTE) 1, 3 AFFICHE CALENDRIER

RÉALISÉE POUR UNE IMPRIMERIE. L'ARTISTE A VOULU TRANSCENDER LA FONCTION PRIMAIRE DU CALENDRIER – INDIQUER DES DATES – ET TRADUIRE L'ÉVOLUTION DU TEMPS QUI PASSE. LA SPIRALE, LES NUAGES ET LA JUXTAPOSITION DU ROUGE ET DU BLEU – LE MATIN ET LE SOIR – SONT LES SYMBOLES DE CETTE DÉMARCHE. LE TROU AU CENTRE SYMBOLISE UN AUTRE ESPACE-TEMPS, UNE DIMENSION QUI NOUS ÉCHAPPE. □ (FOLLOWING SPREAD) 2 ART DIRECTOR/DESIGNER: MARTA IBARRONDO COPYWRITER: TOM GIVONE ADVERTISING AGENCY: FRANKFURT/BALKIND CLIENT: PANTONE COUNTRY: USA ■ (FOLLOWING SPREAD) 2 TO JUSTIFY THE CLIENT'S CLAIM THAT WHEREVER YOU FIND COLOR YOU'LL FIND PANTONE, A STOCK PHOTOGRAPH OF A SUNFLOWER WAS MADE TO LOOK AS IF ITS PETALS WERE PANTONE CHIPS. ● (NÄCHSTE DOPPELSEITE) 2 «PANTONE IST DA, WO DIE FARBE IST.» UM DIESEN ANSPRUCH ZU ILLUSTRIEREN, WURDEN AUS DEN BLÜTENBLÄTTERN DER SONNENBLUME PANTONE-FARBMUSTERKARTEN. ▲ (DOUBLE PAGE SUIVANTE) 2 «LÀ OÙ IL Y A DE LA COULEUR, IL Y A PANTONE.» POUR ILLUSTRER CETTE AFFIRMATION, LES PÉTALES DU TOURNESOL S'APPARENTENT À DES ÉCHANTILLONS PANTONE. □ (FOLLOWING SPREAD) 4 ART DIRECTOR/DESIGNER: DAVID BECK PHOTOGRAPHER: ROBB DEBENPORT DESIGN FIRM: SIBLEY/PETEET DESIGN CLIENT: PADGETT PRINTING COUNTRY: USA ■ (FOLLOWING SPREAD) 4 SELF-PROMOTIONAL POSTER FOR PADGETT AND THEIR NEW EIGHT-COLOR PRESS. ● (NÄCHSTE DOPPELSEITE) 4 EIGENWERBUNG DER DRUCKEREI PADGETT, DIE EINE NEUE ACHTFARBENDRUCKPRESSE BESITZT. ▲ (DOUBLE PAGE SUIVANTE) 4 PUBLICITÉ POUR L'IMPRIMERIE AMÉRICAINE PADGETT ET SA NOUVELLE PRESSE HUIT COULEURS. ■ (FOLLOWING SPREAD) 5 ART DIRECTOR/DESIGNER:

ANDREY LOGVIN DESIGN FIRM: LOGVINDESIGN CLIENT: LINIA GRAFIC COUNTRY: RUSSIA ■ 5 "WE CAN DO WHATEVER YOU HAVE IN MIND," SAYS THIS POSTER FOR A RUSSIAN PRINTER. ● 5 IHRE VORSTELLUNGEN LASSEN SICH VERWIRKLICHEN, VERSPRICHT EINE RUSSISCHE DRUCKEREI IHREN KUNDEN. ▲ 5 «LA RÉALISATION DE VOS IDÉES, C'EST NOTRE AFFAIRE!» VOILÀ CE QUE PROMET UNE IMPRIMERIE RUSSE. □ 6 DESIGNER: MICHAEL KIMMERLE CLIENT: WAGNER SIEBDRUCK GMBH COUNTRY: GERMANY ■ 6 SILKSCREEN PRINT OF A COMPUTER-GENERATED POSTER CELEBRATING 25 YEARS OF A SILKSCREEN PRINTER. THE FACES SYMBOLIZING DIFFERENT EPOCHS AND CULTURES ARE, FROM TOP LEFT TO BOTTOM RIGHT: JANUS HEAD, ANDY WARHOL, RICHARD WAGNER, AND MAO TSE-TUNG. ● 6 SIEBDRUCK EINES MIT HILFE DES COMPUTERS GESTALTETEN PLAKATES ZUM 25JÄHRIGEN BESTEHEN EINER SIEBDRUCKEREI. DIE KÖPFE, DIE VERSCHIEDENE EPOCHEN UND KULTUREN

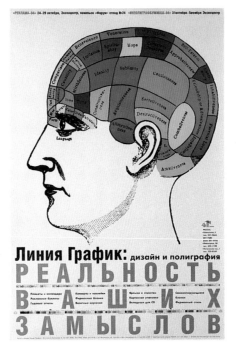
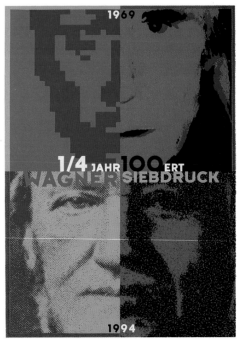

SYMBOLISIEREN, SIND VON OBEN LINKS NACH UNTEN RECHTS: JANUS KOPF, ANDY WARHOL, RICHARD WAGNER UND MAO TSE-TUNG. ▲ 6 AFFICHE CÉLÉBRANT LE 25ᵉ ANNIVERSAIRE D'UNE IMPRIMERIE SPÉCIALISÉE DANS LA SÉRIGRAPHIE. DE GAUCHE À DROITE ET DE HAUT EN BAS, ON RECONNAÎT LES PORTRAITS DE JANUS, D'ANDY WARHOL, DE RICHARD WAGNER ET DE MAO ZEDONG, SYMBOLES DE DIVERSES ÉPOQUES ET CULTURES. □ 7 ART DIRECTOR/DESIGNER: SEYMOUR CHWAST ILLUSTRATOR: SEYMOUR CHWAST STUDIO: PUSHPIN GROUP CLIENT: SERIGRAFI TRYCKT AV BILLES TRYCKERI AB COUNTRY: SWEDEN ■ 7 CREATED FOR A SILKSCREEN COMPANY IN STOCKHOLM, SWEDEN, THIS POSTER ILLUSTRATES THE COMPANY'S PRINTING TECHNIQUE. ● 7 HIER WIRD DIE DRUCKTECHNISCHE QUALITÄT EINER SIEBDRUCKEREI IN STOCKHOLM DEMONSTRIERT. ▲ 7 PUBLICITÉ ILLUSTRANT LA QUALITÉ D'IMPRESSION OFFERTE PAR UNE IMPRIMERIE SUÉDOISE SPÉCIALISÉE DANS LA SÉRIGRAPHIE.

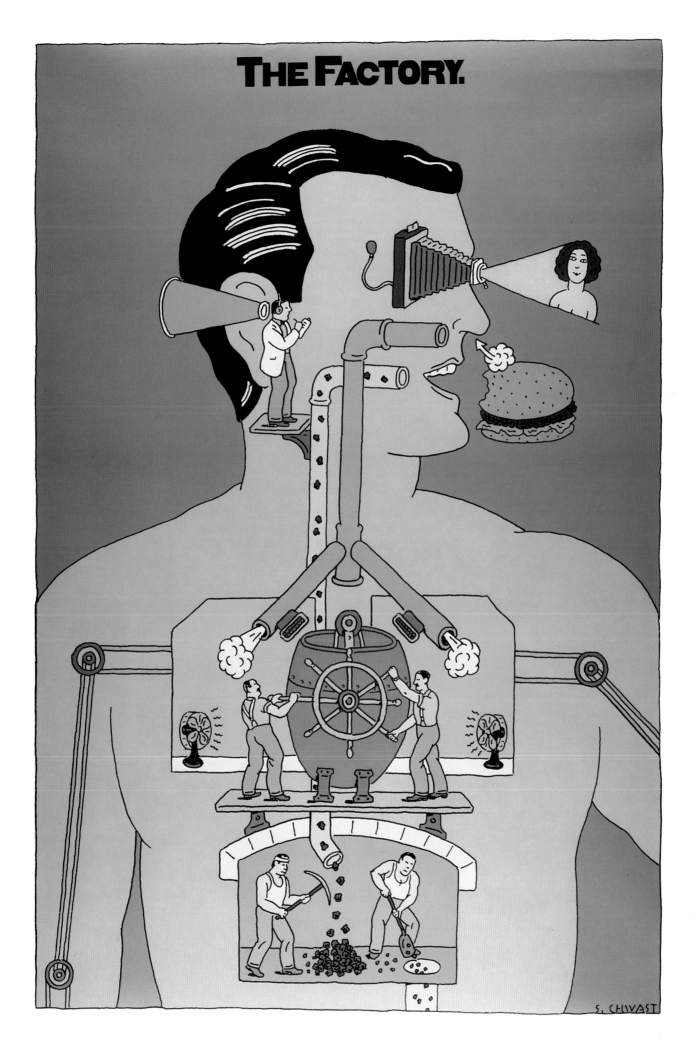

1–4 ART DIRECTOR/COPYWRITER: ANDREI CHELIOUTTO DESIGNERS: ANDREI CHELIOUTTO, IGOR GUROVICH PHOTOGRAPHER: EDUARD BASILIA DESIGN FIRM: PREMIER SV CLIENT: IMA-PRESS COUNTRY: RUSSIA ■ 1–4 POSTERS FOR AN ASSOCIATION OF PAPER MAKERS, PRINTERS, PUBLISHERS, AND DESIGNERS. ● 1–4 PLAKATREIHE FÜR EINEN VERBAND VON PAPIERHER-STELLERN, DRUCKEREIEN, VERLAGEN UND GESTALTERN. ▲ 1–4 SÉRIE D'AFFICHES RÉALISÉES POUR UNE ASSOCIATION RUSSE REGROUPANT FABRICANTS DE PAPIER, IMPRIMERIES, ÉDITEURS ET DESIGNERS. □ 5 ART DIRECTOR/DESIGNER: XU WANG PHOTOGRAPHER: WU HONG ILLUSTRATOR: ZHANG BO DESIGN FIRM: SINO WEST DESIGN CO. CLIENT: EXCHANGE PUBLISH HOUSE COUNTRY: CHINA ■ 5 DESIGN EXCHANGE MAGAZINE ANNOUNCES AN ISSUE DEDICATED TO PARIS DESIGNERS. ● 5 DESIGN EXCHANGE KÜNDIGT EINE AUSGABE AN, DIE BEKANNTEN GRAPHIKERN AUS PARIS GEWIDMET IST. ▲ 5 AFFICHE DU MAGAZINE DESIGN EXCHANGE ANNONÇANT UN NUMÉRO SPÉCIAL CONSACRÉ AUX PLUS GRANDS DESIGNERS PARISIENS. □ 6

ART DIRECTOR/DESIGNER: STEVE MITSCH PHOTOGRAPHER: DAVID BURNETT ADVERTISING AGENCY: ALTSCHILLER + COMPANY CLIENT: *PARENTING* MAGAZINE COUNTRY: USA ■ 6 PART OF A CONSUMER AND TRADE CAMPAIGN THAT REPOSITIONED *PARENTING* MAGAZINE. ● 6 DIE NEUE POSITIONIERUNG DER ELTERNZEITSCHRIFT *PARENTING* WAR GEGENSTAND EINER KONSUMENTEN- UND FACHKAMPAGNE. ▲ 6 AFFICHE D'UNE VASTE CAMPAGNE VISANT AU REPOSITIONNEMENT DU MAGAZINE *PARENTING*. ☐ 7 ART DIRECTOR: PETRULA VRONTIKIS DESIGNER: KIM SAGE STUDIO: VRONTIKIS DESIGN OFFICE CLIENT: TIME WARNER AUDIO BOOKS COUNTRY: USA ■ 7 A PROMOTIONAL POSTER FOR GABRIEL GARCIA MARQUEZ'S *ONE HUNDRED YEARS OF SOLITUDE*, ONE OF MANY SELECTIONS AVAILABLE THROUGH A+ AUDIO, A DIVISION OF TIME WARNER AUDIO BOOKS THAT PRODUCES BOOKS ON AUDIO CASSETTE. ● 7 GABRIEL GARCIA MARQUEZ' *HUNDERT JAHRE EINSAMKEIT* IST EINER DER ZAHLREICHEN TITEL, DIE AUF TONBANDKASSETTEN VON TIME WARNER ERHÄLTLICH SIND. ▲ 7 PUBLICITÉ POUR *CENT ANS DE SOLITUDE* DE GABRIEL GARCIA MARQUEZ, L'UN DES NOMBREUX TITRES PROPOSÉS EN CASSETTE PAR TIME WARNER.

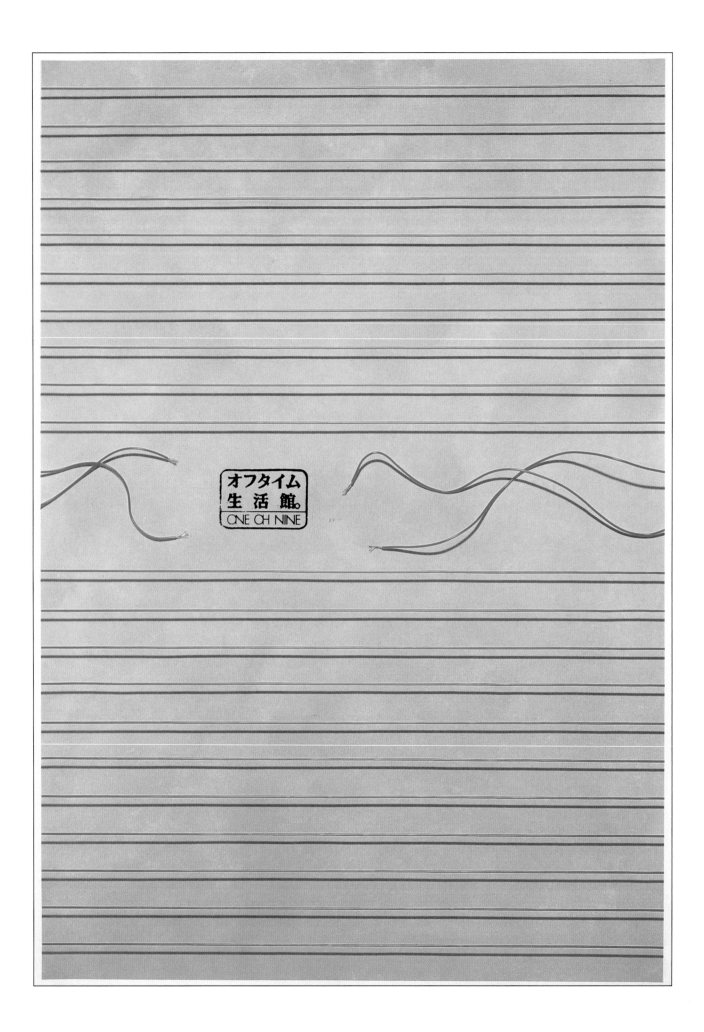

ずーっと息ぬきしないでいると、そりゃあ苦しいです。

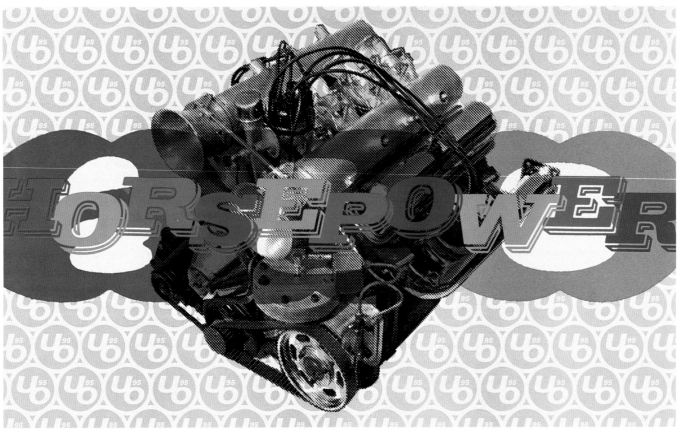

(PRECEDING SPREAD) 1, 2 ART DIRECTOR: SEICHI OHASHI DESIGNERS: ZENICHI IMAI (1), SEICHI OHASHI (2), MIYUKI YAMAZAKI (2) PHOTOGRAPHERS: TOSHIAKI TAKEUCHI (1), DAN MERKEL (2) COPYWRITER: ICHIRO SUGITANI DESIGN FIRM: LES MAINS INC. CLIENT: T.M.D. CO., LTD. COUNTRY: JAPAN ■ (PRECEDING SPREAD) 1, 2 TWO POSTERS FOR A DEPARTMENT STORE EXCLUSIVE-LY DEVOTED TO LEISURE CLOTHING. BOTH MEAN "LET'S TAKE A REST." THE WIRES SYMBOLIZE THE WORLD OF BUSINESS, THE ONES CUT BY THE SYMBOL "ONE OH NINE" STAND FOR BREAKING AWAY. THE DOLPHINS REPRESENT THE NEED TO TAKE A BREATH. ● (VORANGEHENDE DOPPELSEITE) 1, 2 ZWEI PLAKATE FÜR EIN KAUFHAUS, DAS SICH AUF FREIZEITMODE UND -ARTIKEL SPEZIALISIERT HAT. «LASST UNS EINE PAUSE MACHEN» IST DAS MOTTO BEIDER PLAKATE. DIE DRÄHTE SYMBO-LISIEREN DIE BERUFSWELT, DIE VON DEM FIRMENSYMBOL ZERSCHNITTENEN DAS ENTKOMMEN. DAS MOTIV MIT DEN DELPHINEN BEZIEHT SICH AUF DIE NOTWENDIGKEIT, LUFT ZU HOLEN. ▲ (DOUBLE PAGE PRÉCÉDENTE) 1, 2 AFFICHES RÉALI-SÉES POUR UN GRAND MAGASIN SPÉCIALISÉ DANS LA MODE ET LES ARTICLES DE LOISIRS. LE SLOGAN DES DEUX AFFICHES EST LE MÊME: «FAITES UNE PAUSE!». SYMBOLES DU MONDE DU TRAVAIL, LES CÂBLES SONT COUPÉS PAR LE SLOGAN ANNONCIATEUR DU RÉPIT TANT ATTENDU. LES DAUPHINS SYMBOLISENT POUR LEUR PART LA NÉCESSITÉ DE RESPIRER, DE

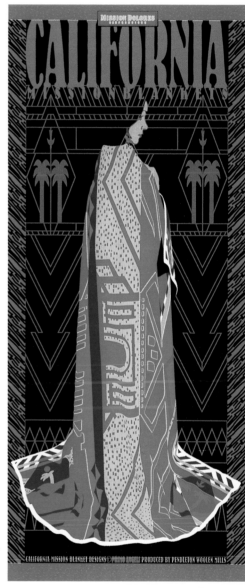

REPRENDRE SON SOUFFLE. □ (THIS SPREAD) 1–3 ART DIRECTOR: HOWARD BROWN DESIGNER: HOWARD BROWN, MIKE CALKINS ILLUSTRATOR: MIKE CALKINS AGENCY: URBAN OUTFITTERS IN-HOUSE CLIENT: URBAN OUTFITTERS COUNTRY: USA ■ 1–3 THESE SEASONAL POSTERS ARE INCORPORATED INTO VARIOUS ASPECTS OF MERCHANDISING AND DISPLAY THROUGHOUT EACH URBAN OUTFITTERS STORE. ● 1–3 DIESE AUF DIE SAISONS ABGESTIMMTEN PLAKATE SIND TEIL DER DEKORATION IN DEN «URBAN OUTFITTERS» LÄDEN. ▲ 1–3 AFFICHES SUR LE THÈME DES SAISONS, UTILISÉES COMME MATÉRIEL DE DÉCORATION DANS LES MAGASINS AMÉRICAINS «URBAN OUTFITTERS». □ 4 CREATIVE DIRECTOR: MICHAEL JAGER ART DIRECTOR: MICHAEL SHEA DESIGNER: ANDREW SZURLEY PHOTOGRAPHER: PETER RICE AGENCY: JAGER DI PAOLA KEMP CLIENT: KARHU U.S.A., INC. COUNTRY: USA ■ 4 A POINT-OF-PURCHASE POSTER INTENDED TO EMPHASIZE THE HIGH PERFORMANCE NATURE OF KOHO'S NEW LINE OF INLINE HOCKEY SKATES. BOLD TYPOGRAPHY, PAIRED WITH TECHNICAL INFORMATION AND TESTIMONIALS WERE ENLISTED TO COMMUNICATE THE SKATES' KEY SELLING FEATURES. ● (VORANGEHENDE DOPPELSEITE) 4 EINE NEUE LINIE ANSPRUCHSVOLLER ROLLERBLADES FÜR HOCKEY IST THEMA DIESES LADENPLAKATES. TECHNISCHE INFORMATIONEN UND ANERKENNENDE KOMMENTARE INFORMIEREN ÜBER DIE HAUPTVORZÜGE DIESER INLINE HOCKEY SKATES. ▲ (DOUBLE PAGE

PRÉCÉDENTE) 4 PUBLICITÉ VANTANT LES QUALITÉS D'UNE NOUVELLE GÉNÉRATION DE PATINS POUR HOCKEYEURS. DONNÉES TECHNIQUES ET TÉMOIGNAGES D'ADEPTES CONVAINCUS INFORMENT DES PRINCIPAUX ATOUTS DE CES PATINS HAUT DE GAMME. □ (PRECEDING SPREAD) 5 ART DIRECTOR/DESIGNER: PRIMO ANGELI PHOTOGRAPHER: JUNE FOUCH COMPUTER ILLUSTRATOR: MARCELO DE FREITAS PRODUCTION MANAGER: ERIC KUBLY CLIENT: PENDLETON (SAN FRANCISCO) COUNTRY: USA ■ (PRECEDING SPREAD) 5 THIS POSTER WAS CREATED TO PUBLICIZE THE CALIFORNIA MISSION BLANKETS DESIGNED BY PRIMO ANGELI AND PRODUCED BY PENDLETON. ● (VORANGEHENDE DOPPELSEITE) 5 WERBUNG FÜR VON PRIMO ANGELI ENTWORFENE UND VON PENDLETON HERGESTELLTE DECKEN. ▲ (DOUBLE PAGE PRÉCÉDENTE) 5 PUBLICITÉ POUR LES COUVERTURES «CALIFORNIA MISSION», UN PRODUIT DE FABRICATION PENDLETON CRÉÉ PAR PRIMO ANGELI. □ (THIS SPREAD) 1 ART DIRECTOR: BILL THORBURN DESIGNER: ALEX TYLEVICH DESIGN FIRM: THORBURN DESIGN CLIENT: BENETTON COUNTRY: ITALY ■ (THIS SPREAD) 1 IN ORDER TO STRENGTHEN THE IMAGE OF THE "UNITED COLORS OF BENETTON" LINE, THIS POSTER EMPLOYS A FLAG-LIKE MOTIF. ● (DIESE DOPPELSEITE) 1 UM DAS IMAGE DER «UNITED COLORS OF BENETTON»-PRODUKTE ZU STÄRKEN, WURDE FÜR DIESES PLAKAT EIN FLAGGENARTIGES MOTIV GEWÄHLT. ▲ 1 LE MOTIF DE L'AFFICHE, QUI RAPPELLE UN DRAPEAU, A ÉTÉ

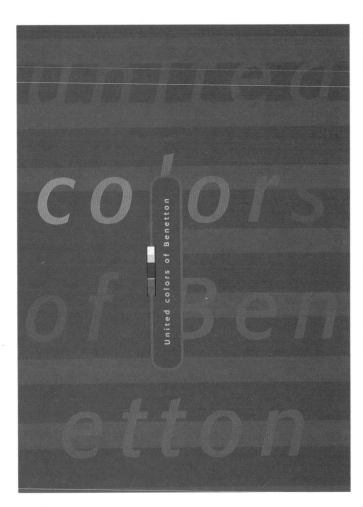

CHOISI POUR RENFORCER L'IMAGE DES PRODUITS «UNITED COLORS OF BENETTON». □ 2 ART DIRECTOR/ DESIGNER: TRACY WONG PHOTOGRAPHER: LARRY PROSOR ADVERTISING AGENCY: WONGDOODY CLIENT: K2 SKIS COUNTRY: USA ■ 2 MEANT TO GENER- ATE EXCITEMENT AMONG AVID SKIERS AND TO POSITION K2 AS THE ALL-TERRAIN SKI, THIS POSTER SHOWS EXTREME-SKIER DOUG COOMBS ON ICE CLIFFS IN ALASKA, USA. ● 2 DER K2-SKI IST ALS EIN FÜR ALLE TERRAINS GEEIGNETER SKI FÜR PAS- SIONIERTE SKILÄUFER POSITIONIERT. GEZEIGT IST DER SKI-ARTIST DOUG COOMBS AUF EISKLIPPEN IN ALASKA. ▲ 2 PUBLICITÉ POUR LES SKIS K2: GRÂCE À CES SKIS TOUT-TERRAIN, LE CRACK DE LA GLISSE AMÉRICAIN DOUG COOMBS PEUT ALLER JUSQU'AU BOUT DE L'EXTRÊME DANS LES GLACES DE L'ALASKA. □ 3 ART DIRECTORS/DESIGNERS: PETER GOOD, CHRISTOPHER HYDE PHOTOGRAPHER: SEAN KERNAN DESIGN FIRM: PETER GOOD GRAPHIC DESIGN CLIENT: ROSSI ENTERPRISES COUNTRY: USA ■ 3 USING A QUINTESSENTIAL AMERICAN OBJECT—THE BASEBALL BAT—THIS POSTER IDENTIFIES THE SEVEN SPECIES OF WOOD EXPORTED BY THE CLIENT, ROSSI ENTERPRISES. ● 3 EIN TYPISCH AMERIKANISCHER GEGENSTAND, DER BASEBALLSCHLÄGER, DIENT HIER ALS ILLUSTRATION VON SIEBEN HOLZSORTEN, DIE ROSSI ENTERPRISES EXPORTIEREN. ▲ 3 UNE BATTE DE BASE-BALL – OBJET CULTE PAR EXCELLENCE DE LA CULTURE AMÉRICAINE – TEL ÉTAIT LE SUJET DE CETTE AFFICHE DESTINÉE À PRÉSENTER LES SEPT QUALITÉS DE BOIS EXPORTÉES PAR LA SOCIÉTÉ ROSSI ENTERPRISES.

1 ART DIRECTORS: JENNIFER HANSEN, JIM GALLAGHER DESIGNER: JENNIFER HANSEN DESIGN FIRM: HANSEN DESIGN CLIENT: HOSHINO U.S.A. INC. COUNTRY: USA ■ 1 IN ORDER TO PROMOTE THE IBANEZ GUITAR "ATK SERIES" IN GUITAR AND MUSIC STORES, THE DESIGN OF THIS POSTER WAS KEPT RAW TO APPEAL TO THE GRUNGE MUSIC MARKET. ● 1 DIESES LADENPLAKAT FÜR DIE «ATK-GITARRENLINIE» VON IBANEZ GUITAR RICHTET SICH MIT SEINEM RUDIMENTÄREN DESIGN AN DEN «GRUNGE MUSIC» MARKT. ▲ 1 PUBLICITÉ POUR LES GUITARES ATK D'IBANEZ GUITAR. CIBLÉ SUR LE MARCHÉ DE LA MUSIQUE GRUNGE,

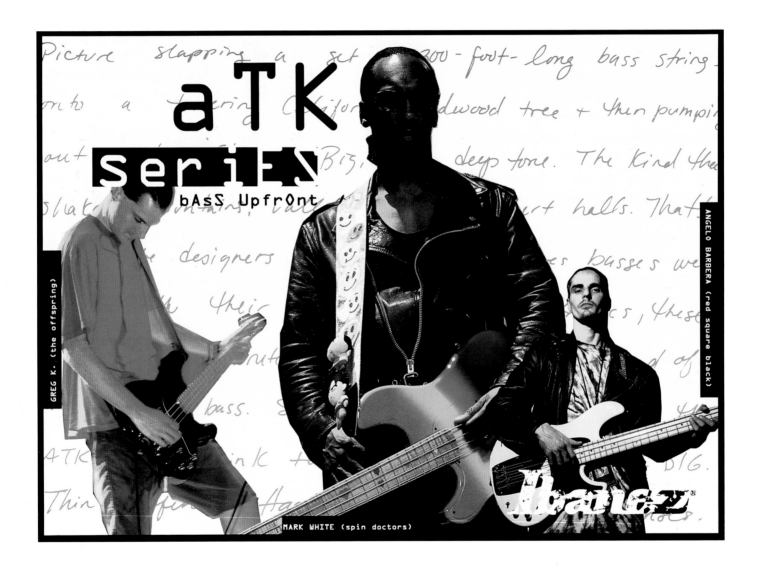

LE GRAPHISME A VOLONTAIREMENT ÉTÉ RÉDUIT À SA FORME LA PLUS BRUTE. ■ 2 ART DIRECTOR/DESIGNER: TAKU SATOH CLIENT: VANCO CO., LTD. COUNTRY: JAPAN ■ 2 THESE POSTERS WERE DESIGNED FOR A JAPANESE COMPANY WHICH PRODUCES DESIGN TOOLS. THEY ARE PART OF A SERIES CREATED FOR DISPLAY IN EXHIBITIONS AND TO PROMOTE THE USE OF DESIGN TOOLS IN PLACE OF THE COMPUTER. ● 2 DIE PLAKATE GEHÖREN ZU EINER SERIE FÜR EINEN HERSTELLER VON GRAPHIKER-WERKZEUGEN. SIE WERDEN BEI AUSSTELLUNGEN UND ALS LADENPLAKATE EINGESETZT. ▲ 2 UTILISÉES POUR DES EXPOSITIONS ET EN TANT QUE P.L.V., CES AFFICHES FONT PARTIE D'UNE SÉRIE COMMANDÉE PAR UN FABRICANT DE MATÉRIEL DESTINÉ AUX GRAPHISTES.

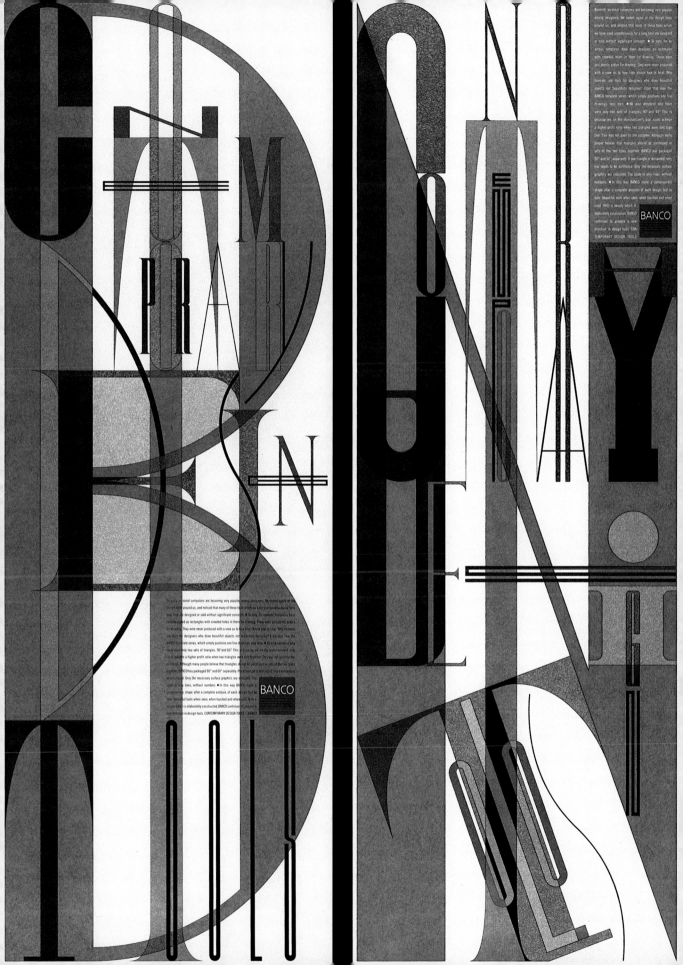

CONTEMPRARY

BANCO

CONTEMPORARY DESIGN TOOLS

Recently personal computers are becoming very popular among designers. We looked again at the design tools around us, and noticed that many of these tools which we have used unostentatiously for a long time are designed or sold without significant concept. • In date, for example, templates have been designed as rectangles with crowded holes in them for drawing. These were just plastic plates for drawing. They were never produced with a view as to how they should look in total. Why however are tools for designers who draw beautiful objects not beautifully designed? From that idea the BANCO template series, which simply positions one line drawings, was born. • We also wondered why there were only two sets of triangles, 90° and 60°. This is because we, on the manufacturer's side, could achieve a higher profit ratio when two triangles were sold together. This was not good to the customer. Although many people believe that triangles should be purchased in sets of the two types together, BANCO has packaged 90° and 60° separately if one triangle is demanded, only that needs to be purchased. Only the necessary surface graphics are indicated. The scale is only lines without numbers. • In this way BANCO made a contemporary shape after a complete analysis of each design tool to date. Beautiful tools when seen, when touched and when used. With a beauty which is elaborately constructed, BANCO continues to propose a new direction in design tools. CONTEMPORARY DESIGN TOOLS.

We pierce anything.

Catalogs 800 RINGS 2 U · New York 212 229 0180 · San Francisco 415 431 3133 · Los Angeles 310 657 6677

We pierce anything.

Catalogs 800 RINGS 2 U · New York 212 229 0180 · San Francisco 415 431 3133 · Los Angeles 310 657 6677

アリよさらば
STARRING
EIKICHI YAZAWA
GOOD BYE, MY ANTS.
START/APRIL·15·FRIDAY·9:00 P.M.

矢沢永吉／長塚京三　茶木良介　岡本信人　湯江健幸　田中広子／木内みどり・松村達雄 ほか
企画・原案／秋元康　主題歌「アリよさらば」矢沢永吉(東芝EMI)
提供／AJINOMOTO、花王〉タイガー魔法瓶　ロッテ
4月15日スタート・金曜よる9時

—Yes, TBS

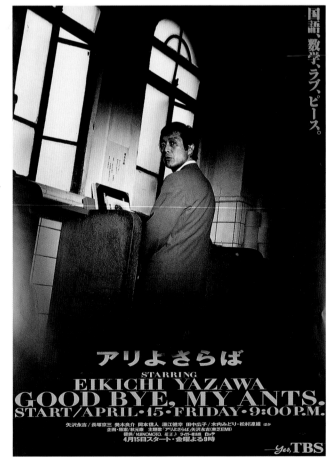

アリよさらば
STARRING
EIKICHI YAZAWA
GOOD BYE, MY ANTS.
START/APRIL·15·FRIDAY·9:00 P.M.

矢沢永吉／長塚京三　茶木良介　岡本信人　湯江健幸　田中広子／木内みどり・松村達雄 ほか
企画・原案／秋元康　主題歌「アリよさらば」矢沢永吉(東芝EMI)
提供／AJINOMOTO、花王〉タイガー魔法瓶　ロッテ
4月15日スタート・金曜よる9時

—Yes, TBS

1, 2 ART DIRECTOR: BOB WEEKS PHOTOGRAPHER: BRUCE DE BOER CLIENT: THE GAUNTLET BODY PIERCING COUNTRY: USA ■ 1, 2 TWO POSTERS FROM A SERIES PRODUCED FOR THE GAUNTLET, A SAN FRANCISCO BODY-PIERCING COMPANY. ● 1, 2 BEISPIELE AUS EINER PLAKATREIHE FÜR EINE PIERCING-FIRMA IN SAN FRANCISCO. ▲ 1, 2 SÉRIE D'AFFICHES D'UNE ENTREPRISE DE BODY-PIERCING À SAN FRANCISCO. □ 3, 4 ART DIRECTOR: KENZO IZUTANI DESIGNERS: KENZO IZUTANI, AKI HIRAI PHOTOGRAPHERS: KAZUYUKI IKENAGA (3), TOHRU KATO (4) COPYWRITER: MITSUHIRO KOIKE DESIGN FIRM: KENZO IZUTANI OFFICE CORPORATION CLIENT: TBS (TOKYO BROADCASTING SYSTEM) COUNTRY: JAPAN ■ 3, 4 A JAPANESE TELEVISION CHANNEL ANNOUNCES A TV DRAMA. ● 3, 4 EIN JAPANISCHER FERNSEHSENDER WIRBT FÜR EINE TV-SPIELFILMSERIE. ▲ 3, 4 PUBLICITÉ D'UNE CHAÎNE DE TÉLÉVISION JAPONAISE POUR UN FEUILLETON. □ 5–8 DESIGNER: BART DE ROOY PHOTOGRAPHER: DIRK

KARSTEN DESIGN FIRM: WEDA DESIGN & PACKAGING CLIENT: WEDA ADVERTISING COUNTRY: NETHERLANDS ■ 5–8 EACH OF THESE POSTERS PROMOTING A DUTCH ADVERTISING AGENCY IS DEDICATED TO A DIFFERENT CLIENT: PATRIMONIUM WONEN, THERMONOORD, AVERO PENSIONEN, OR FRIEDLAND FRICO DOMO. THE BODY PAINTING ON THE MODELS REFERS TO COMPANY LOGOS OR AD CAMPAIGNS. ● 5–8 JEDES DIESER PLAKATE FÜR EINE NIEDERLÄNDISCHE WERBEAGENTUR IST EINEM KUNDEN GEWIDMET: PATRIMONIUM WONEN, THERMONOORD, AVERO PENSIONEN, FRIEDLAND FRICO DOMO. DIE BODYPAINTINGS AUF DEN MODELLEN BEZIEHEN SICH AUF DIE LOGOS ODER ANZEIGEN FÜR DIESE FIRMEN. ▲ 5–8 PROMOTION D'UNE AGENCE DE PUBLICITÉ NÉERLANDAISE. CHAQUE AFFICHE EST DÉDIÉE À UN CLIENT: PATRIMONIUM WONEN, THERMONOORD, AVERO PENSIONEN, FRIEDLAND FRICO DOMO. LES MOTIFS DU BODY-PAINTING S'INSPIRENT DU LOGO OU D'UNE PUBLICITÉ DE CES ENTREPRISES.

The allure of Tahiti, that clutch of mystical French Polynesian islands, is legendary. The personas of Robert Lewis
Stevenson, Clark Gable, Marlon Brando and Captain Cook were all refashioned by Tahiti's unique beauty —
its unsullied beaches, its azure waters, its archaeological intrigue. ✤ Now you, too, have the opportunity to be
transformed by Tahiti's supernatural appeal. Because the KINK Explorers Club's 1995 adventure is a classic.
Tahiti Under Sail. For seven days you'll sweep across the South Pacific on a 51-foot yacht, exploring the exotic

TAHITI

isles of Tahiti, Raiatea, Tahaa and Bora Bora. ✤ Along the way you'll experience the finest foods and the most
luxurious accommodations, including a stay at the world-class Hotel Bora Bora. And you'll discover opportuni-
ties for exploration, relaxation, and photography. ✤ Space is limited to ensure a first-class journey. Your KINK
account executive has all the details regarding the itinerary and qualifications criteria. You'll be contacted soon
to discuss the KINK Explorers Club program. ✤ Tahiti beckons. We look forward to you heeding its call.

1 ART DIRECTOR/DESIGNER: STEVEN SANDSTROM PHOTOGRAPHER: MARK HOOPER ILLUSTRATORS: STEVEN SANDSTROM, JANÉE WARREN DESIGN FIRM: SANDSTROM DESIGN CLIENT: KINK RADIO COUNTRY: USA ■ 1 A SALES PROMOTION FOR KINK RADIO, PRO-MOTING THE KINK EXPLORERS CLUB. THE CLUB SENDS MEMBERS ON ALL-EXPENSES-PAID TRIPS TO EXOTIC LOCATIONS. ● 1 DER KINK EXPLORERS CLUB VON KINK RADIO BIETET SEINEN MITGLIEDERN PAUSCHALREISEN AN EXOTISCHE ORTE. ▲ 1 PUBLICITÉ D'UNE STATION DE RADIO AMÉRICAINE PROPOSANT DES VOYAGES EXOTIQUES AUX MEMBRES DE SON CLUB. □ 2 ART DIRECTOR/DESIGNER: JOHN SAYLES ILLUSTRATOR: JOHN SAYLES DESIGN FIRM: SAYLES GRAPHIC DESIGN CLIENT: FORT DEARBORN LIFE COUNTRY: USA ■ 2 THIS LIMITED EDITION POSTER FEATURES AN ORIGINAL CHARCOAL ILLUSTRATION USING TEN COLORS PRINTED ON A THICK, CLOTH-LIKE PAPER. IT WAS USED TO PROMOTE A TRIP FOR THE CLIENTS TOP PERFORM-ERS. ● 2 IN LIMITIERTER AUFLAGE GEDRUCKTES PLAKAT MIT EINER KOHLEZEICHNUNG, IN SIEBEN FARBEN AUF EIN DICKES,

STOFFARTIGES PAPIER GEDRUCKT. DAS THEMA: EINE REISE FÜR ANGESTELLTE DES AUFTRAGGEBERS ALS BELOHNUNG FÜR BESONDERE LEISTUNGEN. ▲ 2 CETTE AFFICHE AVEC UN DESSIN AU CARBONE A ÉTÉ IMPRIMÉE EN SEPT COULEURS SUR UN PAPIER ÉPAIS, SEMBLABLE À DU TISSU. ÉDITION LIMITÉE. SUJET: UN VOYAGE ORGANISÉ PAR LE CLIENT POUR RÉCOM-PENSER SES MEILLEURS COLLABORATEURS. □ 3 ART DIRECTOR/DESIGNER: KEVIN KEARNS PHOTOGRAPHY: STOCK ILLUSTRATOR: ED KUNZE DESIGN FIRM: HILL, HOLIDAY NEW YORK CLIENT: KILLINGTON LIMITED COUNTRY: USA ■ 3 DESIGNED FOR DISPLAY IN MANHATTAN, THIS POSTER ILLUSTRATES THE SNOW-MAKING CAPABILITIES OF TWO NEARBY SKI AREAS. ● 3 DAS FÜR DEN AUSHANG IN MANHATTAN BESTIMMTE PLAKAT INFORMIERT ÜBER DIE SCHNEEMASCHINEN IN ZWEI NAHEGELEGENEN SKIGEBIE-TEN. ▲ 3 PUBLICITÉ D'UNE CAMPAGNE D'AFFICHAGE DESTINÉE AU QUARTIER DE MANHATTAN. CETTE AFFICHE VISAIT À PROMOU-VOIR DEUX DOMAINES SKIABLES PROCHES DE LA CITÉ NEW-YORKAISE EN MONTRANT LES POSSIBILITÉS DES CANONS À NEIGE.

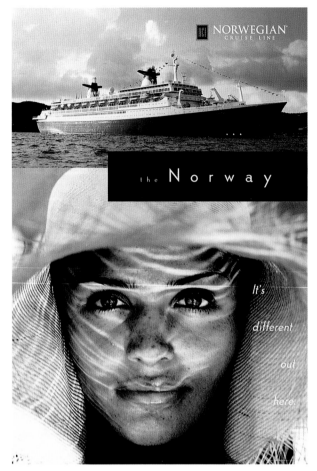

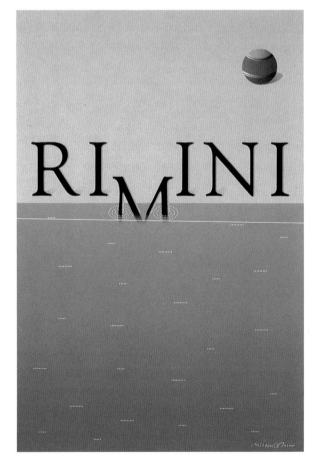

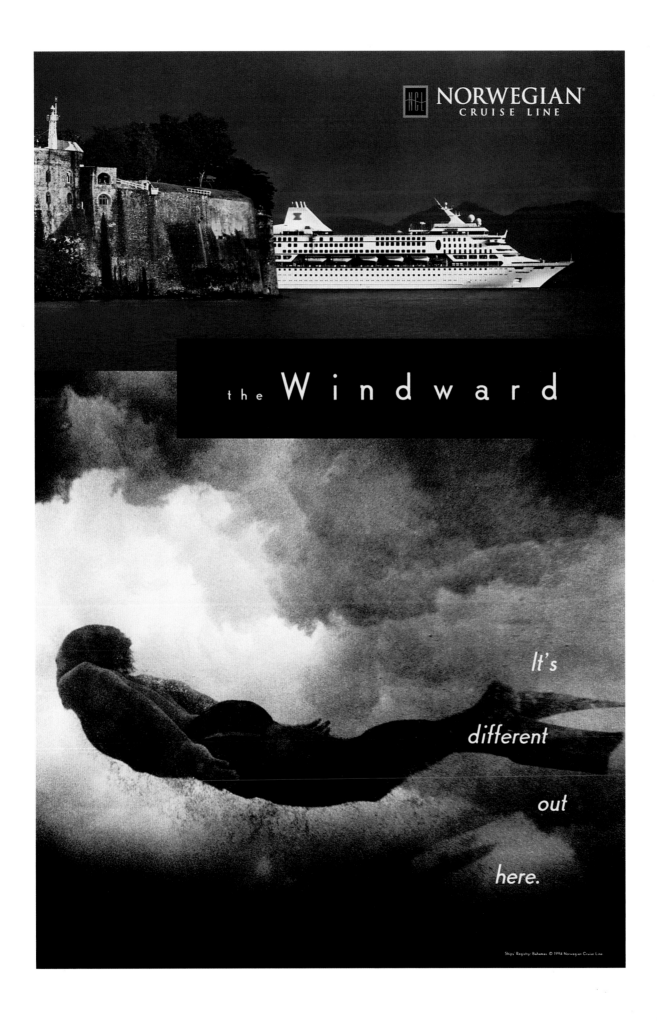

(PRECEDING SPREAD) **1, 2, 5** ART DIRECTORS: PAUL CURIN, DAMON DUREE DESIGNER: DAMON DUREE PHOTOGRAPHERS: JIM ERICKSON, TOM TRACY, HERB RITTS, WAYNE LEVIN DESIGN FIRM: GOODBY SILVERSTEIN + PARTNERS CLIENT: NORWEGIAN CRUISE LINES COUNTRY: USA ■ **1, 2, 5** FOR DISPLAY IN TRAVEL AGENCIES, THIS SERIES OF POSTERS REINFORCES NORWEGIAN CRUISE LINE'S MOTTO: "IT'S DIFFERENT OUT HERE." EACH POSTER REFLECTS A DIFFERENT SHIP'S PERSONALITY OR ITINERARY. ● **1, 2, 5** JEDES DIESER FÜR DEN AUSHANG IN REISEBÜROS BESTIMMTEN PLAKATE BEFASST SICH MIT EINEM BESTIMMTEN SCHIFF DER NORWEGISCHEN REEDEREI NORWEGIAN CRUISE LINE. DAS MOTTO DER LINIE: «HIER DRAUSSEN IST ALLES ANDERS.» ▲ **1, 2, 5** P.L.V. DESTINÉE AUX AGENCES DE VOYAGES ET PRÉSENTANT LES DIFFÉRENTS BATEAUX DE LA COMPAGNIE NORWEGIAN CRUISE LINE. LE SLOGAN PROMET LA DÉCOUVERTE DE NOUVEAUX HORIZONS. □ **3** ART DIRECTOR/DESIGNER: MILTON GLASER ILLUSTRATOR: MILTON GLASER DESIGN FIRM: MILTON GLASER INC. CLIENT: RIMINI COUNTRY: ITALY ■ **3** A PROMOTIONAL POSTER FOR THE 1995 TOURIST SEASON IN RIMINI, AN ITALIAN SEASIDE CITY. ● **3** WERBUNG FÜR DIE SAISON 1995 IN RIMINI. ▲ **3** PUBLICITÉ POUR LA SAISON 1995 À RIMINI. □ **4** DESIGNER: BOZENA JANKOWSKA CLIENT: LANDESHAUPTSTADT MÜNCHEN, FREMDENVERKEHRSAMT COUNTRY: GERMANY ■ **4** THE CITY OF MUNICH ADVERTISES ITS ANNUAL OCTOBER FESTIVAL. THE POSTER IS THE WINNER OF AN ANNUAL COMPETITION. ● **4** DIESES PLAKAT IST DER GEWINNER DES JÄHRLICH FÜR DAS MÜNCHNER OKTOBERFEST AUSGESCHRIEBENEN PLAKATWETTBEWERBS.

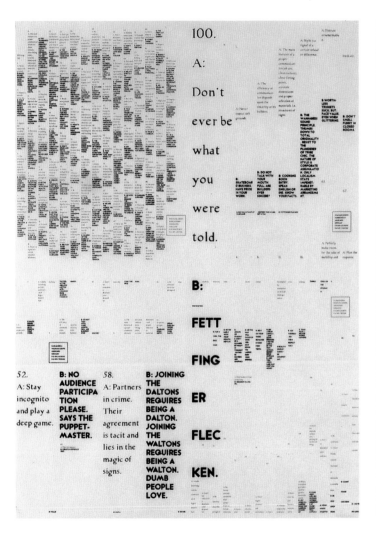

▲ **4** AFFICHE "LAURÉATE", PRIMÉE LORS DU CONCOURS ANNUEL CONSACRÉ AUX MEILLEURES AFFICHES POUR LA FÊTE DE LA BIÈRE À MUNICH. □ (THIS SPREAD) **1** ART DIRECTOR/DESIGNER: CHRIS MAPLE ILLUSTRATORS: JIM HAYES, JOHN FRETZ DESIGN FIRM: MAPLE DESIGN, INC. CLIENT: HOLLAND AMERICA LINE WESTOURS, INC. COUNTRY: USA ■ **1** A POSTER HONORING HOLLAND AMERICA'S AWARD-WINNING QUALITY AND SERVICE, AS WELL AS ITS NEW "WORLD VOYAGE" LINE OF SHIPS. ● **1** DIE NEUEN «WORLD VOYAGE»-SCHIFFE DER HOLLAND AMERICA LINE UND IHRE MIT PREISEN AUSGEZEICHNETE QUALITÄT UND DIENSTLEISTUNGEN SIND DIE THEMEN DIESES PLAKATES. ▲ **1** PUBLICITÉ POUR LES NOUVEAUX BATEAUX «WORLD VOYAGE» DE LA COMPAGNIE HOLLAND AMERICA LINE ET LES PRESTATIONS À BORD, PRIMÉES POUR LEUR EXCELLENCE. □ **2** ART DIRECTORS/DESIGNERS/COPYWRITERS: FLORIAN BÖHM, DR. WOLFGANG SCHEPPE DESIGN FIRM: SCHEPPE BÖHM ASSOCIATES COUNTRY: GERMANY ■ **2** "WRAPRAP BELIEVES," THE GIVE-AWAY PROMOTION OF A TYPOGRAPHER AND A DESIGNER. THE TEAM CREATES SPECIAL TYPEFACES ESPECIALLY DESIGNED FOR THEIR CLIENTS' CORPORATE IDENTITY. THE TWO TYPE FONTS USED HERE ARE CALLED DEPRESS AND VANTA. THE POSTER WAS ALSO DESIGNED TO SERVE AS WRAPPING PAPER FOR THE COMPANY, THUS THE DIFFERENT LAYERS OFFER NEW TYPOGRAPHIC IMAGES AND MEANINGS. ● **2** «WRAPRAP BELIEVES», SELBSTDARSTELLUNG EINES TYPOGRAPHEN-DESIGNER-TEAMS, DEM ES DABEI UM ZURÜCKHALTUNG UND WITZ ZU TUN WAR. DIE AGENTUR ZEICHNET EIGENE SCHRIFTSCHNITTE, DIE OFT EXKLUSIV DEN KUNDEN-CIS ZUGEORDNET WERDEN. HIER SIND

ES DIE FONTS DEPRESS UND VANTA. DAS PLAKAT DIENT NICHT NUR ALS GIVE-AWAY, SONDERN AUCH ALS EINWICKELPAPIER. ES WURDE SO KONZIPIERT, DASS BEIM VERPACKEN REIZVOLLE ÜBERLAGERUNGEN DES TRANSPARENTPAPIERS ENTSTEHEN, WAS ZU NEUEN TYPOGRAPHISCHEN BILDERN UND SINNZUSAMMENHÄNGEN FÜHRT. ▲ 2 «WRAPRAP BELIEVES» OU VARIATIONS SUR UN MÊME THÈME. «PORTRAIT D'AGENCE» HUMORISTIQUE RÉALISÉ PAR UN TYPOGRAPHE ET UN DESIGNER, DÉSIREUX DE PRÉSENTER LEUR TRAVAIL DE MANIÈRE ORIGINALE TOUT EN FAISANT PREUVE D'UNE CERTAINE RETENUE. SPÉCIALISÉE DANS LA CRÉATION DE CARACTÈRES TYPOGRAPHIQUES, L'AGENCE CRÉA NOTAMMENT DIVERS TYPES D'ÉCRITURE POUR L'IDENTITÉ INSTITUTIONNELLE DE LEURS CLIENTS. DANS LE CAS PRÉSENT, LES POLICES UTILISÉES ONT POUR NOM DEPRESS ET VANTA. RÉALISÉE SUR UN SUPPORT TRANSPARENT, L'AFFICHE PEUT AUSSI SERVIR DE PAPIER D'EMBALLAGE (D'OÙ LE TERME ANGLAIS «WRAP»). DANS CE CAS, LA SUPERPOSITION DES COUCHES CRÉE UN NOUVEL AGENCEMENT

DES MOTS QUI, À LEUR TOUR, FORMENT DE NOUVEAUX MOTIFS TYPOGRAPHIQUES. ☐ (PRECEDING SPREAD) 3 DESIGNER: BOB AUFULDISH ILLUSTRATOR: ERIC DONELAN DESIGN FIRM: AUFULDISH & WARINNER CLIENT: EMIGRE COUNTRY: USA ■ 3 A DIRECT-MAIL POSTER DESIGNED TO PROMOTE "BIG CHEESE" — 216 ILLUSTRATIONS IN FONT FORMAT, AVAILABLE FROM EMIGRE. ● 3 EIN FÜR DEN DIREKTVERSAND BESTIMMTES PLAKAT FÜR «BIG CHEESE» – 216 ILLUSTRATIONEN IM FONTFORMAT, DIE BEI DER ZEITSCHRIFT EMIGRE ANGEBOTEN WERDEN ▲ 3 PUBLICITÉ DIRECTE POUR 216 ILLUSTRATIONS «BIG CHEESE», DISPONIBLES AUPRÈS DU MAGAZINE EMIGRE. ☐ (THIS SPREAD) 1, 2 ART DIRECTOR/DESIGNER: CARLOS SEGURA PHOTOGRAPHER: JOHN PAYNE (TIES) ILLUSTRATOR: TONY KLASSEN DESIGN FIRM: SEGURA INC. CLIENT: [T26] DIGITAL TYPE FOUNDRY COUNTRY: USA ■ 1, 2 POSTERS TO PROMOTE T-26, A NEW DIGITAL TYPE FOUNDRY INTENDED TO PROMOTE EXPERIMENTATION. ● 1, 2 WERBUNG FÜR T-26, HERSTELLER NEUER DIGITALER SCHRIFTEN, DER DIE EXPERIMENTIERFREUDIGKEIT FÖRDERN WILL. ▲ 1, 2 PUBLICITÉ POUR DE NOUVELLES POLICES DE CARACTÈRES DIGITALES DESTINÉES À STIMULER LA CRÉATIVITÉ.

1 Art Director/Designer/Illustrator/Design Firm: K. DOMENIC GEISSBÜHLER Client: SCHWEIZERISCHER BANKVEREIN Country: SWITZERLAND ■ 1 ANNOUNCEMENT OF AN EXHIBITION OF THE ARTIST'S POSTERS FOR THE ZURICH OPERA HOUSE, EMPLOYING A MOTIF FROM A BALLET POSTER. ● 1 ANKÜNDIGUNG EINER AUSSTELLUNG VON PLAKATEN DES KÜNSTLERS FÜR DAS OPERNHAUS

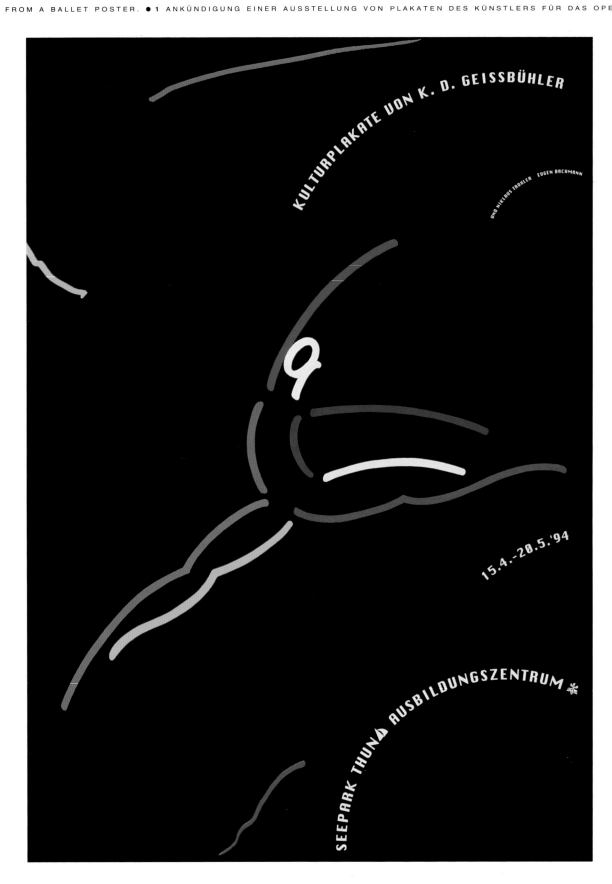

ZÜRICH. DAS MOTIV IST EINEM PLAKAT FÜR EINE BALLETTAUFFÜHRUNG ENTNOMMEN. ▲ 1 EXPOSITION D'UNE SÉRIE D'AFFICHES RÉALISÉES PAR K. DOMENIC GEISSBÜHLER POUR L'OPÉRA DE ZURICH. □ 2–5 Art Director/Designer: JOHN CABALKA Photographer: AL PITZNER Design Firm: CABALKA STUDIO USA Client: STATE BALLET OF MISSOURI Country: USA ■ 2–5 POSTERS TO PROMOTE BALLET AS AN ART FORM. ● 2–5 BALLETT ALS EINE FORM DER KUNST. ▲ 2–5 LE BALLET, ÉLEVÉ AU RANG D'ART.

卒業制作展
2月21日(火)〜26日(日)【前期】
洋画, 日本画, 彫塑, 書, 総合造形
2月28日(火)〜3月5日(日)【後期】
構成, 視覚伝達デザイン, 生産デザイン,
環境デザイン, 建築デザイン

卒業研究発表会
3月7日(火)
芸術学
会場:美術館内2Fアルスホール13:00〜

修了展
3月7日(火)〜12日(日)
洋画, 日本画, 彫塑, 書, 構成, 総合造形,
視覚伝達デザイン, 生産デザイン,
環境デザイン, 建築デザイン

ART
DESIGN

ENVIRONMENTAL DESIGN
CARVING AND MODELLING
SHO-CALLIGRAPHY ART
CONSTRUCTIVE ART
NIHONGA
ARCHITECTURAL DESIGN
PRODUCT DESIGN
PAINTING
THEORY AND HISTORY OF ART
PLASTIC ARTS AND MIXED MEDIA
VISUAL COMMUNICATION DESIGN

平成6年度筑波大学
芸術専門学群卒業制作展
芸術研究科修了展
会場:茨城県つくば美術館 9:30〜17:00(入館は16:30まで)

Invitation days: October 5(Tue)-7(Thu) Public days: October 8(Fri)-9(Sat) Location: Makuhari Messe Show Hours: 10:00a.m. to 5:00p.m. Admission: Adult ¥500/Student ¥300
Sponsor: Electronic Industries Association of Japan Management: Japan Electronics Show Association

Exciting Creations...Yours to Discover

JAPAN ELECTRONICS SHOW '93

(PRECEDING SPREAD LEFT) **1** ART DIRECTOR: MASAYUKI YAMAMOTO DESIGNERS: MASAYUKI YAMAMOTO, AYA KOYANAGI PHOTOGRAPHER: MASANORI KANESHIGE COPYWRITER: TADANOBU HARA DESIGN FIRM: MASAYUKI YAMAMOTO DESIGN STUDIO CLIENT: UNIVERSITY OF TSUKUBA COUNTRY: JAPAN ■ 1 THE TWO HEADS OF THIS CREATURE—MARKED DESIGN AND FINE ART—INDICATE THE VARIOUS DISCIPLINES REPRESENTED IN THIS STUDENT EXHIBITION. ● 1 DIE BEIDEN KÖPFE DIESER KREATUR MIT DER AUFSCHRIFT DESIGN UND KUNST SIND EIN HINWEIS AUF DIE VERSCHIEDENEN DISZIPLINEN, DIE IN DIESER AUSSTELLUNG DER ABSCHLUSSARBEITEN VON STUDENTEN VERTRETEN SIND. ▲ 1 ART ET DESIGN: LES TÊTES DE CETTE CRÉATURE BICÉPHALE FONT ALLUSION AUX DIVERSES DISCIPLINES REPRÉSENTÉES DANS CETTE EXPOSITION, CONSACRÉE AUX TRAVAUX DE FIN D'ÉTUDES DE JEUNES ARTISTES. □ (PRECEDING SPREAD RIGHT) **2** ART DIRECTOR: NORIO KUDO DESIGNER: HARUKO KOTAKA PHOTOGRAPHER: YUKIHIKO UDA COPYWRITER: HIROSHI YAMAZAKI DESIGN FIRM: MAGNA INC. ADVERTISING

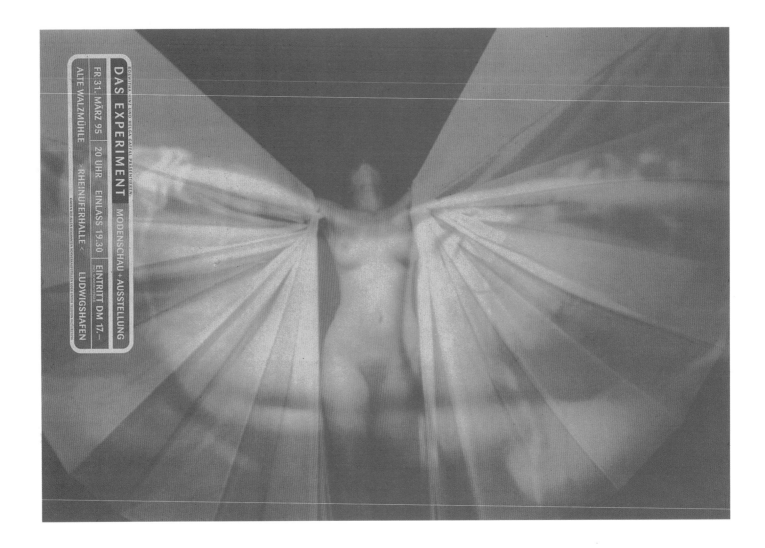

CLIENT: JAPAN ELECTRONICS SHOW ASSOCIATION COUNTRY: JAPAN ■ 2 "EXCITING CREATIONS, YOURS TO DISCOVER"—AT THE JAPAN ELECTRONICS SHOW. ● 2 AUFREGENDE ENTDECKUNGEN VERSPRICHT DIESES PLAKAT DEN BESUCHERN EINER ELEKTRONISCHEN FACHMESSE. ▲ 2 AFFICHE D'UN SALON DE L'ÉLECTRONIQUE JAPONAIS. DÉCOUVERTES PASSIONNANTES GARANTIES. □ (THIS SPREAD) **1** ART DIRECTOR/DESIGNER: ANDREAS OCHS DESIGN FIRM: AGIL CLIENT: GAFFAL/HINZ COUNTRY: GERMANY ■ 1 "THE EXPERIMENT"—A FASHION SHOW AND EXHIBITION. ● 1 ZWEI MODESCHÖPFERINNEN PRÄSENTIEREN IHRE KREATIONEN. ▲ 1 DEUX STYLISTES PRÉSENTENT LEUR COLLECTION. □ **2** ART DIRECTOR/DESIGNER/PHOTOGRAPHER: HOLGER MATTHIES CLIENT: GOETHE INSTITUT COUNTRY: GERMANY ■ 2 THESE "STAIRS" ARE REACHING FOR THE SKY, JUST LIKE THE PIANISTS IN CONCERTS PRESENTED BY A GERMAN CULTURAL INSTITUTE. ● 2 DIESE «HIMMELSTREPPE» STEHT FÜR DIE PIANISTEN ERSTEN RANGES IN DEN KONZERTEN DES GOETHE INSTITUTS. ▲ 2 AFFICHE RÉALISÉE POUR DES RÉCITALS DE

PIANO PATRONNÉS PAR L'INSTITUT GOETHE: LA VIRTUOSITÉ DES INTERPRÈTES EST GAGE D'UNE MUSIQUE CÉLESTE. □ 3
ART DIRECTOR/DESIGNER/PHOTOGRAPHER: HOLGER MATTHIES CLIENT: THEATER GÜTERSLOH COUNTRY: GERMANY ■ 3 POSTER PRO-
MOTING THE CONCERTS PRESENTED BY A THEATER IN THE 1995/96 SEASON. ● 3 SPIELZEITPLAKAT MIT DEM KERNBEREICH
MUSIK. ▲ 3 AFFICHE DE THÉÂTRE PRÉSENTANT LE PROGRAMME DE LA SAISON 95-96. □ 4 ART DIRECTOR/DESIGNER: HOLGER
MATTHIES CLIENT: MUSEUM FÜR KUNST UND GEWERBE HAMBURG COUNTRY: GERMANY ■ 4 ANNOUNCEMENT OF A POSTER EXHI-
BITION PRESENTING THE WORK OF PROMINENT POSTER ARTISTS. ● 4 ANKÜNDIGUNG EINER AUSSTELLUNG DER WICHTIG-
STEN PLAKATGESTALTER. ▲ 4 ANNONCE D'UNE EXPOSITION CONSACRÉE AUX PLUS GRANDS AFFICHISTES. □ 5 ART
DIRECTORS/DESIGNERS: SASCHA LOBE, ANDREAS OCHS DESIGN FIRM: AGIL CLIENT: GALERIE BRÖTZINGER ART COUNTRY:
GERMANY ■ 5 AN EXHIBITION OF UNIQUE DOLLS MADE FROM OLD LOCKERS. ● 5 EINE AUSSTELLUNG GANZ BESONDERER

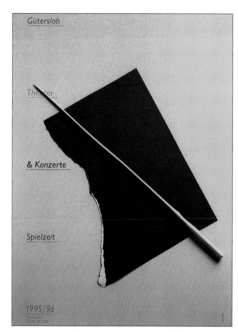
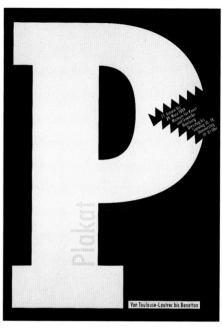

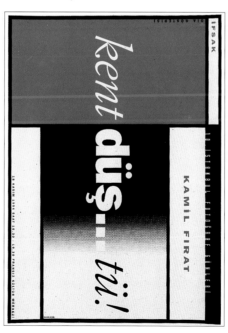

PUPPEN, DIE AUS ALTEN SPINDEN GEMACHT SIND. ▲ 5 EXPOSITION DE POUPÉES ORIGINALES, FABRIQUÉES À PARTIR DE
VIEILLES ARMOIRES. □ 6 ART DIRECTOR/DESIGNER: SAVAS CEKIC DESIGN FIRM: VALÖR TASARIM LTD. STI. CLIENT: KAMIL FIRAT
COUNTRY: TURKEY ■ 6 ANNOUNCEMENT OF A PHOTO EXHIBITION. ● 6 ANKÜNDIGUNG EINER PHOTOAUSSTELLUNG. ▲ 6 AFFICHE
D'UNE EXPOSITION DE PHOTO. □ 7 DESIGNER: DANIEL VOLKART PHOTOGRAPHER: MICHEL VAN GRONDEL CLIENT: MUSEUM FÜR
GESTALTUNG COUNTRY: SWITZERLAND ■ 7 AN EXHIBITION ENTITLED "A CITY AND ITS PROBLEM" REFERS TO A ZURICH DRUG
HANG-OUT WHICH HAS SINCE BEEN BROKEN UP BY THE POLICE. ● 7 DAS PROBLEM DER OFFENEN DROGENSZENE AM
ZÜRCHER LETTENAREAL WAR THEMA DIESER AUSSTELLUNG. DIE SZENE WURDE DURCH EINE POLIZEIAKTION OFFIZIELL
AUFGELÖST. ▲ 7 AFFICHE D'UNE EXPOSITION CONSACRÉE AUX PROBLÈMES POSÉS PAR UNE SCÈNE OUVERTE DE LA DROGUE
QUI S'ÉTAIT IMPLANTÉE DANS UN ARRONDISSEMENT DE ZURICH. ENTRE-TEMPS, L'ENDROIT A ÉTÉ FERMÉ PAR LA POLICE.

(THIS SPREAD) 1, 2 ART DIRECTOR: SEIJU TODA DESIGNERS: SEIJU TODA, KOICHI KUNO PHOTOGRAPHER: SAKATA EIICHIRO COPY-WRITER: JUN MAKI DESIGN FIRM: TODA OFFICE COUNTRY: JAPAN ■ 1, 2 AN EXHIBITION OF SKETCHES BY FILM DIRECTOR AKIRA KUROSAWA IN NEW YORK. THE POLE OF THE US FLAG IS A JAPANESE BOW. THE MOTIF OF THE FLAG IN FIGURE 2 REFERS TO KUROSAWA'S FIRST NAME AKIRA, AS THE CHINESE CHARACTER FOR THIS NAME CAN BE BROKEN DOWN INTO SUN AND MOON. ● 1, 2 AUSSTELLUNG VON SKIZZEN DES JAPANISCHEN FILMREGISSEURS AKIRA KUROSAWA IN NEW YORK. DER MAST DER US-FLAGGE IST EIN JAPANISCHER BOGEN. DAS MOTIV DER FLAGGE IN ABB. 2 BEZIEHT SICH AUF DEN VORNAMEN AKIRA, DA DAS CHINESISCHE SCHRIFTZEICHEN DAFÜR SICH AUS DEN ZEICHEN FÜR SONNE UND MOND ZUSAMMENSETZT. ▲ 1, 2 CETTE EXPO-SITION PRÉSENTAIT LES ESTAMPES D'UN ARTISTE JAPONAIS À NEW YORK. ■ 3–6 ART DIRECTOR/DESIGNER/PHOTOGRAPHER: SEIJU TODA COPYWRITER: JUN MAKI DESIGN FIRM: TODA OFFICE COUNTRY: JAPAN ■ 3–6 NO COMPUTER WAS USED FOR THIS SERIES OF EXHIBITION POSTERS. ● 3–6 FÜR DIESE PLAKATREIHE FÜR EINE AUSSTELLUNG WURDE KEIN COMPUTER VERWENDET. ▲ 3–6 CETTE SÉRIE D'AFFICHES POUR UNE EXPOSITION A ÉTÉ RÉALISÉE SANS L'AIDE DE L'ORDINATEUR. □ (FOLLOWING SPREAD) 1–3 ART DIRECTOR/DESIGNER: KENYA HARA DESIGN FIRM: NIPPON DESIGN CENTER, INC. CLIENT: DAI NIPPON PRINTING CORP. COUNTRY: JAPAN ■ 1–3 A POSTER FOR GRAPHIC DESIGNER KENYA HARA'S ONE-MAN SHOW. THE ILLUSTRATIONS ARE A REFER-ENCE TO THE JAPANESE SPIRIT, SOMETIMES EXPRESSED AS "UTSU," MEANING AN EMPTINESS IN WHICH SOMETHING (PER-HAPS GOD) CAN EXIST. ● 1–3 EINZELAUSSTELLUNG DES DESIGNERS KENYA HARA. HIER GEHT ES UM DEN JAPANISCHEN BEGRIFF «UTSU», DER LEERE BEDEUTET. WENN IN EINEM ZENTRUM NICHTS IST, KANN DIESE LEERE VON ETWAS (VIEL-LEICHT GOTT) EINGENOMMEN WERDEN. ▲ 1–3 EXPOSITION DU DESIGNER KENYA HARA. L'ARTISTE S'INSPIRA D'UNE PHILOSO-PHIE JAPONAISE, PARFOIS RÉSUMÉE PAR LE TERME «UTSU» QUI SIGNIFIE LE VIDE. LORSQU'UN VIDE SUBSISTE AU CENTRE, CE VIDE PEUT ALORS ÊTRE COMBLÉ PAR AUTRE CHOSE (PEUT-ÊTRE DIEU). □ 4–6 ART DIRECTOR/DESIGNER: KENYA HARA DESIGN FIRM: NIPPON DESIGN CENTER, INC. CLIENT: JAPAN DESIGN COMMITTEE COUNTRY: JAPAN ■ 4–6 THIS SERIES WAS DONE FOR AN EXHIBITION WITH "LIFE" AS ITS THEME. THE DESIGNER EXPRESSES "BIRTH OF LIFE," "ENERGY OF LIFE," "PERSISTENCE

AND BEAUTY OF LIFE," THROUGH THE JUXTAPOSITION OF SOFTNESS AND TENSION INHERENT IN THE TRADITIONAL ART OF IKEBANA. ● 4–6 EINE SERIE FÜR EINE AUSSTELLUNG ZUM THEMA «LEBEN». DIE FORMEN IN DIESEN PLAKATEN SIND AUSDRUCK FÜR DIE «GEBURT DES LEBENS», «KRAFT DES LEBENS», «BEHARRLICHKEIT» UND DIE «SCHÖNHEIT DES LEBENS», WOBEI DIE VERBINDUNG VON SANFTHEIT UND SPANNUNG AUF DIE TRADITIONELLE KUNST DES IKEBANA ZURÜCKGEHT. ▲ 4–6 «LA NAISSANCE DE LA VIE», «LA FORCE DE LA VIE», «LA TÉNACITÉ ET LA BEAUTÉ DE LA VIE». SÉRIE D'AFFICHES RÉAL-ISÉES POUR UNE EXPOSITION CONSACRÉE AU THÈME DE LA VIE. LES FORMES CHOISIES PAR L'ARTISTE S'INSPIRENT DE L'IKEBANA (ARRANGEMENTS FLORAUX), UN ART TRADITIONNEL JAPONAIS QUI ALLIE TENSION ET DOUCEUR. □ 7 ART DIRECTOR/DESIGNER: NORMAN MOORE DESIGN FIRM: DESIGN/ART, INC. CLIENT: LAKELORD COUNTRY: USA ■ 7 A POSTER DESIGNED TO PROMOTE AN ECLECTIC ART EXHIBITION IN NEW YORK WHICH FEATURED PAINTINGS, SCULPTURE, AND PHOTOGRAPHY. ● 7 ANKÜNDIGUNG EINER AUSSTELLUNG IN NEW YORK, IN DER GEMÄLDE, SKULPTUREN UND PHOTOGRAPHIEN GEZEIGT WER-DEN. ▲ 7 AFFICHE D'UNE EXPOSITION NEW-YORKAISE PRÉSENTANT PEINTURES, SCULPTURES ET PHOTOGRAPHIES. □ 8 ART DIRECTOR/DESIGNER/ILLUSTRATOR: IKU AKIYAMA CLIENT: THE MAINICHI NEWSPAPERS COUNTRY: JAPAN ■ 8 ANNOUNCEMENT OF A COMMEMORATIVE EXHIBITION DEDICATED TO SHARAKU (KNOWN AS TOSHUSAI), A MASTER OF THE JAPANESE COLORED WOODCUT. ● 8 ANKÜNDIGUNG EINER GEDENKAUSSTELLUNG, DIE EINEM MEISTER DES JAPANISCHEN FARBHOLZSCHNITTS GEWIDMET IST. SHARAKU BENUTZTE DEN KÜNSTLERNAMEN TOSHUSAI UND TRAT ERSTMALS VOR 200 JAHREN MIT SEINEN ARBEITEN IN ERSCHEINUNG. ▲ 8 AFFICHE RÉALISÉE POUR UNE EXPOSITION CONSACRÉE À SHARAKU, GRAND MAÎTRE JAPO-NAIS DE LA GRAVURE SUR BOIS, PLUS CONNU SOUS LE NOM DE TOSHUSAI (18E SIÈCLE). □ 9 ART DIRECTOR/DESIGNER: ERIC CHAN PHOTOGRAPHER: TIM PHOTOGRAPHY DESIGN FIRM: ERIC CHAN DESIGN CO. LTD. CLIENT: HONG KONG DESIGNERS ASSOCIATION COUNTRY: HONG KONG ■ 9 ANNOUNCEMENT OF AN EXHIBITION OF 15 GRAPHIC DESIGNERS FROM HONG KONG. ● 9 ANKÜNDIGUNG EINER AUSSTELLUNG VON 15 GRAPHIK-DESIGNERN AUS HONGKONG. ▲ 9 AFFICHE ANNONÇANT L'EXPOSITION

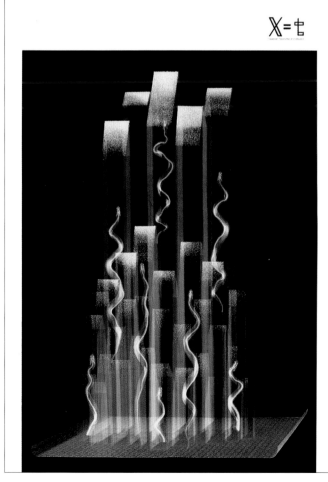

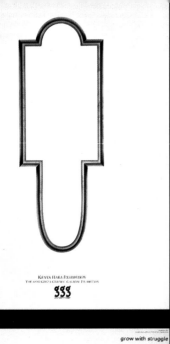

KENYA HARA EXHIBITION
THE 2ND GINZA GRAPHIC GALLERY EXHIBITION
ggg

KENYA HARA EXHIBITION
THE 2ND GINZA GRAPHIC GALLERY EXHIBITION
ggg

KENYA HARA EXHIBITION
THE 2ND GINZA GRAPHIC GALLERY EXHIBITION
ggg

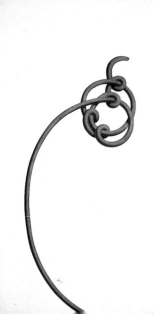
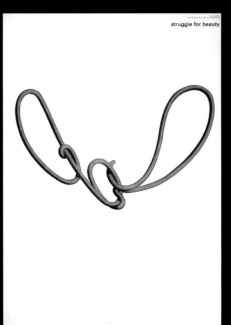

COUNTRY: JAPAN ■ 10 "HAVING REACHED A CLIMAX AT AGE OF «29, I WAS DEAD." AN EXHIBITION BY JAPANESE POSTER ARTIST TADANORI YOKOO. ● 10 «NACHDEM ICH IM ALTER VON 29 JAHREN EINEN HÖHEPUNKT ERREICHT HATTE, WAR ICH TOT.» EINE AUSSTELLUNG DES JAPANISCHEN PLAKATKÜNSTLERS YOKOO TADANORI. ▲ 10 «APRÈS AVOIR ATTEINT LE SOMMET À L'ÂGE DE 29 ANS, JE SUIS MORT.» UNE EXPOSITION DE L'AFFICHISTE JAPONAIS YOKOO TADANORI. □ 11 ART DIRECTOR/DESIGNER: KEIZO MATSUI DESIGN FIRM: KEIZO MATSUI & ASSOCIATES CLIENT: MORISAWA CO., LTD. COUNTRY: JAPAN ■ 11 AN EXHIBITION CELE-BRATING THE 20TH ANNIVERSARY OF THE PUBLIC RELATIONS MAGAZINE OF A TYPESETTING COMPANY WHO PROMOTED IMAGINATION THROUGH LETTERS. TRANSFORMED INTO A KIND OF HIEROGLYPH, THESE ANCIENT CHINESE CHARACTERS SIG-NIFY: SUN, MOON, MOUNTAIN, CLOUD, SEA, AND FISH. ● 11 EINE AUSSTELLUNG ZUM 20JÄHRIGEN BESTEHEN DER

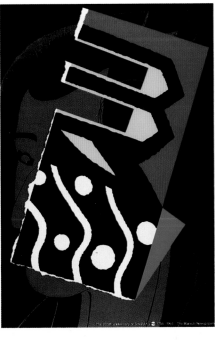

KUNDENZEITSCHRIFT EINER SETZEREI, DEREN THEMA «PHANTASIE UND BUCHSTABEN» WAR. ALTE CHINESISCHE SCHRIFTZEICHEN WURDEN IN EINE ART HIEROGLYPHEN VERWANDELT. IHRE BEDEUTUNG: SONNE, MOND, BERG, WOLKE, MEER UND FISCH. ▲ 11 EXPOSITION À L'OCCASION DU 20ᴱ ANNIVERSAIRE DU MAGAZINE-CLIENTS D'UN ATELIER DE COMPO-SITION SUR LE THÈME «LETTRES ET IMAGINATION». TRANSFORMÉS EN HIÉROGLYPHES, CES ANCIENS CARACTÈRES CHI-NOIS SIGNIFIENT: SOLEIL, LUNE, MONTAGNE, NUAGES, MER ET POISSON. □ 12 ART DIRECTOR/DESIGNER: TADANORI YOKOO COUNTRY: JAPAN ■ 12 "JAPANESE CULTURE, THE 50 POSTWAR YEARS." AN EXHIBITION POSTER EMPLOYING VARIOUS ELE-MENTS THAT SYMBOLIZE DEVELOPMENT IN JAPAN. ● 12 «JAPANISCHE KULTUR, DIE 50 NACHKRIEGSJAHRE.» AUSSTEL-LUNGSPLAKAT MIT VERSCHIEDENEN ELEMENTEN, DIE DIE ENTWICKLUNG IN JAPAN SYMBOLISIEREN. ▲ 12 «LA CULTURE JAPONAISE DURANT LES 50 ANS D'APRÈS-GUERRE.» LES SUJETS DE L'AFFICHE SYMBOLISENT L'ÉVOLUTION DU JAPON.

The 200th anniversary of SHARAKU 1794–1994   The Mainichi Newspapers

(PRECEDING SPREAD) **1** ART DIRECTOR/DESIGNER: TADANORI YOKOO COUNTRY: JAPAN ■**1** THE JAPANESE MASTER OF WOODCUTS SHARAKU, KNOWN AS TOSHUSAI, WORKED IN TOKYO IN 1794/95 CREATING 140 ACTORS' PORTRAITS WITH HIGHLY DECORATIVE EFFECTS. ●**1** SHARAKU, DER ALS TOSHUSAI BEKANNTE MEISTER DES JAPANISCHEN FARBHOLZSCHNITTS, SCHUF 1794/95 IN TOKIO CA. 140 SCHAUSPIELERPORTRÄTS MIT STARKER DEKORATIVER WIRKUNG. ▲**1** PLUS CONNU SOUS SON NOM D'ARTISTE TOSHUSAI, LE GRAND MAÎTRE JAPONAIS DE LA GRAVURE SUR BOIS SHARAKU RÉALISA QUELQUE 140 PORTRAITS DE COMÉDIENS EN L'ESPACE D'UN AN À PEINE (1794–95). ■**2** ART DIRECTOR/DESIGNER/CLIENT: SHIN MATSUNAGA DESIGN FIRM: SHIN MATSUNAGA DESIGN INC. COUNTRY: JAPAN ■**2** ANOTHER EXAMPLE FROM THE SERIES OF POSTERS BY CONTEMPORARY JAPANESE POSTER ARTISTS DEDICATED TO SHARAKU, A MASTER OF JAPANESE COLORED WOODCUTS. ●**2** EIN WEITERES PLAKAT AUS DER REIHE, DIE SHARAKU, DEM MEISTER DES JAPANISCHEN FARBHOLZSCHNITTS GEWIDMET IST. ▲**2** AUTRE EXEMPLE D'UNE SÉRIE D'AFFICHES DÉDIÉES À SHARAKU, GRAND MAÎTRE JAPONAIS DE LA GRAVURE SUR BOIS. □ (THIS SPREAD) **1** ART

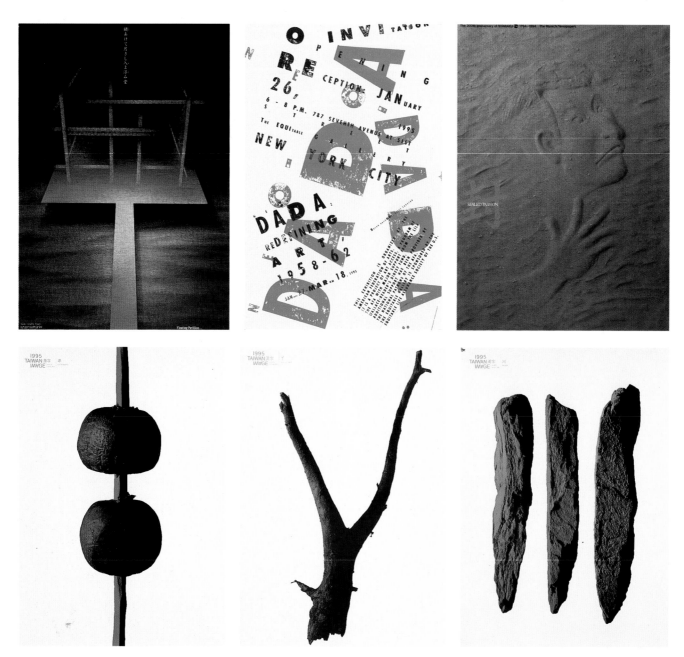

DIRECTOR/DESIGNER: TOYOTSUGU ITOH PHOTOGRAPHER: ISAO TAKAHASHI DESIGN FIRM: DESIGN ROOM ITOH CLIENT: CHUBU CREATORS CLUB COUNTRY: JAPAN ■**1** AN EXHIBITION COMMEMORATING THE 350TH ANNIVERSARY OF THE JAPANESE POET BASHO MATSUO. HE WAS A ZEN MONK, AND HIS HAIKU POEMS ARE SOME OF THE MOST PERFECT. ●**1** GEDENKAUSSTELLUNG ZUM 350. GEBURTSTAG DES JAPANISCHEN DICHTERS BASHO MATSUO, DER, ENG MIT DER NATUR VERBUNDEN, ALS ZEN-MÖNCH LEBTE. SEINE GEDICHTE GEHÖREN ZU DEN VOLLENDETSTEN DER HAIKU-DICHTUNG. ▲**1** EXPOSITION COMMÉMORANT LE 350ᵉ ANNIVER-SAIRE DU POÈTE JAPONAIS BASHO MATSUO. MOINE ZEN, IL VÉCUT EN UNION AVEC LA NATURE, ET SES POÈMES HAIKU COMPTENT PARMI LES PLUS PARFAITS DU GENRE. ■**2** ART DIRECTOR/DESIGNER: TAKAAKI MATSUMOTO DESIGN FIRM: MATSUMOTO INCORPORATED CLIENT: THE EQUITABLE GALLERY COUNTRY: USA ■**2** A RUBBER STAMP WAS USED TO CREATE THE TYPE FOR THIS POSTER, DESIGNED TO PUBLICIZE AN EXHIBITION AT THE EQUITABLE GALLERY IN NEW YORK. ●**2** FÜR DIE BESCHRIFTUNG DIESES AUSSTELLUNGSPLAKATS EINER NEW YORKER GALERIE WURDE EIN GUMMISTEMPEL VERWENDET. ▲**2** AFFICHE D'EXPOSI-

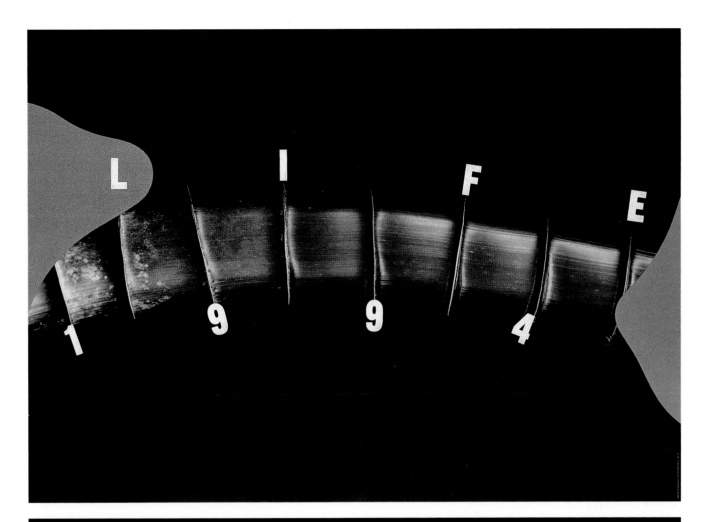

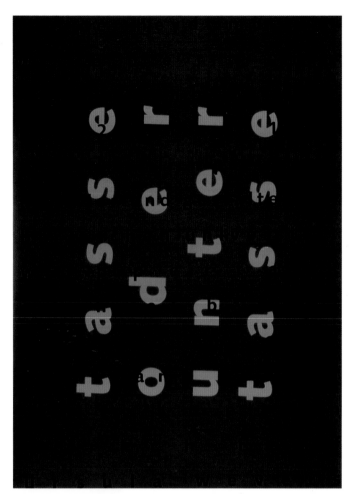

TION D'UNE GALERIE D'ART NEW-YORKAISE. LES CARACTÈRES ONT ÉTÉ IMPRIMÉS À L'AIDE D'UN TAMPON. ■ 3 ART DIRECTOR: TOYOTSUGU ITOH DESIGNER: TOYOTSUGU.ITOH PHOTOGRAPHER: ISAO TAKAHASHI DESIGN FIRM: DESIGN ROOM ITOH CLIENT: MAINICHI NEWSPAPERS CO., LTD. COUNTRY: JAPAN ■ 3 ONE OF A SERIES OF POSTERS BY CONTEMPORARY JAPANESE POSTER ARTISTS COMMEMORATING SHARAKU, A MASTER OF THE JAPANESE WOODCUT. ● 3 BEISPIEL AUS EINER REIHE VON PLAKATEN ZEITGENÖSSISCHER JAPANISCHER PLAKATKÜNSTLER FÜR EINE AUSSTELLUNG IM GEDENKEN AN SHARAKU, EINEM MEISTER DES JAPANISCHEN FARBHOLZSCHNITTS. ▲ 3 EXEMPLE D'UNE SÉRIE D'AFFICHES RÉALISÉES PAR DE JEUNES ARTISTES JAPONAIS POUR UNE EXPOSITION CONSACRÉE À SHARAKU, GRAND MAÎTRE JAPONAIS DE LA GRAVURE SUR BOIS. ■ 4-6 ART DIRECTOR/DESIGNER: XU WANG DESIGN FIRM: SINO WEST DESIGN CO. CLIENT: TAIWAN IMAGE POSTER DESIGN ASSOCIATION COUNTRY: TAIWAN ■ 4-6 POSTERS SHOWING THE ORIGIN OF CHINESE CHARACTERS: SHISH KEBAB, FORK OF TREE, VALLEY. THE ACTUAL CHARACTERS ARE SHOWN IN MINIATURE AT THE TOP. ● 4-6 DER URSPRUNG CHINESISCHER SCHRIFTZEICHEN IST GEGENSTAND DIESES PLAKATES: SHISH KEBAB, ASTGABEL, TAL. DIE ENTSPRECHENDEN ZEICHEN SIND OBEN LINKS GEZEIGT. ▲ 4-6 AFFICHES CONSACRÉES À L'ORIGINE DES CARACTÈRES CHINOIS: CHICHE-KEBAB, FOURCHE, VALLÉE. LES CARACTÈRES MODERNES FIGURENT DANS LE COIN SUPÉRIEUR GAUCHE DE L'AFFICHE. ■ 7, 8 ART DIRECTOR: TAKU SATOH DESIGNER: TAKU SATOH PHOTOGRAPHER: MEGUMU WADA DESIGN FIRM: TAKU SATOH DESIGN OFFICE INC. CLIENT: JAPAN DESIGN COMMITTEE COUNTRY: JAPAN ■ 7, 8 "LIFE 1994" WAS THE THEME OF AN EXHIBITION. BAMBOO SYMBOLIZES A STRONG LIFE FORCE AND THE STAGES OF LIFE. ● 7, 8 «LEBEN 1994» WAR DAS THEMA EINER AUSSTELLUNG. DIE BAMBUSSTÄMME DIENEN ALS SYMBOL FÜR LEBENSKRAFT UND DIE VERSCHIEDENEN LEBENSABSCHNITTE DES MENSCHEN. ▲ 7, 8 AFFICHE RÉALISÉE POUR UNE EXPOSI-

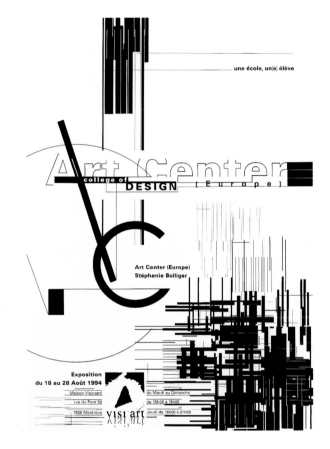

TION INTITULÉE «VIE 1994». LES TIGES DE BAMBOU SYMBOLISENT LA FORCE DE L'ÉNERGIE VITALE ET LES DIFFÉRENTS STADES DE LA VIE. □ (THIS SPREAD) 1 ART DIRECTOR/DESIGNER: UWE LOESCH CLIENT: VON DER HEYDT MUSEUM COUNTRY: GERMANY ■ 1 "CUP OR SAUCER"—MEANING ART AND/OR DESIGN—AN EXHIBITION OF THE WORK OF ART OR DESIGN PROFESSORS AT THE BERGISCHE UNIVERSITÄT WUPPERTAL. ● 1 KUNST UND/ODER DESIGN, DIE ALTE FRAGE NACH DEM UNTERSCHIED BZW. DEREN VERNEINUNG STEHT HINTER DIESEM TITEL. IN DER AUSSTELLUNG WURDEN ARBEITEN VON PROFESSOREN AUS VERSCHIEDENEN FACHBREICHEN DER BERGISCHEN UNIVERSITÄT WUPPERTAL GEZEIGT. ▲ 1 ART ET/OU DESIGN. CETTE EXPOSITION PRÉSENTAIT LES TRAVAUX DE PROFESSEURS D'ARTS PLASTIQUES ET GRAPHIQUES, CHARGÉS DE COURS À L'UNIVERSITÉ DE WUPPERTAL. □ 2 ART DIRECTOR: KEIZO MATSUI DESIGNER: KEIZO MATSUI DESIGN FIRM: KEIZO MATSUI & ASSOCIATES CLIENT: DDD GALLERY COUNTRY: JAPAN ■ 2 THIS ILLUSTRATION FOR A JAPANESE EXHIBITION OF THE GERMAN POSTER ARTIST UWE LOESCH CONSISTS OF TWO POSTERS BY LOESCH ('PUNKTUM' AND A POSTER COMMEMORATING CHERNOBYL). ● 2 DIE ILLUSTRATION DIESES PLAKAT FÜR EINE AUSSTELLUNG DES DEUTSCHEN PLAKATKÜNSTLERS UWE LOESCH IN JAPAN IST EINE ÜBERLAGERUNG ZWEIER SEINER PLAKATE (PUNKTUM UND EIN PLAKAT IM GEDENKEN AN TSCHERNOBYL). ▲ 2 AFFICHE ANNONÇANT UNE EXPOSITION AU JAPON DE L'AFFICHISTE ALLEMAND UWE LOESCH. DEUX AFFICHES DE L'ARTISTE ONT SERVI À SA COMPOSITION («PUNKTUM» ET UNE AFFICHE SUR TCHERNOBYL). □ 3 DESIGNERS: H. + C. WALDVOGEL CLIENT: KUNSTHAUS ZÜRICH COUNTRY: SWITZERLAND ■ 3 A POSTER PROMOTING AN EXHIBITION OF DEGAS' PORTRAITS. HERE, A DETAIL OF HIS PAINTING "VICOMTE LEPIC ET SES FILLES" (CA. 1871). ● 3 DIE ILLUSTRATION DES PLAKATES IST EIN AUSSCHNITT AUS DEGAS GEMÄLDE «VICOMTE LEPIC ET SES FILLES» (CA. 1871) AUS DER SAMMLUNG

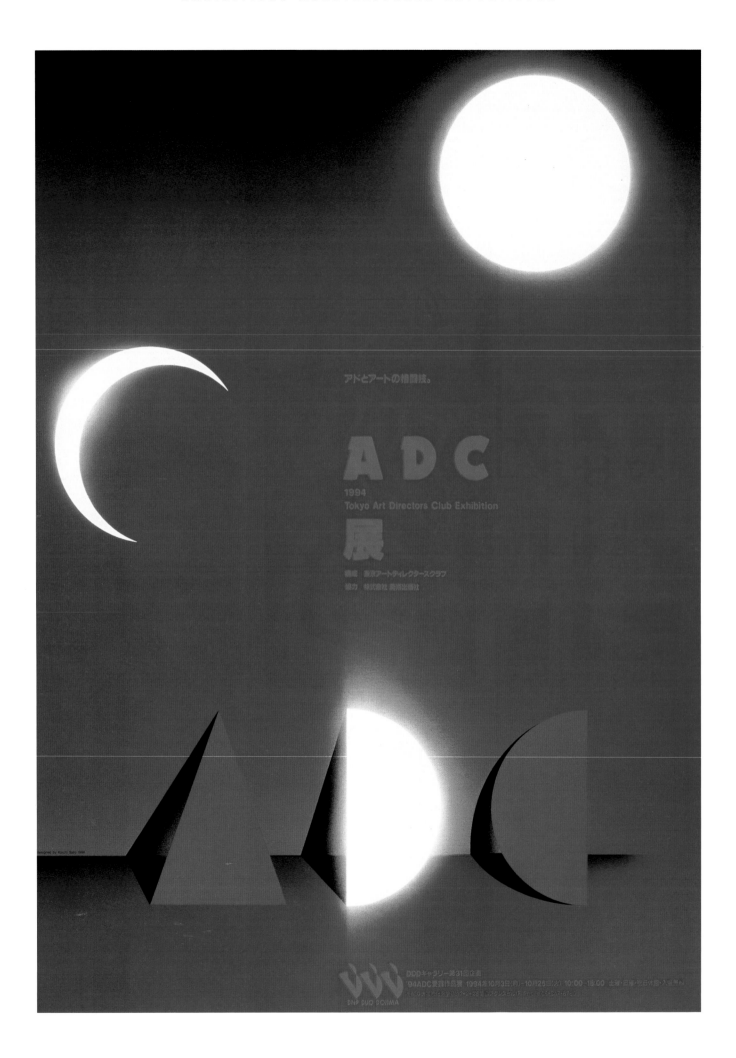

BÜHRLE, ZÜRICH. ▲ 3 AFFICHE POUR UNE EXPOSITION DEGAS (DÉTAIL D'UN TABLEAU DU MAÎTRE INTITULÉ «VICOMTE LEPIC ET SES FILLES», PEINT VERS 1871). □ 4 ART DIRECTOR: FRANZ WERNER COPYWRITER: FRANZ WERNER DESIGNER: J.B. LEVY PHOTOGRAPHER: FRANZ WERNER AGENCY: AND (TRAFIC GRAFIC) DESIGN FIRM/CLIENT: FRANZ WERNER COUNTRY: USA ■ 4 DESIGNED TO PROMOTE THE PHOTOGRAPHER FRANZ WERNER AND ANNOUNCE AN EXHIBITION OF HIS WORK, THIS POSTER DEMONSTRATES THE ARTIST'S CAPACITY FOR STAGED STUDIO PHOTOGRAPY. ● 4 DIESES PLAKAT FÜR EINE AUSSTELLUNG DES PHOTOGAPHEN FRANZ WERNER DEMONSTRIERT SEIN KÖNNEN IM BEREICH INSZENIERTER STUDIOPHOTOGRAPHIE. ▲ 4 RÉALISÉE POUR UNE EXPOSITION DU PHOTOGRAPHE FRANZ WERNER, L'AFFICHE TÉMOIGNE DE LA QUALITÉ SCÉNIQUE DES IMAGES, CARACTÉRISTIQUE DU TRAVAIL DE L'ARTISTE LORS DE SES SÉANCES PHOTO EN STUDIO. □ 5 ART DIRECTOR/DESIGNER: STEPHANIE BOLLIGER CLIENT: ART CENTER (EUROPE) COUNTRY: SWITZERLAND ■ 5 "A SCHOOL, A STUDENT,"—THE FIRST IN A SERIES OF EXHIBITIONS BY THE MONTREUX CULTURAL CENTER PRESENTING ART SCHOOLS THROUGH THE WORK OF ONE STUDENT. THIS POSTER EXAMINES THE STUDENT'S WORK FROM THROUGH-OUT THE TERM. ● 5 «EINE SCHULE, EIN(E) STUDENT(IN)», DIE ERSTE AUSSTELLUNG EINER REIHE, IN WELCHER DAS KULTURZENTRUM VON MONTREUX VERSCHIEDENE SCHULEN DURCH DIE ARBEITEN JEWEILS EINES STUDENTEN ODER EINER STUDENTIN PRÄSENTIERT. DIESES PLAKAT ENTHÄLT TEILE DER ARBEITEN DER STUDENTIN AUS DER GESAMTEN STUDIENZEIT. ▲ 5 «UNE ÉCOLE, UN(E) ÉTUDIANT(E)». PREMIÈRE EXPOSITION D'UNE SÉRIE PATRONNÉE PAR LE CENTRE

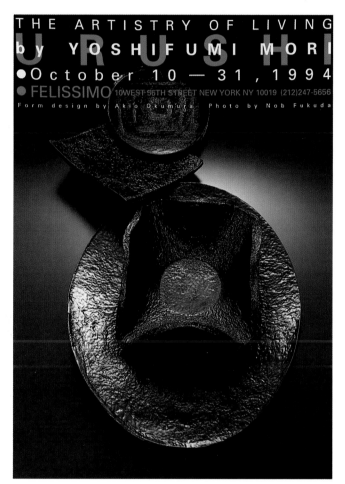 

DE CULTURE DE MONTREUX VISANT À PRÉSENTER DIVERSES ÉCOLES PAR LES TRAVAUX D'UN ÉTUDIANT OU D'UNE ÉTU-DIANTE. L'AFFICHE EST UNE COMPOSITION RÉALISÉE À PARTIR DE DÉTAILS DE DIVERS TRAVAUX DE L'ÉTUDIANTE. □ (THIS SPREAD) 1 ART DIRECTOR/DESIGNER: KOICHI SATO DESIGN FIRM: KOICHI SATO DESIGN STUDIO CLIENT: TOKYO ART DIRECTORS CLUB COUNTRY: JAPAN ■ 1 AN AIRBRUSH POSTER FOR THE ANNUAL SHOW OF THE TOKYO ART DIRECTORS CLUB EXAMINES SUCH WIDE-RANGING SUBJECTS AS THE ALPHABET AND THE MOON, CLASSICAL AND CONTEMPORARY AESTHET-ICS, AND THE OCCIDENT AND THE ORIENT. ● 1 DAS ALPHABET UND DER MOND, KLASSISCHE UND ZEITGENÖSSISCHE ÄSTHETIK, WESTEN UND OSTEN – PLAKAT (AIRBRUSH-TECHNIK) FÜR DIE JAHRESSCHAU DES ADC TOKIO. ▲ 1 L'ALPHABET ET LA LUNE, L'ESTHÉTIQUE CLASSIQUE ET CONTEMPORAINE, L'ORIENT ET L'OCCIDENT. AFFICHE RÉALISÉE POUR L'EXPO-SITION ANNUELLE DE L'ADC DE TOKYO (AIRBRUSH). □ (THIS SPREAD) 2, 3 ART DIRECTOR: AKIO OKUMURA DESIGNER: EMI KAJIHARA PHOTOGRAPHER: NOB FUKUDA ARTIST: YOSHIFUMI MORI DESIGN FIRM: PACKAGING CREATE INC. CLIENT: FELISSIMO CORPORATION COUNTRY: JAPAN ■ 2, 3 AN EXHIBITION OF CONTEMPORARY JAPANESE LACQUER ARTIST YOSHIFUMI MORI. IN HIS WORK HE APPLIES NUMEROUS LAYERS OF LACQUER ON SINGLE SHEETS OF PAPER INSTEAD OF WOOD. ● 2, 3 EINE AUS-STELLUNG DES ZEITGENÖSSISCHEN JAPANISCHEN LACKIERKÜNSTLERS YOSHIFUMI MORI. ES HANDELT SICH DABEI UM EINE SPEZIELLE TECHNIK, ZAHLREICHE LACKSCHICHTEN AUF PAPIER STATT AUF HOLZ AUFZUTRAGEN. ▲ 2, 3 EXPOSITION CON-SACRÉE AUX LAQUES DE L'ARTISTE JAPONAIS YOSHIFUMI MORI. L'ARTISTE UTILISE UNE TECHNIQUE TRÈS SOPHISTIQUÉE, CONSISTANT À APPLIQUER PLUSIEURS COUCHES DE LAQUE SUR UNE SEULE FEUILLE DE PAPIER (ET NON SUR BOIS).

1 ART DIRECTOR/DESIGNER: EDUARD CEHOVIN DESIGN FIRM: A+/-B (IN EXILE) CLIENT: SOROS-SLOVENIA COUNTRY: SLOVENIA ■ 1 AN EXHIBITION OF THE WORK OF A YOUNG SLOVENIAN ARTIST IN BELGRAD. ● 1 AUSSTELLUNG EINES JUNGEN SLOVENISCHEN KÜNSTLERS IN BELGRAD. ▲ 1 EXPOSITION D'UN JEUNE ARTISTE SLOVAQUE À BELGRADE. □ 2 ART DIRECTOR/DESIGNER: BÜLENT ERKMEN CLIENT: KOLEKSIYON COUNTRY: TURKEY ■ 2 THE FOURTH IN A SERIES OF CONTEMPORARY FINE ART EXHIBITIONS. ● 2 DIE VIERTE AUSSTELLUNG EINER REIHE, DIE DER BILDENDEN KUNST GEWIDMET IST. ▲ 2 4ᵉᵐᵉ EXPOSITION D'UNE SÉRIE CON-SACRÉE AUX ARTS PLASTIQUES. □ 3 ART DIRECTOR/DESIGNER/PHOTOGRAPHER: GRANT JORGENSEN DESIGN FIRM: GRANT JORGEN-SEN GRAPHIC DESIGN CLIENT: DESIGN INSTITUTE OF AUSTRALIA (SA CHAPTER) COUNTRY: AUSTRALIA ■ 3 A POSTER PROMOT-ING AN AWARDS PROGRAM FOR INTERIOR DESIGN. THE GOAL WAS TO AVOID THE USE OF LITERAL IMAGERY, SUGGESTING INSTEAD A DESIGNER'S "THOUGHTS" ON SPATIAL ARRANGEMENTS WITH SYMBOLS AND MULTIPLE LAYERS OF GRAPHIC ELE-MENTS. ● 3 EIN WETTBEWERB FÜR INNENARCHITEKTUR UND DIE PREISVERLEIHUNG. STATT REALER BILDER WURDEN DIE

'GEDANKEN' DES DESIGNERS ZUR RÄUMLICHEN GESTALTUNG DARGESTELLT, WOBEI SYMBOLE UND VERSCHIEDENE EBENEN GRAPHISCHER ELEMENTE FÜR DIE PLANUNG UND BEARBEITUNG DREIDIMENSIONALER FORMEN UND DES RAUMS EINGESETZT WURDEN. ▲ 3 CONCOURS DE DÉCORATION D'INTÉRIEUR. EN LIEU ET PLACE D'IMAGES RÉELLES, SEULES LES 'IDÉES' DU DESIGNER EN MATIÈRE D'AMÉNAGEMENT DE L'ESPACE DEVAIENT ÊTRE REPRÉSENTÉES. SYMBOLES ET ÉLÉMENTS GRAPHIQUES ILLUSTRENT LA PLANIFICATION DES FORMES TRIDIMENSIONNELLES ET DE L'ESPACE. □ 4 ART DIRECTORS/DESIGNERS: TOM ANTISTA, THOMAS FAIRCLOUGH DESIGN FIRM/CLIENT: ANTISTA FAIRCLOUGH DESIGN COUNTRY: USA ■ 4 AN EXHI-BITION POSTER FOR ANTISTA DESIGN. THIS IMAGE WAS A RE-INTERPRETATION OF ONE OF THE FIRM'S EARLY POSTERS ENTI-TLED "COAST TO COAST." ● 4 AUSSTELLUNGSPLAKAT FÜR ANTISTA DESIGN. ES IST EINE NEUINTERPRETATION EINES DER FRÜHEN PLAKATE DES STUDIOS MIT DEM TITEL «VON KÜSTE ZU KÜSTE». ▲ 4 AFFICHE D'EXPOSITION DE L'AGENCE ANTISTA DESIGN, PRÉSENTANT UNE NOUVELLE INTERPRÉTATION D'UNE PRÉCÉDENTE AFFICHE, INTITULÉE «DE CÔTE EN CÔTE». □ 5

ART DIRECTOR: TERENCE WINCH DESIGNER: JUDY KIRPICH PHOTOGRAPHER: DAVID HEALD CLIENT: NATIONAL MUSEUM OF THE AMERICAN INDIAN COUNTRY: USA ■ 5 THE CIRCULAR COMPOSITION OF THE FOOTWEAR SHOWN IN THIS POSTER—SELECTED FROM MORE THAN TWO DOZEN INDIAN CULTURES FOR THE 1994 INAUGURAL EXHIBITION AT THE CANADIAN MUSEUM OF CIVILIZATION IN QUEBEC, CANADA—SUGGESTS THE MOVEMENT OF DANCERS IN A "ROUND DANCE," AS WELL AS THE TRADITIONAL NATIVE BELIEF IN THE CONNECTION OF ALL LIFE. ● 5 DIE KREISFÖRMIGE ANORDNUNG DER SCHUHE AUF DIESEM PLAKAT – DIE AUS MEHR ALS ZWEI DUTZEND INDIANISCHEN KULTUREN STAMMEN, IST EINE ANSPIELUNG AUF DEN TRADITIONELLEN «ROUND DANCE» UND AUF DEN GLAUBEN DER UREINWOHNER AN DEN ZUSAMMENHANG ALLEN LEBENS. ▲ 5 L'ARRANGEMENT CIRCULAIRE DES MOCASSINS – REPRÉSENTATIFS D'UNE VINGTAINE DE CULTURES INDIENNES ET SÉLECTIONNÉS POUR L'EXPOSITION D'INAUGURATION 1994 DU MUSÉE CANADIEN DE LA CIVILISATION À QUÉBEC – ÉVOQUE LES DANSES ET LES CROYANCES TRADITIONNELLES INDIENNES SELON LESQUELLES TOUS LES ÉLÉMENTS DE LA NATURE SONT

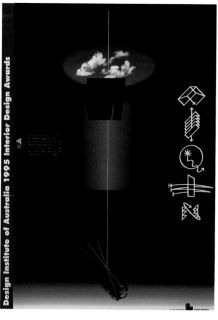 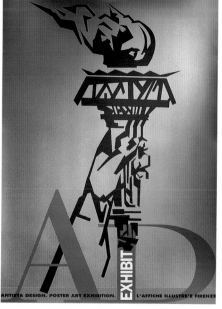 

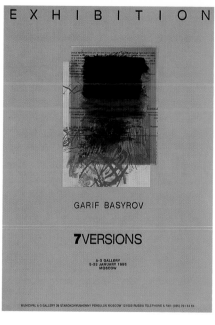  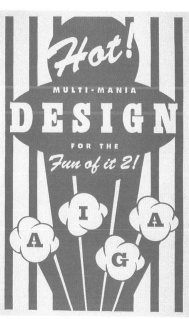

ÉTROITEMENT LIÉS. □ 6 DESIGNER: GARIF BASYROV COUNTRY: RUSSIA ■ 6 EXAMPLE OF A SERIES OF SMALL-SIZE POSTERS THAT WERE DESIGNED AND HANDMADE BY THE ARTIST FOR HIS EXHIBITION. ● 6 BEISPIEL EINER REIHE VON PLAKATEN IM FORMAT A3, DIE DER KÜNSTLER FÜR SEINE AUSSTELLUNG SELBST GESTALTETE UND VON HAND HERSTELLTE. ▲ 6 EXEMPLE D'UNE SÉRIE D'AFFICHES ARTISANALES DE FORMAT A3, CONÇUES ET RÉALISÉES PAR L'ARTISTE POUR SON EXPOSITION. □ 7 ART DIRECTOR/DESIGNER/ILLUSTRATOR: YURIY SURKOV DESIGN FIRM: SURIC DESIGN STUDIO CLIENT: DESIGN GALLERY COUNTRY: RUSSIA ■ 7 AN EXHIBITION AT THE DESIGN GALLERY, MOSCOW. ● 7 EINE AUSSTELLUNG IN DER DESIGN GALERIE, MOSKAU. ▲ 7 EXPOSITION DE LA DESIGN GALLERY À MOSCOU. □ 8 ART DIRECTOR/DESIGNER: NEAL ASHBY ILLUSTRATOR: NEAL ASHBY DESIGN FIRM: RIAA CLIENT: AIGA (WASHINGTON) COUNTRY: USA ■ 8 A POSTER DESIGNED AS AN INVITATION FOR THE AIGA WASHINGTON'S EVENT ON MULTIMEDIA. ● 8 ALS EINLADUNG KONZIPIERTES PLAKAT FÜR EINEN MULTIMEDIA-ANLASS DES AIGA IN WASHINGTON. ▲ 8 AFFICHE INVITANT À PARTICIPER À UNE MANIFESTATION MULTIMÉDIA ORGANISÉE PAR L'AIGA À WASHINGTON.

1, 3 ART DIRECTOR/DESIGNER: YOSHIMARU TAKAHASHI PHOTOGRAPHERS: KOICHI OKUWAKI (1), KAZUO CHIKADA (3) DESIGN FIRM: KOUKOKUMARU INC. CLIENT: OSAKA CONTEMPORARY ART CENTER COUNTRY: JAPAN ■ 1, 3 "DESIGNER TODAY" WAS AN EXHIBITION OF CONTEMPORARY GRAPHIC DESIGN. THESE POSTERS EXPLORE THE SPIRIT AND SEXUALITY OF THE JAPANESE. ● 1, 3 «DESIGNER TODAY» WAR EINE AUSSTELLUNG ZEITGENÖSSISCHEN GRAPHIK-DESIGNS. DAS THEMA DER PLAKATE: GEIST UND SEXUALITÄT DER JAPANER. ▲ 1, 3 «DESIGNER TODAY». EXPOSITION CONSACRÉE AUX ARTS GRAPHIQUES CONTEMPORAINS. LE THÈME DES AFFICHES: L'ESPRIT ET LA SEXUALITÉ DES JAPONAIS. □ 2, 7 ART DIRECTOR/DESIGNER: YOSHIMARU TAKAHASHI

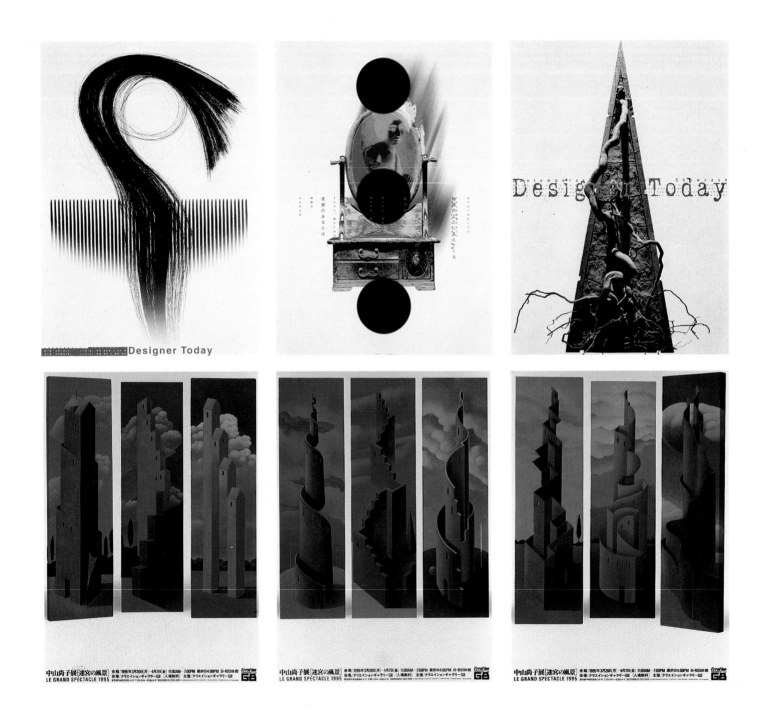

DESIGN FIRM: KOUKOKUMARU INC. CLIENT: CREATIVE TOYAMA IN NEW YORK COUNTRY: JAPAN ■ 2, 7 FOR A JAPANESE POSTER EXHIBITION IN NEW YORK, POSTERS ILLUSTRATING THE CREATIVE CLIMATE OF TOYAMA. ● 2, 7 EINE JAPANISCHE PLAKATAUSSTELLUNG IN NEW YORK. DAS THEMA: DAS KREATIVE KLIMA VON TOYAMA. ▲ 2, 7 EXPOSITION D'AFFICHES JAPONAISE À NEW YORK. THÈME: LE CLIMAT CRÉATIF DE TOYAMA. □ 4-6 ART DIRECTORS: HISAKO NAKAYAMA, SHUZO KATO DESIGNER: SHUZO KATO ILLUSTRATOR: HISAKO NAKAYAMA COPYWRITER: SETSUZI MAEKAWA DESIGN FIRM: STUDIO N'S CLIENT: CREATION GALLERY G8 COUNTRY: JAPAN ■ 4-6 VARIATIONS OF A POSTER ANNOUNCING AN EXHIBITION OF ILLUSTRATIONS. ● 4-6 VARIATIONEN EINES PLAKATES FÜR EINE AUSSTELLUNG VON ILLUSTRATIONEN. ▲ 4-6 TRILOGIE RÉALISÉE POUR UNE EXPOSITION D'ILLUSTRATIONS.

1 ART DIRECTOR/DESIGNER: TAKAHARU MATSUMOTO PHOTOGRAPHER: CHIKAKO OHYAMA COPYWRITER: KOICHI TAKANO DESIGN FIRM: MR. 88 CO., LTD. CLIENT: JAPAN GRAPHIC DESIGNERS ASSOCIATION (JAGDA) COUNTRY: JAPAN ■ 1 "I AM HERE" IS THE TITLE OF THE 1995 JAGDA PEACE AND ENVIRONMENT EXHIBITION, DEDICATED TO HIROSHIMA AND NAGASAKI. ● 1 «I AM HERE» IST DER TITEL DER FRIEDENS- UND UMWELTPLAKATE DER JAGDA. 1995 WAR DIE AUSSTELLUNG HIROSHIMA UND NAGASAKI GEWIDMET. ▲ 1 «I AM HERE». AFFICHE D'EXPOSITION DE LA JAGDA POUR LA PAIX ET L'ENVIRONNEMENT, DÉDIÉE EN 1995 À HIROSHIMA ET À NAGASAKI. □ 2, 3 ART DIRECTOR/DESIGNER: TAKU

SATOH PHOTOGRAPHER: TAMOTSU FUJII DESIGN FIRM: TAKU SATOH DESIGN OFFICE INC. CLIENT: CREATION GALLERY G8 COUNTRY: JAPAN ■ 2, 3 PACKAGE DESIGNS BY KENYA HARA AND TAKU SATOH. THE TITLE "SKELETON" REFERS TO THE MONOCHROME PHOTOGRAPHS OF A CATALOG, HIGHLIGHTING THE STRUCTURE OF ITS DESIGN. ● 2, 3 PACKUNGSGESTALTUNG VON KENYA HARA UND TAKU SATOH. DER TITEL «SKELETON» (GERIPPE) BEZIEHT AUF DIESE SPEZIELLEN MONOCHROMEN AUFNAHMEN EINES KATALOGS, DIE DIE STRUKTUREN DER VERPACKUNGEN HER-VORHEBEN. ▲ 2, 3 LE PACKAGING, VU PAR KENYA HARA ET TAKU SATOH. LE TITRE «SKELETON» FAIT RÉFÉRENCE À LA STRUCTURE DU PACKAGING (LE SQUELETTE), MISE EN RELIEF PAR DES PHOTOS MONOCHROMES.

1–3 ART DIRECTOR/DESIGNER: KAZUMASA NAGAI DESIGN FIRM: NIPPON DESIGN CENTER, INC. CLIENT: RIKUYO-SHA PUBLISHING, INC. COUNTRY: JAPAN ■ 1–3 AN EXHIBITION OF DESIGNER KAZUMASA NAGAI'S "ANIMAL SERIES," IN WHICH HE CLAIMS THAT THE EARTH DOES NOT BELONG TO THE HUMAN BEING ALONE BUT TO EVERY FORM OF LIFE. ● 1–3 EINE AUSSTELLUNG DER 'ANIMAL'-SERIE DES DESIGNERS KAZUMASA NAGAI. DIESE SERIE IST EIN PERSÖNLICHES STATEMENT DES KÜNSTLERS: DIE ERDE GEHÖRT NICHT DEM MENSCHEN, SONDERN JEDER FORM DES LEBENS, WIE DEM GRAS UND DEN TIEREN IN DIESEN BILDERN. ▲ 1–3 EXPOSITION DU DESIGNER KAZUMASA NAGAI, QUI PRÉSENTA UNE SÉRIE INTITULÉE «ANIMAL». LE MESSAGE DE L'ARTISTE: LA TERRE N'APPARTIENT PAS QU'À L'HOMME, MAIS À TOUTES LES FORMES DE VIE VÉGÉTALE OU ANIMALE, SYMBOLISÉES ICI PAR L'HERBE ET LES ANIMAUX. □ 4–6 ART DIRECTOR/DESIGNER: KAZUMASA NAGAI DESIGN FIRM: NIPPON DESIGN CENTER, INC. CLIENT: JAPAN DESIGN COMMITTEE COUNTRY: JAPAN ■ 4–6 THE "LIFE TO SHARE" SERIES BY KAZUMASA NAGAI, CREATED FOR A ONE-MAN EXHIBITION, EXPLORES THE DESTRUCTION OF NATURE AND THE DISTURBANCE OF THE ECOLOGICAL SYSTEM. ● 4–6

 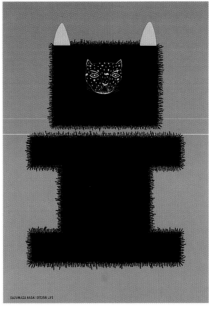 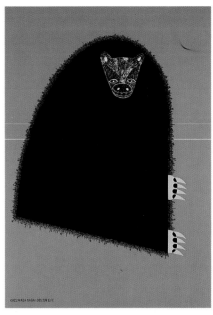

 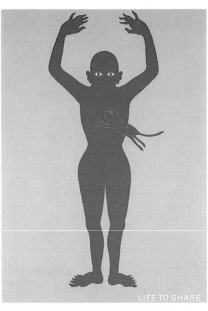 

DIE PLAKATSERIE «LIFE TO SHARE» VON KAZUMASA NAGAI ENTSTAND FÜR EINE EINZELAUSSTELLUNG. SEIN THEMA IST DIE ZERSTÖRUNG DER NATUR DURCH DEN MENSCHEN, DIE STÖRUNG DES ÖKOSYSTEMS UND DIE VERHEERENDEN FOLGEN. SEIN CREDO IST WIE IN DER «ANIMAL SERIES»: DIE ERDE GEHÖRT NICHT DEM MENSCHEN ALLEIN. ▲ 4–6 «LIFE TO SHARE». SÉRIE D'AFFICHES RÉALISÉES PAR KAZUMASA NAGAI POUR UNE EXPOSITION SUR LE THÈME DE LA DESTRUCTION DE LA NATURE PAR L'HOMME ET LES DÉSÉQUILIBRES ÉCOLOGIQUES QUI EN RÉSULTENT. COMME DANS SA SÉRIE «ANIMAL», IL CONJURE L'HOMME DE PARTAGER LA TERRE AVEC TOUS LES ÊTRES VIVANTS. □ 7 ART DIRECTOR/DESIGNER: JOHN BALL ILLUSTRATOR: TRACY SABIN DESIGN FIRM: MIRES DESIGN, INC. CLIENT: COMMUNICATING ARTS GROUP COUNTRY: USA ■ 7 TO PROMOTE AN EVENT FEATURING MCRAY MAGLEBY, THIS POSTER PLAYS ON THE BRITISH TERM "MAC" FOR RAINCOAT, WHICH IS ALSO MAGLEBY'S US NICKNAME. ● 7 DIESES PLAKAT FÜR EINEN VORTRAG DES DESIGNERS MCRAY MAGLEBY BEZIEHT SICH AUF SEINEN SPITZNAMEN «MAC» – IN ENGLAND AUCH DIE BEZEICHNUNG FÜR EINEN REGENMANTEL. ▲ 7 AFFICHE ANNONÇANT UNE CONFÉRENCE DU DESIGNER MCRAY MAGLEBY ET JOUANT SUR LE MOT «MAC», SURNOM DU DESIGNER QUI SIGNIFIE ÉGALEMENT «IMPERMÉABLE» EN ANGLAIS.

M A C

FEW DESIGNERS DO SLICKER WORK
THAN McRAY MAGLEBY. MEET HIM AT
THE NEXT CAG MEETING, DECEMBER 2, AT
THE MARINA VILLAGE CONFERENCE CENTER.
MAKE YOUR RESERVATION NOW AND
AVOID THE DELUGE: 295-5082.

C A
G

3108
FIFTH AVENUE
SUITE I

SAN DIEGO
CALIFORNIA
92103

CZŁOWIEK w OBRAZIE

V FESTIWAL MEDIÓW w ŁODZI   ŁDK, ul. Traugutta 18   26·29·10·1994

1 ART DIRECTOR/DESIGNER: TADEUSZ PIECHURA COPYWRITER: BOGNA WITKOWSKA DESIGN FIRM: ATELIER TADEUSZ PIECHURA CLIENT: LDK – LODZKI DOM KULTURY COUNTRY: POLAND ■ 1 A CULTURAL FESTIVAL OF THE MASS MEDIA. THE POSTER CONSISTS OF TWO PARTS THAT ARE TAPED TOGETHER TO CREATE THE CUT. ● 1 EIN KULTURFESTIVAL DER MASSENMEDIEN. DAS PLAKAT BESTEHT AUS ZWEI TEILEN, DIE SO ZUSAMMENGEKLEBT WERDEN, DASS SICH DER AUSSCHNITT ERGIBT. ▲ 1 FESTIVAL CULTUREL DES MEDIA. L'AFFICHE SE COMPOSE DE DEUX PARTIES, ASSEMBLÉES DE SORTE À FORMER UNE COUPURE. □ 2 ART DIRECTOR: RAINER BAUER DESIGNER: RAINER BAUER CLIENT: ZKM/ZENTRUM FÜR KUNST UND MEDIENTECHNOLOGIE COUNTRY: GERMANY ■ 2 THE 4TH MULTIMEDIALE—AN ANNUAL FESTIVAL FOR CYBER ART—AT THE CENTER FOR ART AND MEDIA TECHNOLOGY OF KARLSRUHE. ● 2 DIE 4. MULTIMEDIALE IN KARLSRUHE, DAS REGELMÄSSIG STATTFINDENDE FESTIVAL DER CYBER-KUNST. ▲ 2 AFFICHE DE LA 4ᴱ MULTIMEDIALE DE KARLSRUHE, FESTIVAL ANNUEL D'ART CYBÉRNÉTIQUE. □ (FOLLOWING SPREAD) 1, 3 ART DIRECTORS/DESIGNERS: SASCHA LOBE, PETER KRAUSS DESIGN FIRM: AGIL CLIENT: KUPFERDÄCHLE COUNTRY: GERMANY ■ 1, 3 A CULTURAL YOUTH CENTER ANNOUNCES A SPECIAL WOMEN'S WEEK AND THE PROGRAM FOR MAY AND JUNE. THESE COMPUTER-GENERATED, LOW BUDGET POSTERS ARE NORMALLY PRINTED IN TWO COLORS AND SERVE ALSO AS BOOKLETS. ● 1, 3 EIN JUGENDKULTURZENTRUM IN PFORZHEIM KÜNDIGT EINE FRAUENKULTURWOCHE (DIESES PLAKAT WURDE MIT HILFE DES COMPUTERS HERGESTELLT) UND DAS PROGRAMM FÜR DIE MONATE MAI UND JUNI AN. NORMALERWEISE WIRD BEI DIESEN ALS PROSPEKTE KONZIPIERTEN PLAKATEN, FÜR DIE NUR EINER KLEINES BUDGET ZUR VERFÜGUNG STEHT, MIT ZWEI DRUCKFARBEN UND FARBIGEM PAPIER GEARBEITET. ▲ 1, 3 UNE MAISON DE LA CULTURE POUR LES JEUNES PRÉSENTE UNE SEMAINE SPÉCIALE CONSACRÉE AUX FEMMES (RÉALISATION SUR ORDINATEUR) AINSI QUE LE PROGRAMME DES MOIS DE MAI

ET JUIN. POUR SATISFAIRE AUX IMPÉRATIFS DE PETITS BUDGETS, CES AFFICHES QUI FONT AUSSI OFFICE DE DÉPLIANTS SONT GÉNÉRALEMENT IMPRIMÉES EN BICHROMIE SUR PAPIER DE COULEUR. □ (FOLLOWING SPREAD) 2 ART DIRECTOR/DESIGNER/ILLUSTRATOR: ADLAI STOCK DESIGN FIRM: A+ DESIGN CLIENT: EMBASSY OF ISRAEL COUNTRY: JAPAN ■ 2 THE VARIOUS EVENTS OF AN ISRAELI CULTURE FESTIVAL IN TOKYO. ● 2 DIE VERSCHIEDENEN VERANSTALTUNGEN IM RAHMEN VON ISRAELISCHEN KULTURTAGEN IN TOKIO. ▲ 2 PRÉSENTATION DE DIVERSES MANIFESTATIONS ORGANISÉES DANS LE CADRE D'UN FESTIVAL DE LA CULTURE ISRAÉLIENNE À TOKYO. □ (FOLLOWING SPREAD) 4, 6 ART DIRECTORS/DESIGNERS: PIETER ROOZEN, MART. WARMERDAM DESIGN FIRM: MART. WARMERDAM CLIENT: HOLLAND FESTIVAL COUNTRY: NETHERLANDS ■ 4, 6 DANCE, MUSIC, OPERA, THEATER, AND FILM PERFORMANCES ARE PART OF THE HOLLAND FESTIVAL. ● 4, 6 TANZ, MUSIK, OPER, THEATER UND FILM GEHÖREN ZUM PROGRAMM DES HOLLAND FESTIVALS. ▲ 4, 6 DANSE, MUSIQUE, OPÉRA, THÉÂTRE ET FILMS SONT AU PROGRAMME DU FESTIVAL DE HOLLANDE QUI A LIEU DANS TOUT LE PAYS, ET PLUS PARTICULIÈREMENT À AMSTERDAM. □ (FOLLOWING SPREAD) 5 ART DIRECTOR/DESIGNER: JAVIER ROMERO ILLUSTRATOR: JAVIER ROMERO DESIGN FIRM: JAVIER ROMERO DESIGN GROUP CLIENT: PRESIDENT OF THE BOROUGH OF QUEENS COUNTRY: USA ■ 5 IN AN EFFORT TO STRESS THE INTERNATIONAL ASPECT OF THE QUEENS FALL FESTIVAL, THIS POSTER ALSO PROMOTED THE 50TH ANNIVERSARY OF THE UNITED NATIONS AND THE 30TH ANNIVERSARY OF THE WORLD'S FAIR. ● 5 UM DIE INTERNATIONALITÄT DES HERBSTFESTES IM NEW YORKER STADTTEIL QUEENS ZU UNTERSTREICHEN, NIMMT DAS PLAKAT BEZUG AUF DAS 50JÄHRIGE BESTEHEN DER VEREINTEN NATIONEN UND DEN 30. JAHRESTAG DER WELTAUSSTELLUNG IN NEW YORK. ▲ 5 AFFICHE DU QUEENS FALL FESTIVAL. POUR SOULIGNER LE CARACTÈRE INTERNATIONAL DE LA MANIFESTATION, L'AFFICHE FAIT RÉFÉRENCE AU

CINQUANTENAIRE DES NATIONS UNIES ET AU 30ᴱ ANNIVERSAIRE DE L'EXPOSITION MONDIALE À NEW YORK. □ 7 DESIGNER/PHOTOGRAPHER: GABOR BAKSAY DESIGN FIRM: PIXEL PRODUKTION CLIENT: GZM-GESELLSCHAFT FÜR ZEITG. MUSIK COUNTRY: GERMANY ■ 7 A FESTIVAL OF CONTEMPORARY MUSIC FROM HOLLAND, BELGIUM, AND GERMANY AT LUDWIG FORUM OF AACHEN. ● 7 EIN FESTIVAL ZEITGENÖSSISCHER MUSIK IM DREILÄNDERECK, DAS IM LUDWIG FORUM FÜR INTERNATIONALE KUNST IN AACHEN STATTFINDET. ▲ 7 FESTIVAL DE MUSIQUE CONTEMPORAINE PRÉSENTANT DES ARTISTES HOLLANDAIS, BELGES ET ALLEMANDS AU LUDWIG FORUM D'AIX-LA-CHAPELLE. □ 8 DESIGNER: MICHEL BOUVET CLIENT: FESTIVAL D'AFFICHES DE CHAUMONT COUNTRY: FRANCE ■ 8 THE 1995 POSTER FESTIVAL IN CHAUMONT, FRANCE, FOCUSED ON SOCIAL AND POLITICAL POSTERS, AND MICHEL BOUVET'S ILLUSTRATION THEREFORE REFERS TO REVOLUTION AND PROPAGANDA. THE SIMPLE RENDERING WITH CUT PAPER AND PLAIN COLORS IS AN HOMAGE TO THE POSTER ARTISTS OF THE ATELIER DE L'ECOLE DES BEAUX-ARTS, PARIS, DURING THE EVENTS OF MAY 1968 AS WELL AS TO THE GREAT FRENCH POSTER ARTIST SAVIGNAC. ● 8 DAS POSTER FESTIVAL IN CHAUMONT, FRANKREICH, WAR 1995 DEM POLITISCHEN UND SOZIALEN PLAKAT GEWIDMET. MICHEL BOUVETS THEMA IST DAHER REVOLUTION UND PROPAGANDA, DIE ERHOBENE FAUST UNIVERSELLER AUSDRUCK FÜR FORDERUNGEN. GLEICHZEITIG SPIELT SEINE ILLUSTRATION AUF DIE MENSCHENRECHTE AN, AUF SOZIALE GERECHTIGKEIT UND FREIHEIT. DER SCHERENSCHNITT UND DIE KLAREN FARBEN SIND EINE HOMMAGE AN DIE ARBEIT DER PLAKATKÜNSTLER DES ATELIER DE L'ECOLE DES BEAUX-ARTS, PARIS, IM MAI 1968, UND AN DEN GROSSEN FRANZÖSISCHEN PLAKATKÜNSTLER SAVIGNAC. ▲ 8 LE FESTIVAL D'AFFICHES DE CHAUMONT, CONSACRÉ EN 1995 AUX AFFICHES POLITIQUES ET SOCIALES. L'ARTISTE, MICHEL BOUVET, A MIS L'ACCENT SUR LA REVENDICATION, L'ASPECT «RÉVOLUTION» ET PROPAGANDE. LE POING LEVÉ EST L'EXPRESSION UNIVERSELLE DE LA REVENDICATION. IL ÉVOQUE AINSI LES DROITS DE L'HOMME, LA JUSTICE SOCIALE, LES LIBERTÉS. LE TRAVAIL SIMPLE DU PAPIER DÉCOUPÉ ET DES COULEURS DIRECTES REND HOMMAGE AUX AFFICHES DE L'ATELIER DE L'ECOLE DES BEAUX-ARTS DE PARIS PENDANT LES ÉVÉNEMENTS DE MAI 1968 AINSI QU'AU GRAND

 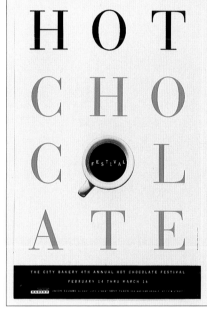 

AFFICHISTE FRANÇAIS SAVIGNAC. □ 9 DESIGNER: JOHN CLARK PHOTOGRAPHER: DON MILLER DESIGN FIRM: LOOKING CLIENT: UCLA, DEPT. OF ITALIAN COUNTRY: USA ■ 9 BY LINKING AN ORANGE—THE SYMBOL FOR LOS ANGELES—AND IMAGES OF MANUSCRIPTS, THIS POSTER BOTH ANNOUCES THE TRIENNIAL EVENT, POETRY ITALY-USA, AND SERVES AS ITS EVENT IDENTITY. ● 9 ANKÜNDIGUNG DES ALLE DREI JAHRE STATTFINDENDEN POESIE-FESTIVALS ITALIEN-USA. DIE KOMBINATION DER ORANGE, SYMBOL FÜR LOS ANGELES, UND DER MANUSKRIPTE WURDE AUCH ZUM LOGO FÜR DIESE VERANSTALTUNG. ▲ 9 AFFICHE D'UN FESTIVAL DE LA POÉSIE ITALO-AMÉRICAIN QUI A LIEU TOUS LES TROIS ANS À LOS ANGELES. LE SUJET DE L'AFFICHE - QUI COMBINE L'ORANGE, SYMBOLE DE LA VILLE, ET LES TEXTES DES POÈMES – SERVIT ÉGALEMENT DE LOGO. □ 10 ART DIRECTOR/DESIGNER/ILLUSTRATOR: ROLF JANSSON DESIGN FIRM: ROLF JANSSON – DESIGN CLIENT: TANGEN GRAFISKE COUNTRY: NORWAY ■ 10 A FESTIVAL FOR YOUNG PEOPLE. ● 10 EIN FESTIVAL FÜR JUNGE MENSCHEN. ▲ 10 AFFICHE D'UN FESTIVAL POUR LA JEUNESSE. □ 11 ART DIRECTOR/DESIGNER: MICHAEL IAN KAYE PHOTOGRAPHER: MICHAEL IAN KAYE CLIENT: THE CITY BAKERY COUNTRY: USA ■ 11 DESIGNED FOR DISPLAY ON THE STREETS OF NEW YORK AND AS A PROMOTIONAL GIVEAWAY FOR THE CITY BAKERY, THIS POSTER FOR THE HOT CHOCOLATE FESTIVAL IS A RESPONSE TO THE SERIOUSNESS WITH WHICH THE BAKERY REGARDS FOOD, JUXTAPOSED TO THE PLAYFULNESS OF THE SUBJECT. ● 11 DAS PLAKAT FÜR DAS HOT CHOCOLATE FESTIVAL WAR FÜR DEN STRASSENAUSHANG UND ALS KUNDENGESCHENK BESTIMMT. HIER GEHT ES EINERSEITS UM DIE ACHTUNG DER CITY BAKERY VOR LEBENSMITTELN, ANDERERSEITS UM EINEN FRÖHLICHEN ANLASS. ▲ 11 PLACARDÉE DANS LES RUES DE NEW YORK, L'AFFICHE DU «HOT CHOCOLATE FESTIVAL» A AUSSI ÉTÉ OFFERTE EN GUISE DE CADEAU PUBLICITAIRE. THE CITY BAKERY ENTENDAIT SOULIGNER AINSI SON SOUCI CONSTANT DE LA QUALITÉ ET METTRE EN AVANT LE CARACTÈRE JOYEUX DU FESTIVAL. □ 12 ART DIRECTOR/DESIGNER: KEN MIKI DESIGN FIRM: KEN MIKI & ASSOCIATES CLIENT: TENJIN BARCA COMMITTEE COUNTRY: JAPAN ■ 12 THE TENJIN FESTIVAL IN JAPAN IS A 1200-YEAR TRADITION. TENJIN BARCA IS A DESIGN SYMPOSIUM. ● 12 DAS TENJIN FESTIVAL IN JAPAN HAT EINE TRADITION VON 1200 JAHREN. TENJIN BARCA IST EIN DESIGN-SYMPOSIUM. ▲ 12 LE FESTIVAL TENJIN AU JAPON EST FORT D'UNE TRADITION MILLÉNAIRE. TENJIN BARCA EST UN COLLOQUE SUR LE DESIGN.

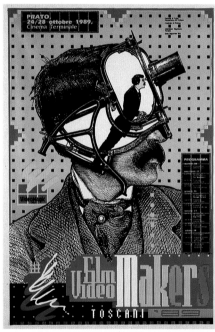

1 ART DIRECTOR/DESIGNER: JACQUES AUGER PHOTOGRAPHER: IRAN ISSA-KHAN DESIGN FIRM: JACQUES AUGER DESIGN ASSOCIATES, INC. CLIENT: COMITES COUNTRY: USA ■ 1 TO PROMOTE THE FIRST MIAMI ITALIAN FILM FESTIVAL, STARK GRAPHIC PHOTOGRAPHY EVOKES THE MYSTERY AND SENSUALITY OF CLASSIC BLACK-AND-WHITE ITALIAN FILMS. ● 1 DIE SINNLICHKEIT KLASSISCHER ITALIENISCHER SPIELFILME IN SCHWARZWEISS WAR AUSGANGSPUNKT FÜR DIESES PLAKAT, DAS EIN ITALIENISCHES FILMFESTIVAL IN MIAMI ANKÜNDIGT. ▲ 1 INSPIRÉE DU MYSTERE ET DE LA SENSUALITÉ DES GRANDS CLASSIQUES ITALIENS EN NOIR ET BLANC, CETTE AFFICHE ANNONCE UN FESTIVAL DU FILM À MIAMI. □ 2 ART DIRECTOR/DESIGNER: CARTER WEITZ ILLUSTRATOR: M. JOHN ENGLISH COPYWRITER: MITCH KOCH DESIGN FIRM: BAILEY LAUERMAN & ASSOCIATES CLIENT: WESTERN PAPER COMPANY COUNTRY: USA ■ 2 A PRODUCT EXHIBITION FOR THE PAPER AND PRINTING INDUSTRY. ● 2 EINE AUSSTELLUNG DER PAPIER- UND DRUCKINDUSTRIE. ▲ 2 AFFICHE D'UNE EXPOSITION PRÉSENTÉE PAR LES INDUSTRIES GRAPHIQUE ET PAPETIÈRE. □ 3 ART DIRECTORS: PRIMO ANGELI, CARLO PAGODA DESIGNER: PRIMO ANGELI COMPUTER ILLUSTRATORS: MARCELO DE FREITAS, PAUL TERRILL PRODUCTION MANAGER: ERIC KUBLY DESIGN FIRM: PRIMO ANGELI, INC. CLIENT: SAN FRANCISCO FILM SOCIETY COUNTRY: USA ■ 3 A PROMOTIONAL POSTER FOR THE SAN FRANCISCO FILM SOCIETY'S 38TH INTERNATIONAL FILM FESTIVAL CELEBRATES 100 YEARS OF CINEMA, FROM 1895 TO 1995. ● 3 100 JAHRE KINO SIND DAS THEMA DIESES PLAKATES FÜR DAS 38. INTERNATIONALE FILMFESTIVAL DER SAN FRANCISCO FILM SOCIETY. ▲ 3 «CENT ANS DE CINÉMA». AFFICHE DU 38ᵉ FESTIVAL INTERNATIONAL DU FILM ORGANISÉ PAR LA SAN FRANCISCO FILM SOCIETY. □ 4 ART DIRECTOR/DESIGNER: EMO RISALITI ILLUSTRATOR: EMO RISALITI DESIGN FIRM: EMO RISALITI GRAPHIC DESIGNER CLIENT: COMUNE DI PRATO COUNTRY: ITALY ■ 4 A FESTIVAL OF VIDEO FILMMAKERS IN WHICH THE INTERNAL AND EXTERNAL WORLDS ARE OBSERVED WITH A TECHNOLOGICAL EYE. ● 4 EIN FESTIVAL DER VIDEOFILMER: BEI DIESER

TÄTIGKEIT WERDEN FAKTEN UND REALITÄTEN DER INNEREN UND ÄUSSEREN WELT NICHT DIREKT, SONDERN MIT HILFE EINES INSTRUMENTS GESEHEN, EINEM TECHNOLOGISCHEN AUGE. ▲ 4 FESTIVAL TOSCAN DE LA VIDÉO: DANS SON TRAVAIL, LE RÉALISATEUR DE FILMS VIDÉO NE PERÇOIT PAS DIRECTEMENT LES FAITS ET LA RÉALITÉ DU MONDE INTÉRIEUR ET EXTÉRIEUR, MAIS AU TRAVERS D'UN INSTRUMENT, UN «ŒIL TECHNOLOGIQUE». □ 5 ART DIRECTOR/DESIGNER: VITTORIO COSTARELLA ILLUSTRATOR: VITTORIO COSTARELLA DESIGN FIRM: MODERN DOG CLIENT: THE RAINY STATES FILM FESTIVAL COUNTRY: USA ■ 5 A POSTER FOR AN INDEPENDENT FILM FESTIVAL IN SEATTLE. MANY INDEPENDENT FILMMAKERS USE 16 MM CAMERAS, WHICH HAPPEN TO RESEMBLE THE HUMAN HEAD. THUS, "THE 16 MILLIMETER MAN." ● 5 ANKÜNDIGUNG EINES FESTIVALS FÜR UNABHÄNGIGE FILMEMACHER. DA VIELE VON IHNEN 16MM-KAMERAS BENUTZEN, IST DER TITEL «DER 16MM-MANN». ▲ 5 «L'HOMME 16 MM». AFFICHE D'UN FESTIVAL CONSACRÉ AUX RÉALISATEURS INDÉPENDANTS, QUI TRAVAILLENT

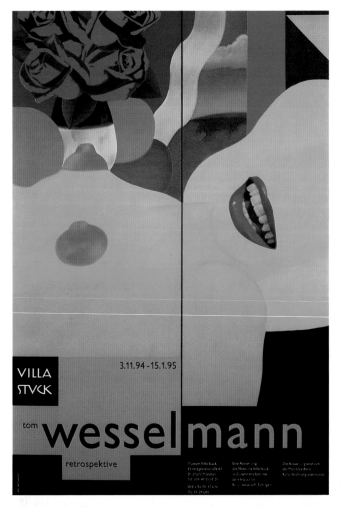

SOUVENT AVEC UNE CAMÉRA 16 MM. □ 6 ART DIRECTOR/DESIGNER: MARTA IBARRONDO COPYWRITER: TOM GIVONE ADVERTISING AGENCY: FRANKFURT/BALKIND CLIENT: AMERICAN FILM INSTITUTE/STEVEN SPIELBERG COUNTRY: USA ■ 6 A POSTER COMMEMO-RATING STEVEN SPIELBERG'S ACCEPTANCE OF THE AMERICAN FILM INSTITUTE'S 23RD LIFE ACHIEVEMENT AWARD. ● 6 DER STEVEN SPIELBERG VERLIEHENE PREIS DES AMERIKANISCHEN FILMINSTITUTS FÜR SEIN LEBENSWERK IST THEMA DIESES PLAKATES. ▲ 6 AFFICHE COMMÉMORANT LA CONSÉCRATION DE STEVEN SPIELBERG PAR L'INSTITUT DU FILM AMÉRICAIN. □ 7 ART DIRECTOR/DESIGNER: JOHN MULLER PHOTOGRAPHER: HALLMARK STAFF DESIGN FIRM: MULLER + COMPANY CLIENT: HALLMARK COUNTRY: USA ■ 7 ANNOUNCEMENT OF A HALLMARK HALL OF FAME MADE-FOR-TV MOVIE. ● 7 «DIE RÜCKKEHR DES EINGE-BORENEN» – DIE AUFFÜHRUNG EINES ROMANTISCHEN KLASSIKERS AM FERNSEHEN. ▲ 7 «LE RETOUR AU PAYS NATAL». ROMAN DE THOMAS HARDY PORTÉ AU PETIT ÉCRAN. □ 8 ART DIRECTOR/DESIGNER: TADANORI YOKOO COUNTRY: JAPAN ■ 8 AFTER "BLUE" AND "WHITE," "RED" CONCLUDES A FILM TRILOGY BY KRZYSZTOF KIESLOWSKI. THE REFERENCE IS TO THE COLORS OF THE FRENCH FLAG. ● 8 NACH «BLEU» UND «BLANC» ENDET DIE FILMTRILOGIE VON KRZYSZTOF KIESLOWSKI MIT «ROUGE». (ANSPIELUNG AUF DIE FRANZÖSISCHE FLAGGE.) ▲ 8 AFFICHE DE CINÉMA. APRÈS «BLEU» ET «BLANC», «ROUGE» BOUCLA LA TRILOGIE DU RÉALISATEUR POLONAIS KRZYSZTOF KIESLOWSKI. □ 9 ART DIRECTOR/DESIGNER: DAN LONG ILLUSTRATOR: ANGEL MUÑEZ DESIGN FIRM: LONG ADVERTISING CLIENT: IWERKS ENTERTAINMENT COUNTRY: USA ■ 9 THE "ALIENS"

POSTER WAS COMPUTER GENERATED TO PROMOTE THE IWERKS ENTERTAINMENT MOTION-SIMULATION RIDE BASED ON THE SCI-FI THRILLER MOVIE OF THE SAME NAME. ● 9 DER SCIENCE-FICTION FILM *ALIENS* DIENTE ALS THEMA DIESES COMPUTER-GENERIERTEN PLAKATES FÜR IWERKS ENTERTAINMENT, SPEZIALISTEN FÜR COMPUTERSIMULATIONEN. ▲ 9 PUBLICITÉ D'IWERKS ENTERTAINMENT, SPÉCIALISTE DE LA SIMULATION. LE FILM DE SCIENCE-FICTION *ALIEN* ÉTAIT LE THÈME DE CETTE AFFICHE RÉALISÉE SUR ORDINATEUR. ■ 10 ART DIRECTOR: PAUL YUNG KIN WANG DESIGNER: PAUL YUNG KIN WANG DESIGN FIRM: XPRESS DESIGN & PRINTING SERVICE CLIENT: ECKOXA FILM PRODUCTION CO., LTD. COUNTRY: HONG KONG ■ 10 ANNOUNCEMENT OF A CHINESE FILM. ● 10 ANKÜNDIGUNG EINES CHINESISCHEN FILMS. ▲ 10 AFFICHE D'UN FILM CHINOIS. □ (THIS SPREAD) 1 ART DIRECTOR: KNUT MAIERHOFER DESIGNERS: TOM FERRARO, KNUT MAIERHOFER DESIGN FIRM: KMS-TEAM CLIENT: VILLA STUCK COUNTRY: GERMANY ■ 1 A WESSELMANN RETROSPECTIVE AT THE VILLA STUCK IN MUNICH. SHOWN HERE, A DETAIL OF THE PAINTING "GREAT AMERICAN NUDE NO. 43." ● 1 EINE WESSELMANN-RETROSPEKTIVE IN DER VILLA STUCK IN MÜNCHEN. GEZEIGT IST EIN AUSSCHNITT DES BILDES «GREAT AMERICAN NUDE NO. 43». ▲ 1 RÉTROSPECTIVE WESSELMANN À LA VILLA STUCK (MUNICH). LE SUJET DE L'AFFICHE EST UN DÉTAIL DU TABLEAU «GREAT AMERICAN NUDE NO. 43». □ 2 ART DIRECTOR/DESIGNER: CLAUDE KUHN CLIENT: NATURHISTORISCHES MUSEUM DER BÜRGERGEMEINDE BERN COUNTRY: SWITZERLAND ■ 2 "THE DOMESTICATED CAT," A SCIENTIFIC EXHIBITION AT THE MUSEUM OF NATURAL HISTORY IN BERNE. ● 2 «DIE HAUSKATZE», EIN POPULÄRES THEMA, WISSENSCHAFTLICH BEHANDELT. ▲ 2 «LE CHAT DOMESTIQUE». AFFICHE D'EXPOSITION

DU MUSÉE D'HISTOIRE NATURELLE DE BERNE. □ 3 ART DIRECTOR: KENZO IZUTANI DESIGNERS: KENZO IZUTANI, AKI HIRAI PHOTOGRAPHERS: YASUYUKI AMAZUTSUMI, ZIGEN (PHOTO OF STATUE) SCULPTOR: KATSURA FUNAKOSHI DESIGN FIRM: KENZO IZUTANI OFFICE CORPORATION CLIENT: PLATINUM GUILD INTERNATIONAL COUNTRY: JAPAN ■ 3 INTRODUCTION OF THE FIRST ISSUE OF THE PLATINUM GUILD'S QUARTERLY MAGAZINE. ● 3 EINFÜHRUNG DER ERSTEN AUSGABEN EINER QUARTALSWEISE ERSCHEINENDEN ZEITSCHRIFT DER PLATIN-GILDE. DURCH DIE ÜBERLAGERUNG EINER AUFNAHME VON BEWEGTEM WASSER UND TROPFEN WURDE DER HÖLZERNEN STATUE (VON KATSURA FUNAKOSHI) LEBEN EINGEGEBEN. ▲ 3 CETTE AFFICHE ANNONCE LA SORTIE D'UN TOUT NOUVEAU MAGAZINE TRIMESTRIEL INTITULÉ PLATINO. L'ARTISTE DONNA VIE À LA STATUE DE BOIS (UNE SCULPTURE DE KATSURA FUNAKOSHI) EN SUPERPOSANT UNE PHOTO D'EAU AGITÉE ET DE GOUTTELETTES. □ 4 ART DIRECTORS/DESIGNERS: DIETER FEHSECKE, HEIKE GREBIN, ANDREAS TROGISCH, TILMAN WENDLAND PHOTOGRAPHERS: GRAPPA KOLLEKTIV, FRITZ LANG (1928) DESIGN FIRM: GRAPPA DESIGN CLIENT: FILMMUSEUM POTSDAM COUNTRY: GERMANY ■ 4 INSPIRATION FOR THIS POSTER FOR A MUSEUM'S PERMANENT FILM COLLECTION COMES FROM FRITZ LANG'S SCIENCE FIC-TION MOVIE "WOMAN IN THE MOON" (1928/29), STARRING GERDA MAURUS. ● 4 DAS HAUPTMOTIV DIESES PLAKATES STAMMT AUS FRITZ LANGS SCIENCE-FICTION-FILM «FRAU IM MOND» VON 1928/29 MIT GERDA MAURUS IN DER HAUPTROLLE. DIE KLEINEN FIGUREN SIND SCHAUSPIELER DER UFA UND DEFA (FILMPRODUKTIONS- UND VERLEIHGESELLSCHAFT DER EHEMALI-GEN DDR). ▲ 4 AFFICHE REPRÉSENTANT UNE SCÈNE DE «LA FEMME SUR LA LUNE», FILM DE SCIENCE-FICTION RÉALISÉ EN 1928–29 PAR FRITZ LANG AVEC GERDA MAURUS DANS LE RÔLE PRINCIPAL. LES PERSONNAGES MINIATURES SONT DES ACTEURS DE L'UFA ET DE LA DEFA, COMPAGNIES CINÉMATOGRAPHIQUES ALLEMANDES. □ 5 ART DIRECTOR/DESIGNER: PIERRE MENDELL DESIGN FIRM: MENDELL & OBERER CLIENT: DIE NEUE SAMMLUNG COUNTRY: GERMANY ■ 5 "CHURCH AND ART," AN EXHI-BITION IN MUNICH. ● 5 SYMBOLIK UND FARBEN DIESES PLAKATES SPRECHEN FÜR SICH. ▲ 5 «L'EGLISE ET L'ART». EXPOSITION PRÉSENTÉE À MUNICH. □ 6 ART DIRECTOR/DESIGNER: PIERRE MENDELL DESIGN FIRM: MENDELL & OBERER PHOTOGRAPHER: KLAUS

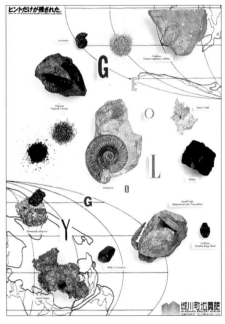

OBERER CLIENT: DIE NEUE SAMMLUNG COUNTRY: GERMANY ■ 6 A VARIATION OF THE SWISS FLAG SERVES TO ANNOUNCE AN EXHIBITION ON SWISS BOOK DESIGN. ● 6 EINE VARIATION DER SCHWEIZER FLAGGE DIENT ALS ANKÜNDIGUNG DIESER AUSSTELLUNG. ▲ 6 AFFICHE RÉALISÉE POUR UNE EXPOSITION SUR L'ÉDITION SUISSE ET S'INSPIRANT DU DRAPEAU SUISSE. □ (THIS SPREAD) 1 ART DIRECTOR: MICHAEL CRONAN DESIGNER: MICHAEL CRONAN, ANTHONY YELL ILLUSTRATOR: MICHAEL CRONAN DESIGN FIRM: CRONAN DESIGN, INC. CLIENT: SAN FRANCISCO MUSEUM OF MODERN ART COUNTRY: USA ■ 1 POSTER COMMEMO-RATING THE NEW SAN FRANCISCO MUSEUM OF MODERN ART (SFMOMA) BUILDING, AS WELL AS THE MUSEUM'S 16TH ANNIVER-SARY. ● 1 DAS 16JÄHRIGE BESTEHEN UND DAS NEUE GEBÄUDE DES SAN FRANCISCO MUSEUM OF MODERN ART SIND DIE THEMEN DIESES PLAKATES. ▲ 1 AFFICHE RÉALISÉE POUR L'INAUGURATION D'UN NOUVEAU BÂTIMENT DU MUSÉE D'ART MO-DERNE DE SAN FRANCISCO, QUI CÉLÉBRAIT AUSSI SON 16E ANNIVERSAIRE. □ 2 ART DIRECTOR: GAKU OKUBO DESIGNERS: GAKU OKUBO, KAZUMI YOSHINO PHOTOGRAPHER: SEIKI NINOMLYA COPYWRITER: JUNKO WADA DESIGN FIRM: OKUBO DESIGN STUDIO CLIENT: SHIROKAWA GEOLOGY MUSEUM COUNTRY: JAPAN ■ 2 "ONLY CLUES ARE LEFT." CHARACTERISTIC EXHIBITS FROM THE SHIROKAWA GEOLOGY MUSEUM REMIND THE VISITOR OF THE BILLIONS OF YEARS THAT MAKE UP THE GEOLOGICAL HISTORY OF THE EARTH. ● 2 «ES BLEIBEN NUR HINWEISE.» DIE HIER GEZEIGTEN ELEMENTE SIND TYPISCH FÜR DAS GEOLOGISCHE MUSEUM. DER BESUCHER WIRD AN DIE ABERMILLIONEN JAHRE DER EXISTENZ DER ERDE ERINNERT, VON DENEN DIE GEOLO-GISCHEN FUNDE ZEUGEN. ▲ 2 «LES VESTIGES DU PASSÉ». AFFICHE DU MUSÉE DE GÉOLOGIE DE SHIROKAWA. L'EXPOSITION RETRACE L'HISTOIRE DE LA TERRE ET LES TRANSFORMATIONS QU'ELLE A SUBIES AU COURS DE MILLIONS D'ANNÉES, DONT TÉMOIGNENT ROCHES ET FOSSILES. □ 3 ART DIRECTOR: RUSTY KAY DESIGNER/ILLUSTRATOR: DAVE CHAPPLE DESIGN FIRM: RUSTY KAY & ASSOCIATES CLIENT: PETERSEN AUTOMOTIVE MUSEUM COUNTRY: USA ■ 3 POSTER FOR THE GRAND OPENING OF THE PETERSEN AUTOMOTIVE MUSEUM, A DIVISION OF THE LOS ANGELES COUNTY MUSEUM OF NATURAL HISTORY. ● 3 ANKÜNDI-GUNG DER ERÖFFNUNG DES AUTO-MUSEUMS DES LOS ANGELES COUNTY MUSEUM OF NATURAL HISTORY. ▲ 3 AFFICHE ANNONÇANT L'OUVERTURE D'UN MUSÉE DE L'AUTOMOBILE, INTÉGRÉ AU MUSÉE D'HISTOIRE NATURELLE DE LOS ANGELES.

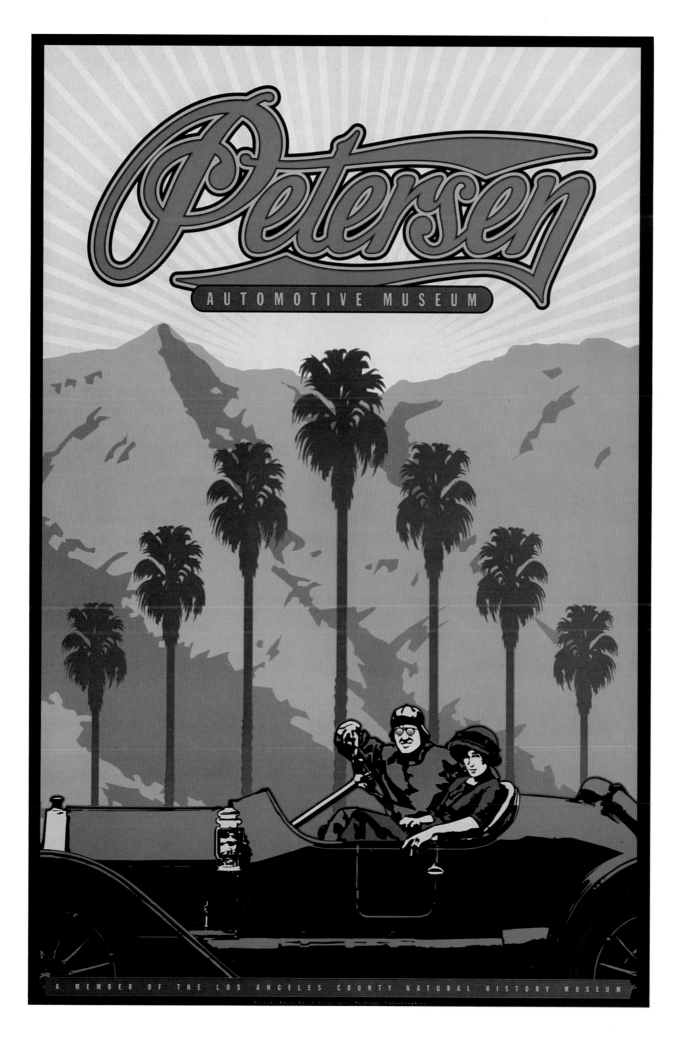

ERIC CLAPTON

★ THE NEW ALBUM ★ IN STORES NOW ★

FROM THE CRADLE

— featuring: —

I'M TORE DOWN

MOTHERLESS CHILD

HOOCHIE COOCHIE MAN

BLUES BEFORE SUNRISE

— And 12 More! —

(PRECEDING SPREAD) **1** ART DIRECTOR: LINDA COBB DESIGNER: LINDA COBB PHOTOGRAPHER: THE DOUGLAS BROTHERS LETTERING: ROWAN MOORE CLIENT: REPRISE RECORDS COUNTRY: USA ■ **1** USED TO PROMOTE ERIC CLAPTON'S ALBUM "FROM THE CRADLE"—A COLLECTION OF BLUES TRACKS—THIS POSTER USES WOOD-CUT TYPE TO CREATE THE FEEL OF AN OLD BLUES POSTER. ● **1** DURCH DIE VERWENDUNG VON HOLZSCHNITTBUCHSTABEN ENTSPRICHT DER STIL DIESES PLAKATES FÜR ERIC CLAPTONS BLUES-ALBUM «FROM THE CRADLE» DEM ALTER BLUESPLAKATE. ▲ **1** PUBLICITÉ POUR L'ALBUM «FROM THE CRADLE» D'ERIC CLAPTON S'INSPIRANT DES ANCIENNES AFFICHES DE BLUES. LA TYPOGRAPHIE EST RÉALISÉE À L'AIDE DE CARACTÈRES D'IMPRIMERIE EN BOIS. □ (PRECEDING SPREAD) **2** ART DIRECTOR: TOM WAITS, CHRISTIE RIXFORD DESIGNER: CHRISTIE RIXFORD ILLUSTRATOR: CHRISTIE RIXFORD CLIENT: TOM WAITS/ISLAND RECORDS, INC. COUNTRY: USA ■ **2** DISTRIBUTED BY ISLAND RECORDS TO RECORD STORES THROUGHOUT THE US AND EUROPE, THIS POSTER PROMOTES SINGER/SONGWRITER TOM WAITS'S ALBUM "THE BLACK RIDER." ● **2** FÜR SCHALLPLATTENLÄDEN IN DEN USA UND EUROPA BESTIMMTES PLAKAT ALS WERBUNG FÜR TOM WAITS' ALBUM «THE BLACK RIDER». ▲ **2** AFFICHE PUBLICITAIRE POUR UN ALBUM DE TOM WAITS, DESTINÉE AUX MAGASINS DE DISQUES AMÉRICAINS ET EUROPÉENS. □ (THIS SPREAD) **1** ART

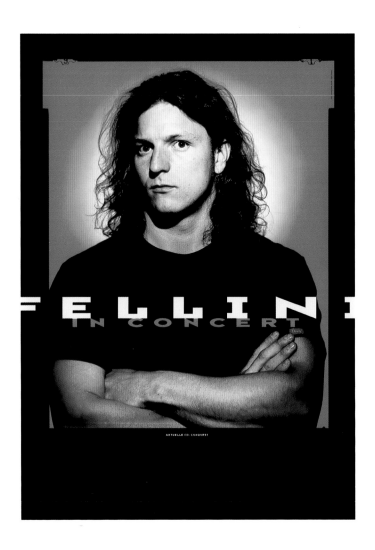

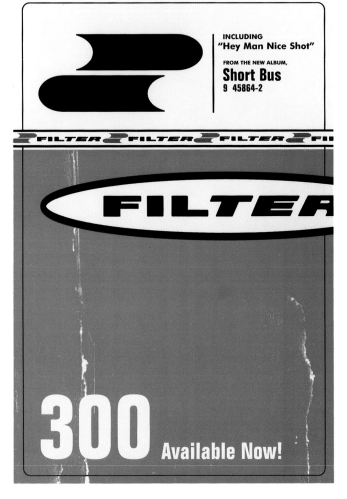

DIRECTOR: PETER FELDER DESIGNERS: PETER FELDER, RENÉ DALPRA PHOTOGRAPHER: GÜNTHER PARTH DESIGN FIRM: FELDER GRAFIK DESIGN CLIENT: KLAUS TSCHANETT COUNTRY: AUSTRIA ■ **1** THIS POSTER ALLOWS FOR INSERTS OF VARIOUS CONCERT DATES. ● **1** DIESES PLAKAT ERMÖGLICH DEN EINDRUCK VERSCHIEDENER KONZERTDATEN. ▲ **1** AFFICHE PERMETTANT L'INSERTION DE PLUSIEURS DATES DE CONCERT. □ (THIS SPREAD) **2** ART DIRECTOR/DESIGNER: DEBORAH NORCROSS CLIENT: REPRISE RECORDS COUNTRY: USA □ (THIS SPREAD) **3–6** ART DIRECTOR/DESIGNER: BÜLENT ERKMEN CLIENT: ISTANBUL FOUNDATION FOR CULTURE AND ARTS COUNTRY: TURKEY ■ **3–6** THE THEME OF THESE POSTERS FOR FOUR SUCCESSIVE FESTIVALS IS "ISTANBUL." THE SEPARATION OF THE WORD ISTANBUL INTO FOUR PARTS INDICATES THE WAY THE POSTERS SHOULD BE HUNG. THE NUMBERS REFER TO THE FESTIVAL IN QUESTION. ● **3–6** ISTANBUL WAR DAS MOTTO DIESER PLAKATE FÜR VIER AUFEINANDER FOLGENDE FESTIVALS. DIE AUFTEILUNG DES WORTES ISTANBUL IN VIER TEILE BESTIMMTE DIE REIHENFOLGE DER PLAKATE. DIE NUMMERN BEZIEHEN SICH AUF DIE EINZELNEN VERANSTALTUNGEN. ▲ (CI-CONTRE) **3–6** SÉRIE DE QUATRE AFFICHES RÉALISÉES POUR DIVERS FESTIVALS À ISTANBUL (JUXTAPOSÉES, ELLES FORMENT LE MOT «ISTANBUL»). LE CHIFFRE FAIT RÉFÉRENCE AU GENRE DU FESTIVAL (13ᵉᵐᵉ FESTIVAL DU FILM, 6ᵉᵐᵉ FESTIVAL DU THÉÂTRE, ETC.)

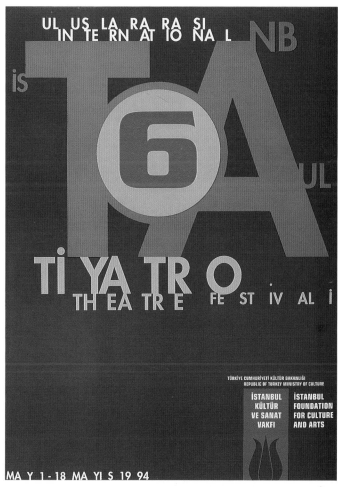

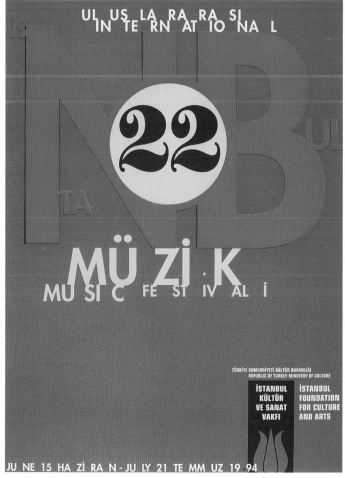

1 ART DIRECTOR/DESIGNER/PHOTOGRAPHER: HOLGER MATTHIES CLIENT: NIEDERSÄCHSISCHE STAATSOPER HANNOVER COUNTRY: GERMANY ■ 1 A PERFORMANCE OF "THE TALES OF HOFFMANN" AT THE OPERA HOUSE OF HANOVER. HERE, MEN'S FANTASIES ARE PROJECTED ON A FEMALE BODY. ● 1 MÄNNERPHANTASIEN, PROJIZIERT AUF EINEN EINZIGEN WEIBLICHEN KÖRPER. ▲ 1 LES FANTASMES MASCULINS PROJETÉS SUR LE CORPS D'UNE FEMME. AFFICHE DE L'OPÉRA D'HANOVRE POUR LES CONTES D'HOFFMANN. □ 2 ART DIRECTOR/DESIGNER/PHOTOGRAPHER: HOLGER MATTHIES CLIENT: GOETHE-INSTITUT COUNTRY: GERMANY ■ 2 THE SYNERGY OF THE MUSICIAN AND HIS INSTRUMENT IS THE SUBJECT OF THIS POSTER FOR A SERIES OF PIANO CONCERTS. ● 2 DIE SYNERGIE ZWISCHEN INSTRUMENT UND KÜNSTLER IST DAS THEMA DIESES PLAKATES FÜR EINE REIHE VON KLAVIERKONZERTEN. ▲ 2 L'ARTISTE ET SON INSTRUMENT EN SYMBIOSE, TEL EST LE THÈME DE CETTE AFFICHE RÉALISÉE POUR UNE SÉRIE DE RÉCITALS. □ (OPPOSITE PAGE) 3–8 ART DIRECTOR/DESIGNER: MARK L. ARMINSKI PHOTOGRAPHERS: MARK L. ARMINSKI (5), STEPHEN APICELLA-HITCHCOCK (8) ILLUSTRATOR: MARK L. ARMINSKI (5–7) DESIGN FIRM: MARK L. ARMINSKI CLIENTS: RITUAL PRODUCTIONS (3), PRISM PRODUCTIONS (4, 6, 7), ARTROCK (5), FIRST AVENUE (8) COUNTRY: USA ■ 3–8

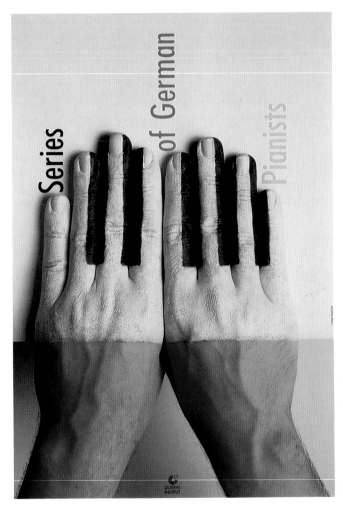

SILKSCREEN POSTERS TO PROMOTE A NUMBER OF CONTEMPORARY MUSICAL ARTISTS. ● 3–8 SIEBDRUCKPLAKATE FÜR VERSCHIEDENE MODERNE MUSIKER. ▲ 3–8 SÉRIGRAPHIES PRÉSENTANT DIVERS MUSICIENS. □ (FOLLOWING SPREAD) 1 ART DIRECTOR/DESIGNER: THOMAS G. FOWLER ILLUSTRATORS: THOMAS G. FOWLER, SAMUEL TOH DESIGN FIRM: TOM G. FOWLER INC. CLIENT: CONNECTICUT GRAND OPERA & ORCHESTRA COUNTRY: USA ■ 1 ANNOUNCEMENT OF AN ALL-RUSSIAN CONCERT PROGRAM PERFORMED BY THE CONNECTICUT GRAND OPERA AND ORCHESTRA. ● 1 ANKÜNDIGUNG EINES GANZ DER RUSSISCHEN MUSIK GEWIDMETEN KONZERTES. ▲ 1 AFFICHE D'UN CONCERT DE MUSIQUE RUSSE INTERPRÉTÉ PAR LE CONNECTICUT GRAND OPERA AND ORCHESTRA. □ (FOLLOWING SPREAD) 2 ART DIRECTOR/DESIGNER: SHINNOSKE SUGISAKI DESIGN FIRM: SHINNOSKE INC. CLIENT: BLUE NOTE OSAKA COUNTRY: JAPAN ■ 2 MICHI FUJII IS A JAZZ TRUMPET PLAYER. THE MOSTLY COMPUTER-GENERATED POSTER, ANNOUNCING HER FIRST CONCERT IN JAPAN, INTERPRETS THE SOUND OF HER INSTRUMENT. ● 2 MICHI FUJII IST EINE AUSGEZEICHNETE JUNGE JAZZ-TROMPETERIN. DAS GRÖSSTENTEILS MIT DEM COMPUTER HERGESTELLTE PLAKAT INTERPRETIERT DEN KLANG IHRES INSTRUMENTS. ▲ 2 AFFICHE DU 1ER CONCERT DE MICHI FUJII, JEUNE TROMPETTISTE DE JAZZ SURDOUÉE. RÉALISÉE EN GRANDE PARTIE SUR ORDINATEUR, L'AFFICHE ÉVOQUE LE SON DE L'INSTRUMENT.

FUJII MICHI

FIRST BLOW FROM OSAKA

10/30 SUNDAY

OSAKA BLUE NOTE

1–6 ART DIRECTOR: NIKLAUS TROXLER DESIGNER: NIKLAUS TROXLER ILLUSTRATOR: NIKLAUS TROXLER DESIGN FIRM: NIKLAUS TROXLER GRAFIK CLIENT: JAZZ IN WILLISAU COUNTRY: SWITZERLAND ■ 1–6 VARIOUS CONCERTS OF THE ANNUAL JAZZ FESTIVAL OF WILLISAU, SWITZERLAND, ARE ANNOUNCED. THE DESIGNER OF THE POSTER IS ALSO THE ORGANIZER OF THE FESTIVAL. ● 1–6 VERSCHIEDENE KONZERTE AM INTERNATIONALEN JAZZFESTIVAL VON WILLISAU, SCHWEIZ, WERDEN HIER ANGEKÜNDIGT. DER GESTALTER DER PLAKATE IST GLEICHZEITIG AUCH ORGANISATOR UND INITIATOR DIESES FESTIVALS. ▲

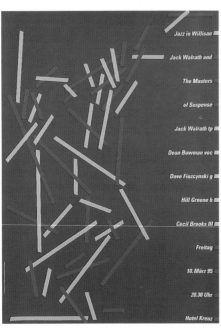

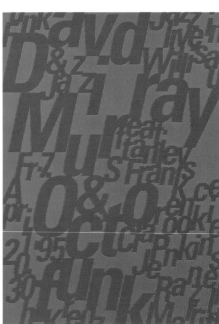

1–6 AFFICHES DU FESTIVAL DE JAZZ DE WILLISAU (SUISSE), RÉALISÉES PAR L'ORGANISATEUR DU FESTIVAL. ☐ 7 ART DIRECTOR: JERRY KETEL DESIGNER: ADAM BRONSON MCISAAC PHOTOGRAPHER: RAFAEL ASTORGA DESIGN FIRM: THE FELT HAT CLIENT: PIONEER COURTHOUSE SQUARE COUNTRY: USA ■ 7 DESIGNED TO PROMOTE AWARENESS OF THE BLUE NOTE JAZZ ALBUM COVERS OF REID MILES. ● 7 REID MILES' PLATTENHÜLLEN FÜR DIE BLUE-NOTE-JAZZ-SERIE SIND GEGENSTAND DIESES PLAKATES. ▲ 7 AFFICHE DÉDIÉE AUX POCHETTES DE DISQUES DE LA SÉRIE JAZZ BLUE NOTE DE REID MILES.

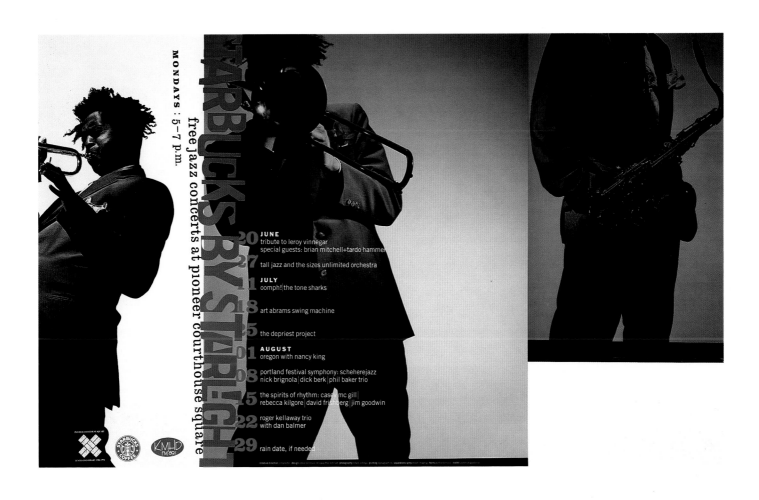

1, 2 ART DIRECTOR/DESIGNER: ANTHONY SELLARI PHOTOGRAPHER: FRANK DRIGGS COLLECTION CLIENT: COLUMBIA/LEGACY COUNTRY: USA ■ 1, 2 POSTERS TO PROMOTE TWO BOXED SETS OF FRANK SINATRA'S MUSIC. ● 1, 2 WERBUNG FÜR ZWEI FRANK-SINATRA-CD-KOLLEKTIONEN. ▲ 1, 2 PUBLICITÉ POUR DES CASSETTES DE FRANK SINATRA. □ 3 DESIGNERS: JOHN CLARK, MARIANNE THOMPSON DESIGN FIRM: LOOKING CLIENT: MARSILIO PUBLISHERS COUNTRY: USA ■ 3 USED INITIALLY AS A BOOK FAIR PROMOTION OF AMIRI BARAKA'S BOOK, THIS POSTER WAS LATER USED AS THE BOOK'S COVER. ● 3 URSPÜNG-LICH ALS MESSEWERBUNG FÜR AMIRI BARAKAS BUCH ENTWORFEN, WURDE DAS PLAKATE SPÄTER ALS BUCHUMSCHLAG VER-WENDET. ▲ 3 INITIALEMENT RÉALISÉE POUR PRÉSENTER UN OUVRAGE D'AMIRI BARAKA LORS D'UN SALON DU LIVRE, CETTE

AFFICHE SERVIT ENSUITE DE JAQUETTE. □ (FOLLOWING SPREAD) 1 ART DIRECTOR/DESIGNER: TOM NUIJENS PHOTOGRAPHER: ALAN GOVENAR DESIGN FIRM: ROBIN SHEPHERD STUDIOS CLIENT: SPRINGING THE BLUES FEST COUNTRY: USA ■ 1 CREATED AND PRODUCED ON A LIMITED BUDGET, THIS POSTER PROMOTED A FLORIDA BLUES FESTIVAL. ● 1 FÜR DAS PLAKAT DES FLORIDA BLUES FESTIVALS STAND NUR EIN KLEINER ETAT ZUR VERFÜGUNG. ▲ 1 AFFICHE PETIT BUDGET D'UN FESTIVAL DE BLUES EN FLORIDE. □ (FOLLOWING SPREAD) 2 ART DIRECTOR/DESIGNER: TOM RECCHION PHOTOGRAPHER: DENNIS KEELEY CLIENT: REPRISE RECORDS COUNTRY: USA ■ 2 THE CREAM-COLORED UNCOATED STOCK OF THIS PROMOTIONAL POSTER GIVES IT AN "OLD" FEEL. ● 2 DAS CREMEFARBENE, UNBESCHICHTETE PAPIER VERLEIHT DIESEM PROMOTIONSPLAKAT EINEN NOSTALGISCHEN TOUCH. ▲ 2 CE PAPIER CRÈME BRUT CONFÈRE UNE PETITE TOUCHE «RÉTRO» À CETTE AFFICHE.

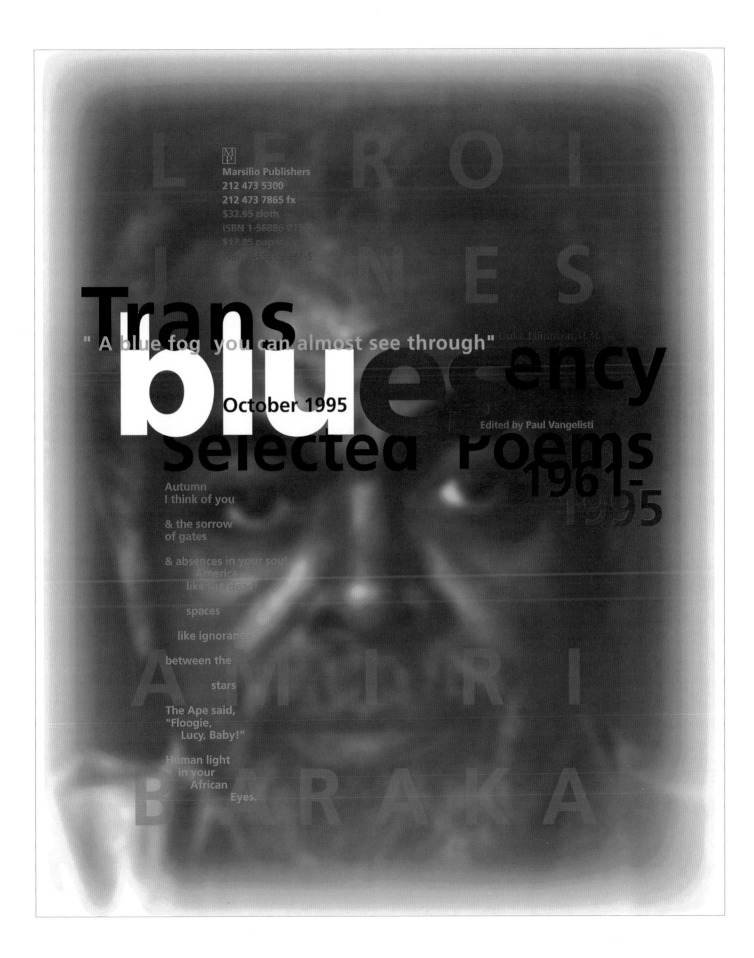

LEROI JONES

Marsilio Publishers
212 473 5300
212 473 7865 fx
$32.95 cloth
ISBN 1-56886-012-7
$17.85 paper
ISBN 1-55586-011-5

Trans
blue
"A blue fog you can almost see through"
October 1995
ency
Edited by Paul Vangelisti
Selected Poems
1961-
1995

Autumn
I think of you

& the sorrow
of gates

& absences in your soul
America
like the dead

spaces

like ignorance

between the

stars

The Ape said,
"Floogie,
Lucy, Baby!"

Human light
in your
African

Eyes.

AMIRI

BARAKA

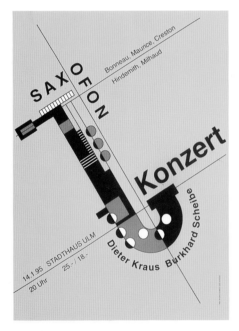

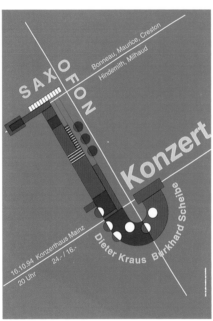

1 ART DIRECTOR/DESIGNER: SIMON SERNEC CLIENT: TATJANA & NINA MOLE COUNTRY: SLOVENIA ■1 ANNOUNCEMENT OF A PIANO CONCERT. ●1 ANKÜNDIGUNG EINES KLAVIERKONZERTES. ▲1 AFFICHE D' UN RÉCITAL DE PIANO. □2 ART DIRECTOR: ALLEN WEINBERG DESIGNER: ALLEN WEINBERG PHOTOGRAPHER: KAREN KUEHN CLIENT: SONY MUSIC COUNTRY: USA ■2 IN-STORE PROMOTIONAL POSTER FOR TONY BENNETT ON "MTV UNPLUGGED." ●2 LADENPLAKAT ALS PROMOTION FÜR DEN SÄNGER TONY BENNETT IN DER TV-SENDUNG «MTV UNPLUGGED». ▲2 PUBLICITÉ POUR TONY BENNETT, INVITÉ SPÉCIAL DE L'ÉMISSION «MTV UNPLUGGED». □3 ART DIRECTOR: LAURA MESEGUER DESIGNERS: LAURA MESEGUER, JUAN DAVILA DESIGN FIRM: COSMIC CLIENT: SANT ANDREU TEATRE COUNTRY: SPAIN ■3 POSTER ANNOUNCING THREE CONCERTS. ●3 ANKÜNDIGUNG VON DREI KONZERTEN. ▲3 ANNONCE DE TROIS CONCERTS. □4–6 ART DIRECTOR/DESIGNER: KARSTEN SCHWEIZER ILLUSTRATOR: JAN WILKER DESIGN FIRM: BÜRO FÜR ALLES KREAKTIVE UND VERRÜCKTE CLIENT: DIETER KRAUS COUNTRY: GERMANY ■4–6 VARIATIONS OF A POSTER ANNOUNCING A CONCERT IN THREE DIFFERENT CITIES. ●4–6 VARIATIONEN EINES PLAKATES FÜR DIE BEKANNTGABE EINES KONZERTES IN DREI VERSCHIEDENEN STÄDTEN. ▲4–6 VARIATIONS SUR UN MÊME AIR POUR L'AFFICHE D'UN CONCERT DONNÉ DANS TROIS VILLES DIFFÉRENTES. □7 ART DIRECTORS: GAYE LOCKWOOD, JOHN HOLDER DESIGNER/ILLUSTRATOR: GAYE LOCKWOOD DESIGN FIRM: THE STUDIO CLIENT: CAMBRIDGE CITY COUNCIL COUNTRY: GREAT BRITAIN ■7 ANNOUNCEMENT OF A FOLK FESTIVAL IN GREAT BRITAIN. ●7 ANKÜNDIGUNG EINES FOLK-FESTIVALS IN GROSSBRITANNIEN. ▲7 AFFICHE D'UN FESTIVAL FOLK EN GRANDE-BRETAGNE. □8 ART DIRECTOR/DESIGNER: TODD COATS PHOTOGRAPHER: BOB BRIDGES ILLUSTRATOR: TODD COATS DESIGN FIRM: GLAXO CORPORATE CREATIVE SERVICES CLIENT: GLAXO HEALTH PROMOTIONS COUNTRY: USA ■8 THIS POSTER TO PROMOTE A

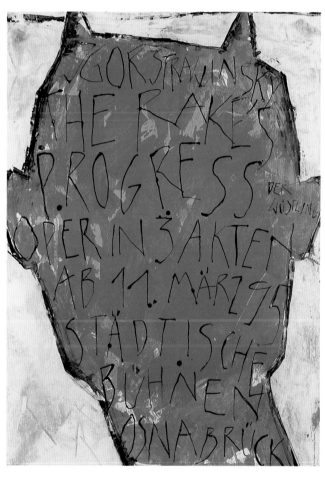

HOLIDAY CONCERT EMPHASIZES HOLIDAY SINGING WITHOUT BEING RELIGIOUS IN NATURE. ●8 ANKÜNDIGUNG EINES FESTTAGSKONZERTES. DIE BOTSCHAFT: UM AN FESTTAGEN ZU SINGEN, MUSS MAN NICHT UNBEDINGT RELIGIÖS SEIN. ▲8 AFFICHE D'UN CONCERT DONNÉ À L'OCCASION D'UNE FÊTE RELIGIEUSE, INDIQUANT QU'IL N'EST PAS NÉCESSAIRE D'ÊTRE PRATIQUANT POUR CHANTER. □9 ART DIRECTOR/ DESIGNER: JEAN-BENOÎT LÉVY PHOTOGRAPHER: JEAN-PASCAL IMSAND DESIGN FIRM: AND (TRAFIC GRAFIC) CLIENT: LES VENDREDIS DE LA CATHÉDRALE/MARIE-CATHERINE BLATTER, JEAN-CHRISTOPHE GEISER COUNTRY: SWITZERLAND ■9 A PHOTOMONTAGE OF LAKE GENEVA SUGGESTS A VISIT TO THE ORGAN CONCERTS AT A CATHEDRAL IN LAUSANNE. THE VARIOUS DATES ARE PRINTED SEPARATELY. ●9 EINE PHOTOMONTAGE MIT DEM GENFER SEE LÄDT ZU EINEM BESUCH DER ORGELKONZERTE IN EINER KATHEDRALE IN LAUSANNE EIN. DIE VERSCHIEDENEN VERANSTALTUNGSDATEN WERDEN JEWEILS SEPARAT EINGEDRUCKT. ▲9 AFFICHE RÉALISÉE POUR UN CONCERT D'ORGUE DANS LA CATHÉDRALE DE LAUSANNE (PHOTOMONTAGE). ON RECONNAÎT LES RIVES DU LAC LÉMAN ET LA CATHÉDRALE. □10 DESIGNER: JÜRGEN HAUFE CLIENT: JAZZCLUB TONNE E.V. COUNTRY: GERMANY ■10 A POSTER PROMOTING A CALVIN RUSSELL ROCK CONCERT. ●10 EIN KONZERT DES ROCKMUSIKERS CALVIN RUSSELL. ▲10 AFFICHE D'UN CONCERT ROCK. □11 ART DIRECTOR: BERND BEXTE DESIGNER/ILLUSTRATOR: NINA PAGALIES CLIENT: STÄDTISCHE BÜHNEN OSNABRÜCK COUNTRY: GERMANY ■11 A PERFORMANCE OF STRAVINSKY'S OPERA "THE RAKE'S PROGRESS" (1951) AFTER "THE LIFE OF THE RAKE" BY W. HOGARTH. ●11 EINE AUFFÜHRUNG VON STRAWINSKYS OPER «THE RAKE'S PROGRESS» (1951) NACH «DAS LEBEN DES WÜSTLINGS» VON W. HOGARTH. ▲11 AFFICHE «THE RAKE'S PROGRESS OU LE LIBERTIN», OPÉRA EN 3 ACTES DE STRAVINSKY (1951) DONNÉ AUX STÄDTISCHE BÜHNEN D'OSNABRÜCK.

1 ART DIRECTOR/DESIGNER/ILLUSTRATOR: PETER HORLACHER CLIENT: WÜRTEMBERGISCHE LANDESBÜHNE ESSLINGEN COUNTRY: GERMANY ■ 1 A THEATER'S PROGRAM FOR THE 1994/95 SEASON. ● 1 DAS PROGRAMM DER WÜRTEMBERGISCHEN LANDESBÜHNE ESSLINGEN FÜR DIE SPIELZEIT 1994/95. ▲ 1 AFFICHE DE THÉÂTRE ANNONÇANT LE PROGRAMME DE LA SAISON 1994-95. □ 2 ART DIRECTOR/DESIGNER: RAFAEL WEIL PHOTOGRAPHER: JEREMY SHATAN PROPS STYLISTS: BRIAN STANLAKE, LISA FAEY CLIENT: YALE REPERTORY THEATRE COUNTRY: USA ■ 2 TO PROMOTE "LE BOURGEOIS AVANT-GARDE," THIS POSTER MOCKED SOME OF THE INTELLECTUAL CONCEPTS AT THE PLAY'S CORE. ● 2 ANKÜNDIGUNG EINER AUFFÜHRUNG DES STÜCKES «LE BOURGEOIS AVANT-GARDE» MIT IRONISCHER ANSPIELUNG AUF EINIGE INTELLEKTUELLE KONZEPTE, UM DIE ES IN DEM STÜCK GEHT. ▲ 2 AFFICHE D'UNE PIÈCE DE THÉÂTRE INTITULÉE «LE BOURGEOIS AVANT-GARDE» FAISANT UNE ALLUSION IRONIQUE À CERTAINS CONCEPTS INTELLECTUELS, OBJETS DE LA PIÈCE. □ 3, 4 ART DIRECTOR/DESIGNER: HOLGER MATTHIES ILLUSTRATOR: HOLGER MATTHIES CLIENT: BAYERISCHES STAATSSCHAUSPIEL COUNTRY: GERMANY ■ 3, 4 PERFORMANCES OF DIFFERENT MUNICH THEATERS. THE SQUARE AND THE LOGO, USED IN EACH POSTER, MAKES FOR A UNIFIED GRAPHIC IDENTITY. ● 3, 4 AUFFÜHRUNGEN VERSCHIEDENER MÜNCHENER THEATER. DAS QUADRAT UND DAS LOGO SORGEN FÜR EINEN HOMOGENEN AUFTRITT. FÜR DAS ZAZOU PLAKAT WURDEN SCHAUSPIELERPHOTOS VERWENDET. ▲ 3, 4

AFFICHES DU BAYERISCHES STAATSSCHAUSPIEL DE MUNICH. LE CARRÉ ET LE LOGO, RÉCURRENTS DANS TOUTE LA SÉRIE, ASSURENT LA COHÉRENCE GRAPHIQUE DES AFFICHES. □ 5, 6 ART DIRECTOR/DESIGNER/ILLUSTRATOR/DESIGN FIRM: K. DOMENIC GEISSBÜHLER CLIENT: OPERNHAUS ZÜRICH COUNTRY: SWITZERLAND ■ 5, 6 FOR THE ANNOUNCEMENT OF "NORMA" (BELLINI), THE DESIGNER EMPLOYED ELEMENTS FROM THE STAGE SET. THE BALLET POSTER REFERS TO VARIOUS PERFORMANCES. ● 5, 6 FÜR DIE ANKÜNDIGUNG DES SINGSPIELS NORMA (BELLINI) ARBEITETE DER GESTALTER MIT ELEMENTEN DES BÜHNENBILDES. DAS BALLETT-PLAKAT DIENTE DER ANKÜNDIGUNG MEHRERER AUFFÜHRUNGEN. ▲ 5, 6 AFFICHES DE L'OPÉRA DE ZURICH. L'AFFICHE DE NORMA REPRÉSENTE DES ÉLÉMENTS DE LA SCÈNE. LA SECONDE AFFICHE PRÉSENTE DIVERS BALLETS. □ (FOLLOWING SPREAD LEFT) 1 ART DIRECTOR/DESIGNER/ILLUSTRATOR: HANS HEINRICH SURES COUNTRY: GERMANY ■ 1 A STUDENT PROJECT RELATING TO A MODERN PLAY. ● 1 EIN STUDENTENPROJEKT, BEI DEM ES UM EIN MODERNES THEATERSTÜCK GEHT. ▲ 1 PROJET D'UN ÉTUDIANT CONSACRÉ À UNE PIÈCE DE THÉÂTRE MODERNE. □ (FOLLOWING SPREAD RIGHT) 2 ART DIRECTOR/DESIGNER: TOYOTSUGU ITOH ILLUSTRATOR: TOYOTSUGU ITOH PHOTOGRAPHER: ISAO TAKAHASHI CLIENT: EXECUTIVE COMMITTEE FOR THE 9TH NATIONAL CULTURE FESTIVAL COUNTRY: JAPAN ■ 2 A CULTURAL FESTIVAL OF THE MIE PREFECTURE IN JAPAN. ● 2 EIN KULTUR-FESTIVAL DER MIE-PRÄFEKTUR IN JAPAN. ▲ 2 AFFICHE D'UN FESTIVAL DE LA CULTURE AU JAPON.

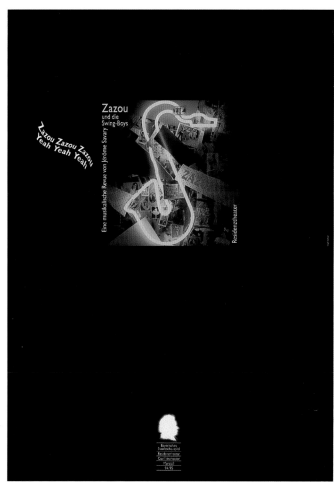

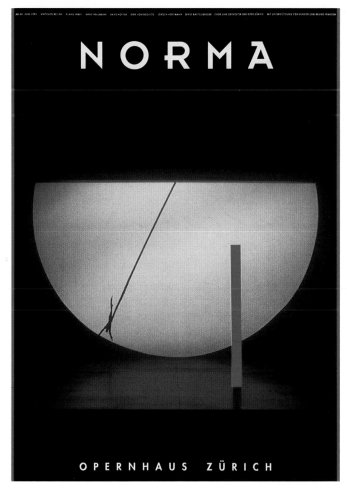

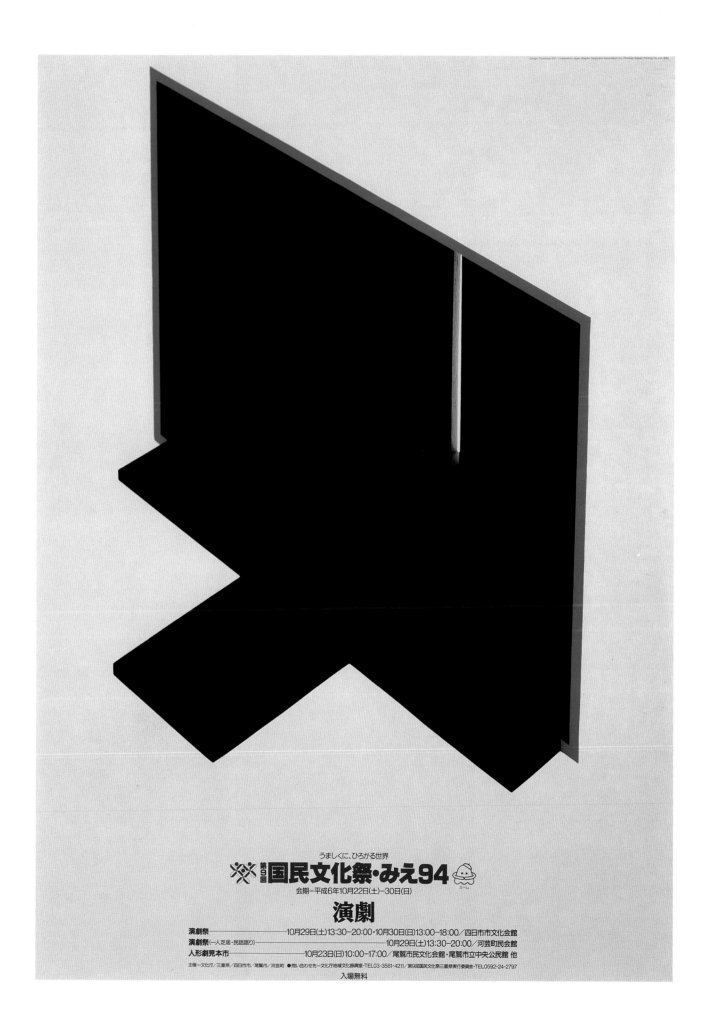

うましくに、ひろがる世界
第9回 国民文化祭・みえ94
会期=平成6年10月22日(土)-30日(日)

演劇

演劇祭━━━━━━━━━━━━10月29日(土)13:30-20:00・10月30日(日)13:00-18:00／四日市市文化会館
演劇祭(一人芝居・民話語り)━━━━━━━━━━━━10月29日(土)13:30-20:00／河芸町民会館
人形劇見本市━━━━━━━━━━━━10月23日(日)10:00-17:00／尾鷲市民文化会館・尾鷲市立中央公民館 他

主催=文化庁／三重県／四日市市／尾鷲市／河芸町　●問い合わせ先=文化庁地域文化振興室・TEL03-3581-4211／第9回国民文化祭三重県実行委員会・TEL0592-24-2797

入場無料

1–3 ART DIRECTOR: HELMUT ROTTKE DESIGNER: NICOLE ELSENBACH PHOTOGRAPHERS: KLAUS LEFEBVRE (1, 3), GUDRUN BUBLITZ (2) COPYWRITER: W. REINHOLD DESIGN FIRM: ROTTKE WERBUNG CLIENT: SCHAUSPIEL ESSEN COUNTRY: GERMANY ■ 1–3 THE PROGRAM FOR THE NEW SEASON AT A THEATER IN ESSEN. THE HEADLINES ARE MEANT TO PORTRAY THE THEATER AS A PLACE WHERE PEOPLE CAN FIND ANSWERS TO EVERYDAY PROBLEMS. ● 1–3 DAS PROGRAMM FÜR DIE NEUE SAISON AM SCHAUSPIEL ESSEN. DIE HEADLINES SOLLEN INTERESSE WECKEN UND DEM PUBLIKUM SAGEN, DASS ES AM THEATER UM SEINE EIGENEN PROBLEME GEHT. ▲ 1–3 AFFICHES DU THÉÂTRE D'ESSEN (ALLEMAGNE), ANNONÇANT LE PROGRAMME DE LA NOUVELLE SAISON. LE TEXTE DES HEADLINES FAIT ALLUSION À DES PROBLÈMES DE LA VIE QUOTIDIENNE, DANS LESQUELS CHACUN PEUT SE RECONNAÎTRE. □ 4 DESIGNER: WIESLAW ROSOCHA COUNTRY: POLAND ■ 4 POSTER ANNOUNCING THE PLAY *SIX CHARACTERS IN SEARCH OF AN AUTHOR.* ● 4 ANKÜNDIGUNG DES THEATERSTÜCKES *SECHS PERSONEN SUCHEN EINEN AUTOR.* ▲ 4 AFFICHE POUR LA PIÈCE DE THÉÂTRE *SIX PERSONNES À LA RECHERCHE D'UN AUTEUR.* □ 5 ART

DIRECTOR/DESIGNER: LEO RAYMUNDO DESIGN FIRM: NBBJ GRAPHIC DESIGN CLIENT: EMPTY SPACE THEATRE COUNTRY: USA ■ 5 A POSTER TO PROMOTE A ONE-WOMAN PLAY. SET IN THE AMERICAN WILD WEST, IT DOCUMENTS AN ENGLISH WOMAN'S STRUGGLE AGAINST DAUNTING PHYSICAL AND SOCIAL HARDSHIPS. ● 5 ANKÜNDIGUNG EINES THEATERSTÜCKS FÜR EINE DARSTELLERIN. ES SPIELT IM WILDEN WESTEN AMERIKAS UND DOKUMENTIERT DEN KAMPF EINER AUS ENGLAND STAM- MENDEN FRAU GEGEN DIE HARTE KÖRPERLICHE ARBEIT UND DIE SCHWEREN SOZIALEN BEDINGUNGEN. ▲ 5 AFFICHE D'UN ONE-WOMAN-SHOW AMÉRICAIN SUR L'HISTOIRE D'UNE PIONNIÈRE ANGLAISE CONFRONTÉE À L'UNIVERS IMPITOYABLE DU FAR WEST. □ 6 ART DIRECTOR/DESIGNER: KARI PIIPPO DESIGN FIRM: KARI PIIPPO OY CLIENT: MIKKELIN TEATTERI COUNTRY: FINLAND ■ 6 "SÄRKELÄ HIMSELF," A COMEDY, REVEALS THE SIMPLICITY OF HUMAN NATURE. ● 6 «SÄRKELÄ SELBST», EINE WITZIGE KOMÖDIE, DIE AUFZEIGT, WIE SIMPEL DIE MENSCHLICHE NATUR IST. ▲ 6 «SÄRKELÄ EN PERSONNE». COMÉDIE GRINÇANTE SUR LA NATURE HUMAINE. □ 7, 8 ART DIRECTOR/DESIGNER: BÜLENT ERKMEN PHOTOGRAPHER: TÜLIN ALTILAR CLIENT:

katkılarıyl.
Nişantaşı
Kız Lisesi
Tiyatro
Salonu'nda
Maçka
Caddesi 8
230 16 18

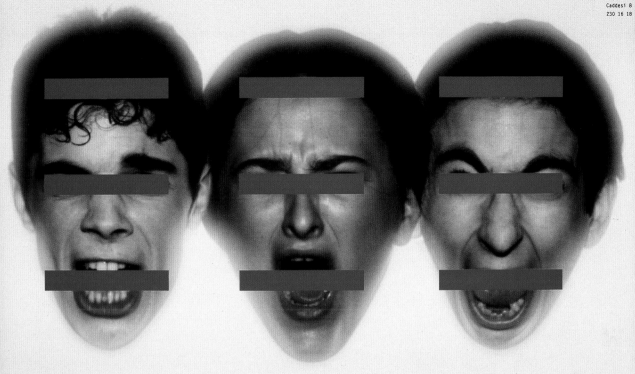

tiyatro²

yazan FRANCA RAME/DARIO FO çeviren FÜSUN DEMİREL yöneten CEYSU KOÇAK yapımcı NEDİM SABAN

CADILAR ZAMANI (DENİZ TÜRKALİ)

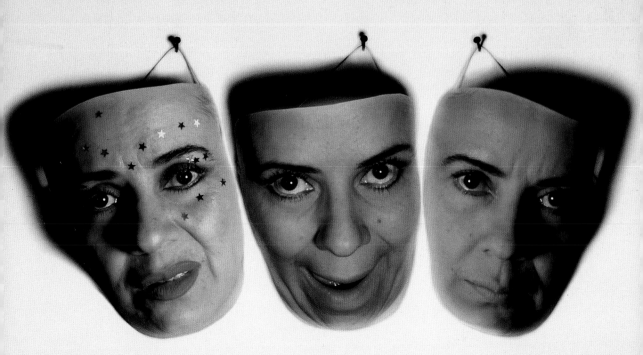

tiyatro²

Nişantaşı
Kız Lisesi
Tiyatro
Salonu
Maçka
Caddesi 8
230 16 18

THEATRE SQUARE Country: TURKEY ■ 7, 8 PERFORMANCES OF PLAYS BY FRANK WEDEKIND AND BY DARIO FO. "SPRING AWAKENING" TRACES THREE YOUNG PROTAGONISTS' REVOLT AGAINST SOCIETY'S RESTRICTIONS. "TIME OF THE WITCHES" BY DARIO FO CONSISTS OF THREE ONE-WOMAN PLAYS PERFORMED BY ONE ACTRESS. ● 7, 8 AUFFÜHRUNGEN VON ZWEI THEATERSTÜCKEN. DAS PLAKAT FÜR FRANK WEDEKINDS «FRÜHLINGS ERWACHEN» BEZIEHT SICH AUF DIE REVOLTE DER DREI JUNGEN PROTAGONISTEN GEGEN DIE BÜRGERLICHE MORAL. «ZEIT DER HEXEN» VON DARIO FO BESTEHT AUS DREI STÜCKEN FÜR EINE SCHAUSPIELERIN. ▲ 7, 8 LA PREMIÈRE AFFICHE PRÉSENTE «L'EVEIL DU PRINTEMPS», UNE PIÈCE DE FRANK WEDEKIND DANS LAQUELLE TROIS JEUNES GENS SE RÉVOLTENT CONTRE LA MORALE BOURGEOISE. «LE TEMPS DES SORCIÈRES» DE DARIO FO SE COMPOSE DE TROIS ONE-WOMAN-SHOWS INTERPRÉTÉS PAR LA MÊME COMÉDIENNE. (THIS SPREAD) 1 ART DIRECTOR: MICHAEL CRONAN DESIGNER: MICHAEL CRONAN ILLUSTRATOR: MICHAEL CRONAN DESIGN FIRM:

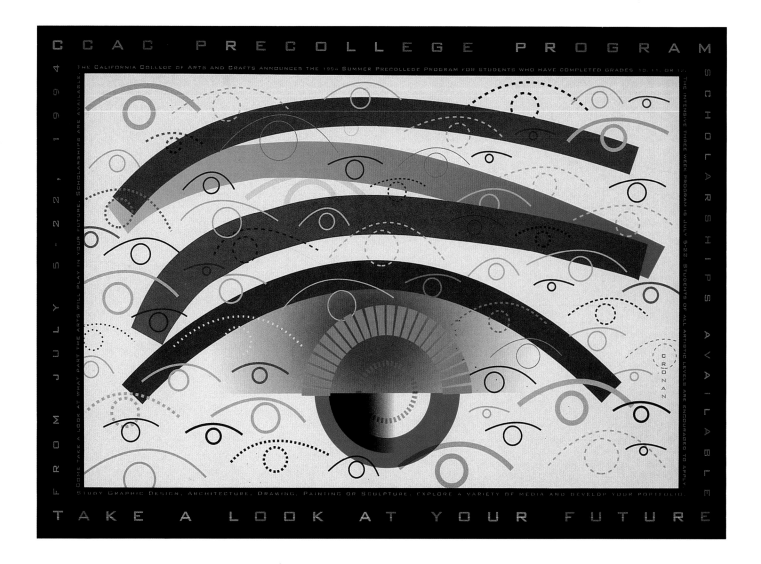

CRONAN DESIGN, INC. CLIENT: CALIFORNIA COLLEGE OF ARTS COUNTRY: USA ■ 1 POSTER ANNOUNCING THE 1994 PRE-COLLEGE PROGRAM AT THE CALIFORNIA COLLEGE OF ARTS AND CRAFTS. ● 1 ANKÜNDIGUNG DER VORKURSE DES CALIFORNIA COLLEGE OF ARTS AND CRAFTS. ▲ 1 AFFICHE PRÉSENTANT LE PROGRAMME DE L'ANNÉE PRÉPARATOIRE AU CONSERVATOIRE DES ARTS ET MÉTIERS DE CALIFORNIE. □ 2 ART DIRECTOR: J. CHARLES WALKER, JOHN B. BUCHANAN DESIGNER: JASON EPLAWY PHOTOGRAPHER: JASON EPLAWY, TOM ROSSINO ILLUSTRATOR: JASON EPLAWY DESIGN FIRM: GLYPHIX CLIENT: KSUCDA/KENT BLOSSOM COUNTRY: USA ■ 2 AN ANNOUNCEMENT FOR A SERIES OF SUMMER WORKSHOPS IN ILLUSTRATION, LETTERPRESS/BOOK ARTS, AND GRAPHIC AND COMPUTER-GENERATED DESIGN FOR STUDENTS AND DESIGN PROFESSIONALS. ● 2 EINE REIHE VON SOMMERKURSEN FÜR ILLUSTRATION, DRUCK- UND BUCHKUNST SOWIE GRAPHIK UND COMPUTER-GRAPHIK FÜR STUDENTEN UND PRAKTIKER SIND GEGENSTAND DIESES PLAKATES. ▲ 2 AFFICHE PRÉSENTANT LE PROGRAMME D'ÉTÉ DE DIVERS COURS POUR ÉTUDIANTS ET DESIGNERS PROFESSIONNELS (ILLUSTRATION, TYPOGRAPHIE, RELIURE, ARTS GRAPHIQUES ET C.A.O.).

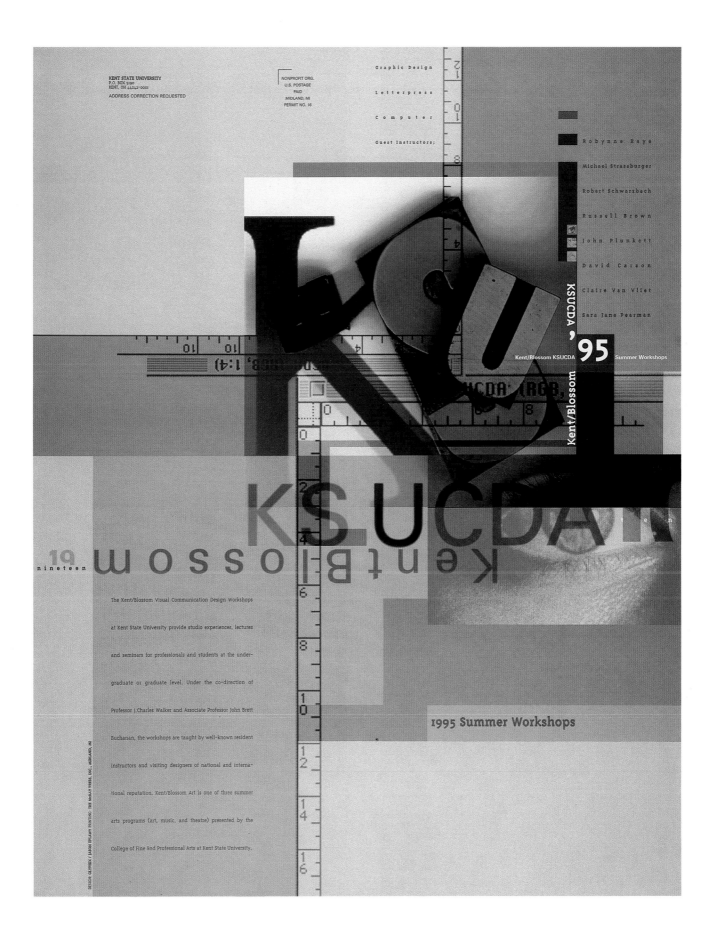

KENT STATE UNIVERSITY
P.O. BOX 5190
KENT, OH 44242-0001
ADDRESS CORRECTION REQUESTED

NONPROFIT ORG.
U.S. POSTAGE
PAID
MIDLAND, MI
PERMIT NO. 16

Graphic Design

Letterpress

Computer

Guest Instructors;

Robynne Raye

Michael Strassburger

Robert Schwarzbach

Russell Brown

John Plunkett

David Carson

Claire Van Vliet

Sara Jane Pearman

KSUCDA, '95

Kent/Blossom KSUCDA   Summer Workshops

Kent/Blossom

KSUCDA

KentBlossom

nineteen

The Kent/Blossom Visual Communication Design Workshops

at Kent State University provide studio experiences, lectures

and seminars for professionals and students at the under-

graduate or graduate level. Under the co-direction of

Professor J.Charles Walker and Associate Professor John Brett

Buchanan, the workshops are taught by well-known resident

instructors and visiting designers of national and interna-

tional reputation. Kent/Blossom Art is one of three summer

arts programs (art, music, and theatre) presented by the

College of Fine And Professional Arts at Kent State University.

1995 Summer Workshops

DESIGN: CLYBECK / JASON EPLAWY PRINTING: THE McKAY PRESS, INC., MIDLAND, MI

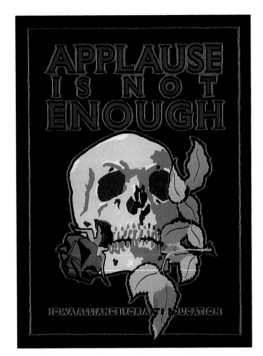

1 ART DIRECTOR/DESIGNER/ILLUSTRATOR: DAVID LANCE GOINES DESIGN FIRM: ST. HIERONYMUS PRESS CLIENT: IOWA ALLIANCE FOR ARTS EDUCATION COUNTRY: USA ■1 IN AN EFFORT TO EMPHASIZE THE IMPORTANCE OF FUNDING FOR ARTS EDUCATION, THIS POSTER ADDRESSES THE CRUCIAL NATURE OF ART ITSELF. ●1 THEMA DES PLAKATES IST DIE NOTWENDIGKEIT DER KUNSTFÖRDERUNG. ▲1 AFFICHE SOULIGNANT L'IMPORTANCE CRUCIALE DE L'ART ET LA NÉCESSITÉ D'ENCOURAGER LA CRÉATION ARTISTIQUE SOUS TOUTES SES FORMES. ☐2 ART DIRECTOR/DESIGNER: ARIEL PINTOS DESIGN FIRM/CLIENT: ASOCIACION PRO DISENO COUNTRY: VENEZUELA ■2 POSTER FOR A DESIGN SCHOOL WITH (MORE OR LESS SERIOUS) CITATIONS AND QUESTIONS ON THE SUBJECT OF DESIGN. ●2 PLAKAT FÜR EINE DESIGN-SCHULE MIT (MEHR ODER WENIGER ERNSTHAFTEN) ZITATEN UND FRAGEN ZUM THEMA DESIGN. ▲2 AFFICHE D'UNE ÉCOLE D'ARTS GRAPHIQUES AVEC DES CITATIONS ET DES QUESTIONS PLUS OU MOINS FARFELUES SUR LE THÈME DU DESIGN. ☐3 DESIGNER/PHOTOGRAPHER/DESIGN FIRM: FRANZ WERNER CLIENT: RHODE ISLAND SCHOOL OF DESIGN COUNTRY: USA ■3 THIS POSTER FOR THE RHODE ISLAND SCHOOL OF DESIGN PROMOTES THE SCHOOL'S SUMMER CLASSES IN GRAPHIC DESIGN. ●3 DIE SOMMER-GRAPHIKKURSE DER RHODE ISLAND SCHOOL OF DESIGN. ▲3 AFFICHE PRÉSENTANT LE PROGRAMME DES COURS D'ÉTÉ DE LA RHODE ISLAND SCHOOL OF DESIGN. ☐4 ART DIRECTOR/DESIGNER/

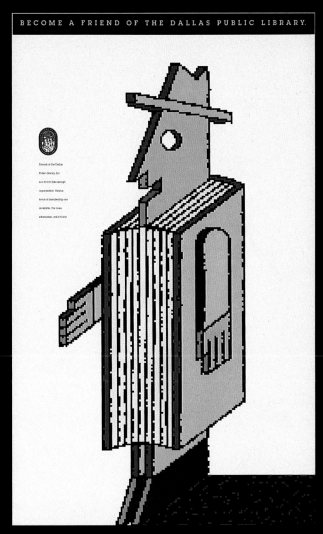

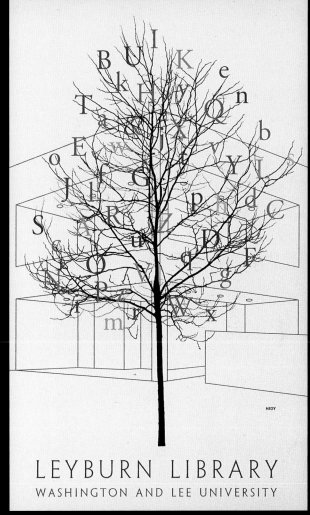

ILLUSTRATOR/DESIGN FIRM: OLE FLYV CHRISTENSEN CLIENT: AALBORG UNIVERSITET COUNTRY: DENMARK ■4 "THE AALBORG UNIVERSE"—RECRUITMENT POSTER FOR THE UNIVERSITY OF AALBORG, DENMARK. ●4 «DAS UNIVERSUM VON AALBORG...» DAS MOTIV DIESES PLAKATES FÜR DIE UNIVERSITÄT WURDE AUCH FÜR ANZEIGEN, POSTKARTEN UND T-SHIRTS VERWENDET. ▲4 «L'UNIVERSITÉ D'AALBORG...» (DANEMARK). LE MOTIF DE CETTE AFFICHE A ÉGALEMENT ÉTÉ REPRODUIT SUR DES ANNONCES, DES CARTES POSTALES ET DES T-SHIRTS. ☐5 ART DIRECTOR/DESIGNER: ART GARCIA DESIGN FIRM: SULLIVAN PERKINS CLIENT: FRIENDS OF THE DALLAS PUBLIC LIBRARY COUNTRY: USA ■5 IN A POSTER PROMOTING THE FRIENDS OF THE DALLAS PUBLIC LIBRARY, AN EXTENDED ARM BECOMES A METAPHOR FOR FRIENDSHIP. ●5 DER AUSGESTRECKTE ARM ALS SYMBOL DER FREUNDSCHAFT – EIN PLAKAT DER «FREUNDE DER ÖFFENTLICHEN BIBLIOTHEK VON DALLAS». ▲5 LA MAIN TENDUE, SYMBOLE DE L'AMITIÉ. AFFICHE DES «AMIS DE LA BIBLIOTHÈQUE MUNICIPALE DE DALLAS». ☐6 DESIGNER: LANCE HIDY CLIENT: LEYBURN LIBRARY, WASHINGTON & LEE UNIVERSITY COUNTRY: USA ■6 A POSTER COMMEMORATING THE NAMING OF LEYBURN LIBRARY AT WASHINGTON & LEE UNIVERSITY IN LEXINGTON, VIRGINIA. ●6 DIE NAMENSGEBUNG DER LEYBURN-BIBLIOTHEK AN DER WASHINGTON & LEE UNIVERSITY IST THEMA DIESES PLAKATES. ▲6 AFFICHE DÉDIÉE AU BAPTÉME DE LA BIBLIOTHÈQUE D'UNE UNIVERSITÉ.

1 ART DIRECTOR/DESIGNER/PHOTOGRAPHER/ILLUSTRATOR: MATUSCHKA DESIGN FIRM: MIRROR IMAGE CLIENT: GREENPEACE COUNTRY: USA ■1 CREATED TO BRING ATTENTION TO THE LINK BETWEEN THE ENVIRONMENT AND CANCER, "TIME FOR PREVENTION" IS CALLED A SELF PORTRAIT. ● 1 «ZEIT FÜR VORBEUGUNG» – DIESES PLAKAT MACHT AUF DIE VERBINDUNG VON KREBSERKRANKUNGEN UND UMWELTBELASTUNG AUFMERKSAM. ▲1 «LE TEMPS DE LA PRÉVENTION». AFFICHE GREENPEACE INSINUANT UNE CORRÉLATION ENTRE LES MALADIES CANCÉREUSES ET LA POLLUTION. □ 2 ART DIRECTOR/DESIGNER: YOSHIMARU TAKAHASHI DESIGN FIRM: KOUKOKUMARU INC. CLIENT: JAPAN GRAPHIC DESIGNERS ASSOCIATION (JAGDA) COUNTRY: JAPAN ■2 POSTER FROM THE ENVIRONMENTAL SERIES "I AM HERE," AN APPEAL TO PROTECT AND PRESERVE NATURE. HERE, THE ENDANGERED ELEPHANT. ● 2 BEISPIEL AUS DER «I AM HERE» PLAKATREIHE, IN DER ES UM DEN SCHUTZ DER NATUR UND ALLER LEBEWESEN GEHT, HIER UM DEN BEDROHTEN ELEFANTEN. ▲2 AFFICHE DE LA SÉRIE «I AM HERE», APPELANT À LA PROTECTION DE LA NATURE ET DES ESPÈCES MENACÉES, ICI LES ÉLÉPHANTS. □ 3 ART DIRECTOR/DESIGNER: DEBBIE KLONK DESIGN FIRM: CORN FED ADVERTISING CLIENT: EARTH GENERAL COUNTRY: USA ■3 EARTH GENERAL SELLS ONLY ENVIRONMENTALLY FRIENDLY AND HEALTHY PERSONAL CARE AND HOUSEHOLD ITEMS. THE IN-STORE POSTER WAS CREATED BY PRINTING A MESSAGE ON AN EARTH GENERAL CLOTH DIAPER. ● 3 EARTH GENERAL VERKAUFT NUR UMWELTFREUNDLICHE UND GESUNDE KÖRPERPFLEGE- UND HAUSHALTPRODUKTE. DAS LADENPLAKAT IST EINE BEDRUCKTE STOFFWINDEL DER FIRMA. ▲3 PUBLICITÉ IMPRIMÉE SUR UNE COUCHE-CULOTTE POUR DES PRODUITS DE SOINS ET D'ENTRETIEN ÉCOLOGIQUES. □ 4 ART DIRECTOR: JENNIFER MORLA DESIGNERS: JENNIFER MORLA, PETRA GEIGER PHOTOGRAPHERS: HOLLY STEWART AND

STOCK PHOTOGRAPHY ILLUSTRATOR: JENNIFER MORLA DESIGN FIRM: MORLA DESIGN CLIENT: THE PUSHPIN GROUP COUNTRY: USA ■4 THE COLLAGE OF BLACK-AND-WHITE PHOTOGRAPHS IN THE BACKGROUND OF THIS POSTER CELEBRATES THE DIVERSITY OF NATURAL ELEMENTS WHILE ALLUDING TO THEIR DISAPPEARANCE. THE BRIGHT COLORS, PATTERNS, AND ILLUSTRATIONS ON THE SURFACE INVITE THE VIEWER TO BECOME REACQUAINTED WITH THE EARTH AND PARTAKE IN ITS RICHNESS AND BEAUTY. ● 4 DIE COLLAGE AUS SCHWARZWEISSPHOTOGRAPHIEN IM HINTERGRUND DES PLAKATES BEZIEHT SICH AUF DIE VIELFALT DER NATUR UND DEREN BEDROHUNG. DIE LEUCHTENDEN FARBEN, MUSTER UND ILLUSTRATION IM VORDERGRUND FORDERN DEN BETRACHTER AUF, WIEDER EIN ENGERES VERHÄLTNIS ZUR NATUR ZU FINDEN UND AN IHREM REICHTUM UND IHRER SCHÖNHEIT TEILZUHABEN. ▲4 LE COLLAGE DE PHOTOS NOIR ET BLANC À L'ARRIÈRE-PLAN DE L'AFFICHE SYMBOLISE LA DIVERSITÉ DE LA NATURE ET L'ASPECT MENAÇANT DES ÉLÉMENTS NATURELS. AU PREMIER PLAN, LES COULEURS LUMINEUSES, LES MOTIFS ET LES ILLUSTRATIONS INVITENT L'OBSERVATEUR À SE RÉCONCILIER AVEC LA NATURE POUR APPRÉCIER SA RICHESSE ET SA BEAUTÉ. □ 5, 6 ART DIRECTOR: WADE KONLAKOWSKY COPYWRITER: KIRK GENTRY PHOTOGRAPHER: PETER SAMUELS, STEVE SHERMAN DESIGN FIRM: DGWB CLIENT: SURFERS ENVIRONMENTAL ALLIANCE COUNTRY: USA ■5, 6 POSTERS PLACED IN WEST COAST SURF SHOPS TO REMIND SURFERS OF THEIR NEED TO GET INVOLVED IN THE FIGHT AGAINST OCEAN POLLUTION. ● 5, 6 FÜR SURF-LÄDEN AN DER WESTKÜSTE BESTIMMTE PLAKATE, DIE SURFER AUFFORDERN, SICH IM KAMPF GEGEN DIE VERSCHMUTZUNG DER OZEANE ZU ENGAGIEREN. ▲5, 6 DESTINÉES AUX MAGASINS DE SURF DE LA CÔTE OUEST, CES AFFICHES INVITENT LES SURFERS À LUTTER ACTIVEMENT CONTRE LA POLLUTION DE L'OCÉAN.

1 Art Director: MICHAEL CRONAN Designer: MICHAEL CRONAN, LISA VAN ZANDT, MARGIE GOODMAN DRECHSEL Illustrator: MICHAEL CRONAN Design Firm: CRONAN DESIGN, INC. Client: NEWMEDIA MAGAZINE Country: USA ■ **1** MEANT TO CALL ATTENTION TO AN INTERNATIONAL MULTIMEDIA DESIGN COMPETITION, THIS POSTER STRESSES NOTIONS OF SPACE AND MOVEMENT INHERENT IN THE DISCIPLINE. ● **1** ALS EINLADUNG ZUR TEILNAHME AN EINEM INTERNATIONALEN MULTIMEDIA-DESIGN-WETTBE-WERB STELLT DIESES PLAKAT VORSTELLUNGEN VON RAUM UND BEWEGUNG IN DEN VORDERGRUND, DIE FÜR DIESEN BEREICH

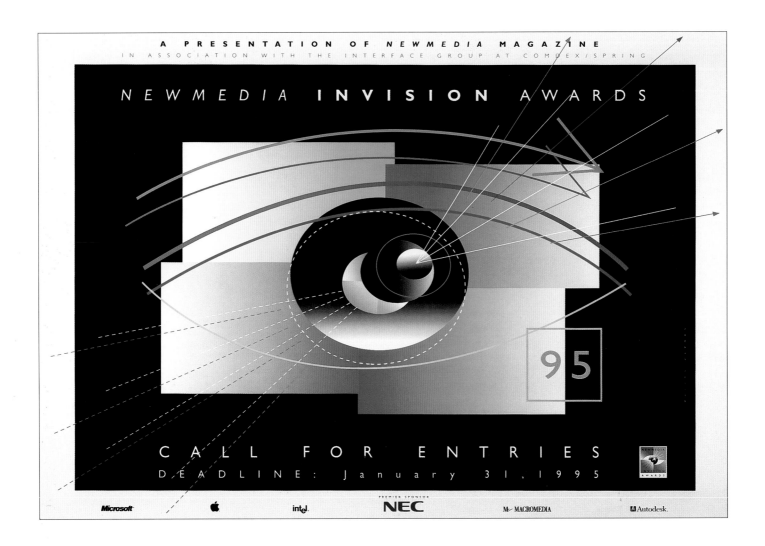

BEZEICHNEND SIND. ▲ **1** AFFICHE D'UN CONCOURS INTERNATIONAL DE DESIGN MULTIMÉDIA. LES REPRÉSENTATIONS DE L'ESPACE ET DU MOUVEMENT – SUJETS DE L'AFFICHE – SONT CARACTÉRISTIQUES DE CETTE DISCIPLINE. □ **2, 3** Art Director: SEIJU TODA Designers: SEIJU TODA, KOICHI KUNO Photographer: KAZUMI KURIGAMI Design Firm: TODA OFFICE Client: SEIO PRINTING Country: JAPAN ■ **2, 3** A PRINTING COMPANY CELEBRATES 40 YEARS OF EXISTENCE. ● **2, 3** EINE DRUCKEREI FEIERT IHR VIERZIGJÄHRIGES BESTEHEN. ▲ **2, 3** AFFICHES CÉLÉBRANT LE 40ᵉᵐᵉ ANNIVERSAIRE D'UNE IMPRIMERIE JAPONAISE.

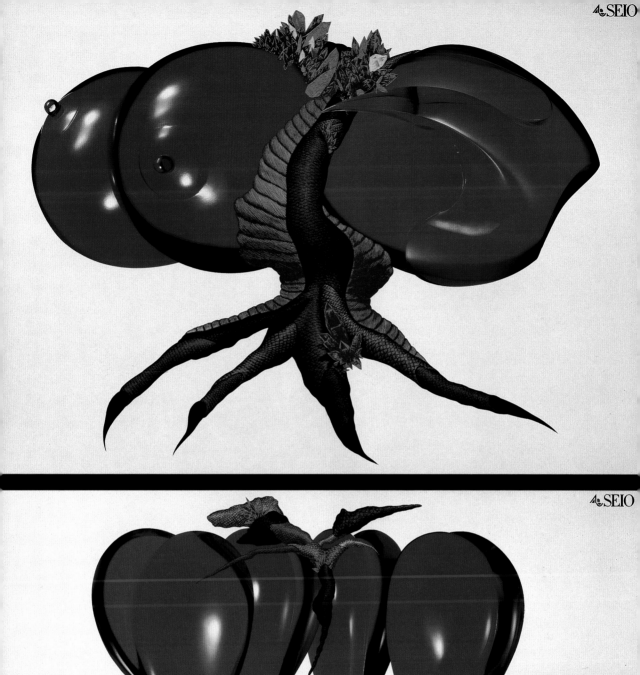

(PRECEDING SPREAD) **1** ART DIRECTORS/DESIGNERS/ILLUSTRATORS: JAMIE SHEEHAN, ART CHANTRY DESIGN FIRMS: ART CHANTRY DESIGN, SHEEHAN DESIGN CLIENT: SEATTLE PEACE HEATHENS COUNTRY: USA ■ **1** TO PROMOTE THE RE-LEGALIZATION OF HEMP IN THE UNITED STATES, THIS POSTER PUBLICIZES A RALLY WHICH EDUCATES THE PUBLIC AS TO THE USES OF THE PLANT. ● **1** ANKÜNDIGUNG EINER RALLY, BEI DER DIE ÖFFENTLICHKEIT ÜBER DIE HANFPLANZE INFORMIERT WIRD. ES GEHT DABEI UM DIE FRAGE DER LEGALISIERUNG VON HANF IN DEN USA. ▲ **1** ANNONCE D'UN RALLYE VISANT À INFORMER LA POPULATION SUR LES DIVERSES UTILISATIONS DU CHANVRE ET À EN PROMOUVOIR LA LÉGALISATION AUX ÉTATS-UNIS. □ (PRECEDING SPREAD) **2** ART DIRECTOR/DESIGNER: NEAL ASHBY ILLUSTRATOR: NEAL ASHBY DESIGN FIRM: RIAA CLIENT: AIGA (WASHINGTON) COUNTRY: USA ■ **2** DESIGNED AS AN INVITATION FOR THE AIGA WASHINGTON'S EVENT ON MULTIMEDIA, THIS POSTER USES ONLY TWO-COLOR PRINTING DUE TO THE BUDGET CONSTRAINTS. ● **2** EINLADUNG FÜR EINE VERANSTALTUNG DES AIGA IN WASHINGTON ZUM THEMA MULTIMEDIA. DER BESCHRÄNKTE ETAT ERLAUBTE NUR EINEN ZWEIFARBENDRUCK. ▲ **2** INVITATION À UNE MANIFESTA-TION DE L'AIGA À WASHINGTON CONSACRÉE AU MULTIMÉDIA. L'AFFICHE A ÉTÉ IMPRIMÉE EN DEUX COULEURS POUR DES RAISONS DE BUDGET. □ (THIS SPREAD) **1** ART DIRECTORS: JEFF JAHN, MARTIN WILLIAMS PHOTOGRAPHER: CHRIS SHEEHAN/PARALLEL PRODUCTIONS COUNTRY: USA ■ **1** CREATED FOR USE IN THE MINNEAPOLIS ADVERTISING FEDERATION AWARDS SHOW AS A "CALL FOR ENTRIES" POSTER. ● **1** WETTBEWERBSPLAKAT DER WERBEVEREINIGUNG VON MINNEAPOLIS. ▲ **1** AFFICHE D'UN CONCOURS ORGANISÉ PAR LA FÉDÉRATION DE LA PUBLICITÉ DE MINNEAPOLIS. □ (THIS SPREAD) **2** ART DIRECTOR/DESIGNER: STEPHEN DOYLE PHOTOGRAPHER: VICTOR SCHRAGER DESIGN FIRM: DRENTTEL DOYLE PARTNERS CLIENT: AIGA

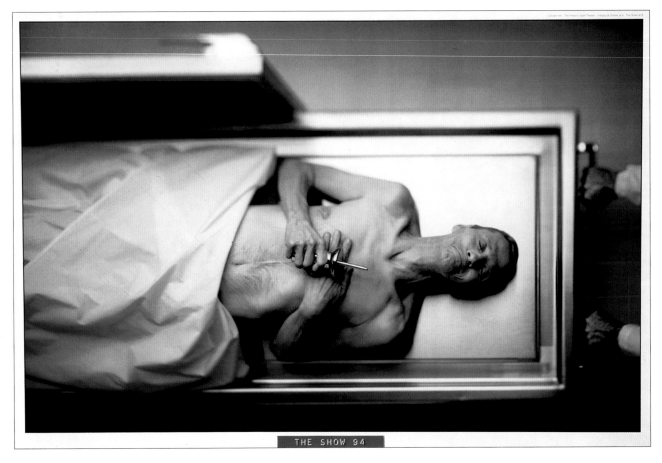

LOS ANGELES COUNTRY: USA ■ **2** A POSTER TO PROMOTE A LECTURE AT THE AMERICAN INSTITUTE OF GRAPHIC ARTS/LOS ANGELES. ● **2** ANKÜNDIGUNG EINES REFERATS AM AMERICAN INSTITUTE OF GRAPHIC ARTS IN LOS ANGELES. ▲ **2** AFFICHE ANNONÇANT UNE CONFÉRENCE À L'INSTITUT AMÉRICAIN DES ARTS GRAPHIQUES DE LOS ANGELES. □ (FOLLOWING SPREAD) **1** ART DIRECTOR/DESIGNER/PHOTOGRAPHER/ILLUSTRATOR: TODD HOUSER DESIGN FIRM: PINKHAUS DESIGN CLIENT: HOWARD SHUSTERMAN COUNTRY: USA ■ **1** A BAR MITZVAH INVITATION POSTER FOR JARED LOREN SHUSTERMAN. ● **1** EINLADUNG ZU EINEM JÜDISCHEN FEST. ▲ **1** INVITATION À UNE FÊTE JUIVE. □ (FOLLOWING SPREAD) **2** ART DIRECTOR/ DESIGNER: KIT HINRICHS PHOTOGRAPHER: BOB ESPARZA DESIGN FIRM: PENTAGRAM DESIGN CLIENT: PACIFIC DESIGN CENTER COUNTRY: USA ■ **2** AN EXHIBITION POSTER DESIGNED TO ANNOUNCE THE PERSONAL COLLECTION OF KIT HINRICHS. "STARS & STRIPES" CELEBRATES THE AMERICAN FLAG IN ITS MANY FORMS. ● **2** EINE AUSSTELLUNG ALLER MÖGLICHEN ERSCHEINUNGSFORMEN DER AMERIKANISCHEN FLAGGE, DIE PERSÖNLICHE SAMMLUNG DES DESIGNERS KIT HINRICHS. ▲ **2** «STARS & STRIPES», OU LE DRAPEAU AMÉRICAIN SOUS TOUTES SES FORMES. AFFICHE ANNONÇANT L'EXPOSITION DE LA COLLECTION PRIVÉE DU DESIGNER KIT HINRICHS. □ (FOLLOWING SPREAD) **3** ART DIRECTOR: KIT HINRICHS DESIGNER: LISA MILLER ILLUSTRATION: OLD ENGRAVING DESIGN FIRM: PENTAGRAM DESIGN CLIENT: SQUARE ONE RESTAURANT COUNTRY: USA ■ **3** THE "SQUARE ONE TENTH ANNIVERSARY" POSTER, DESIGNED BY PENTAGRAM DESIGN TO PLACEMAT DIMENSIONS, CELEBRATES TEN YEARS OF EXCELLENCE AT JOYCE GOLDSTEIN'S FAMOUS SAN FRANCISCO RESTAURANT. ● **3** EIN BERÜHMTES RESTAURANT IN SAN FRANCISCO FEIERT SEIN ZEHNJÄHRIGES BESTEHEN. DAS PLAKAT HAT DAS FORMAT VON TISCH-SETS. ▲ **3** PRÉSENTÉE SOUS FORME D'UN SET DE TABLE, CETTE AFFICHE CÉLÉBRE LE 10ᵉ ANNIVERSAIRE D'UN GRAND RESTAURANT DE SAN FRANCISCO.

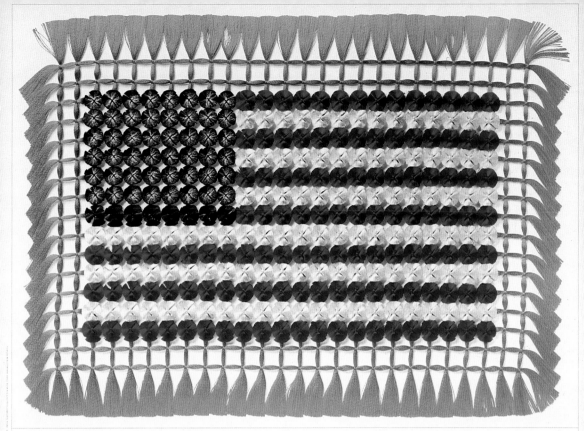

STARS & STRIPES: A Celebration of the American Flag in All Its Forms: Buttons, Ties, Fans, Spoons, Folk Art, Weavings, Postcards, Toys, Quilts, Jewelry, Tobacciana, Ribbons, Ice Cream Molds, Shoes, Political Memorabilia, Books, Pillows, Stamps and Posters. From the Collection of Kit Hinrichs. Sponsored by Pentagram Design. June 14 through July 30, 1994 Exhibition Hours: Tuesday through Saturday 12:00 p.m. to 6:00 p.m. Murray Feldman Gallery at **PACIFIC DESIGN CENTER**

SQUARE ONE

ANNIVERSARY

TENTH

EAGLETHON

HARLEY-DAVIDSON MOTOR COMPANY

SUNDAY, SEPT. 11 - 1994

11:00 A. M. - 5:00 P. M.

CAPITOL DRIVE ENGINE & TRANSMISSION PLANT

11700 WEST CAPITOL DRIVE

Activities include: entertainment, music, children's area, fashion show, plant tours, H-D memorabilia auction, new motorcycle displays, motorcycle raffle.

•

ADMISSION $5.00

Includes commemorative Eaglethon Pin and motorcycle raffle ticket

•

ALL PROCEEDS TO MDA

THIS POSTER WAS MADE POSSIBLE THROUGH THE GENEROUS DONATIONS FROM THE FOLLOWING HARLEY-DAVIDSON "SUPPLIER/PARTNERS"
DESIGN: VSA PARTNERS, INC.   PRINTING: HM GRAPHICS, INC.   PAPER: CHAMPION CARNIVAL® SMOOTH TEXT, SOFT WHITE/70LB.

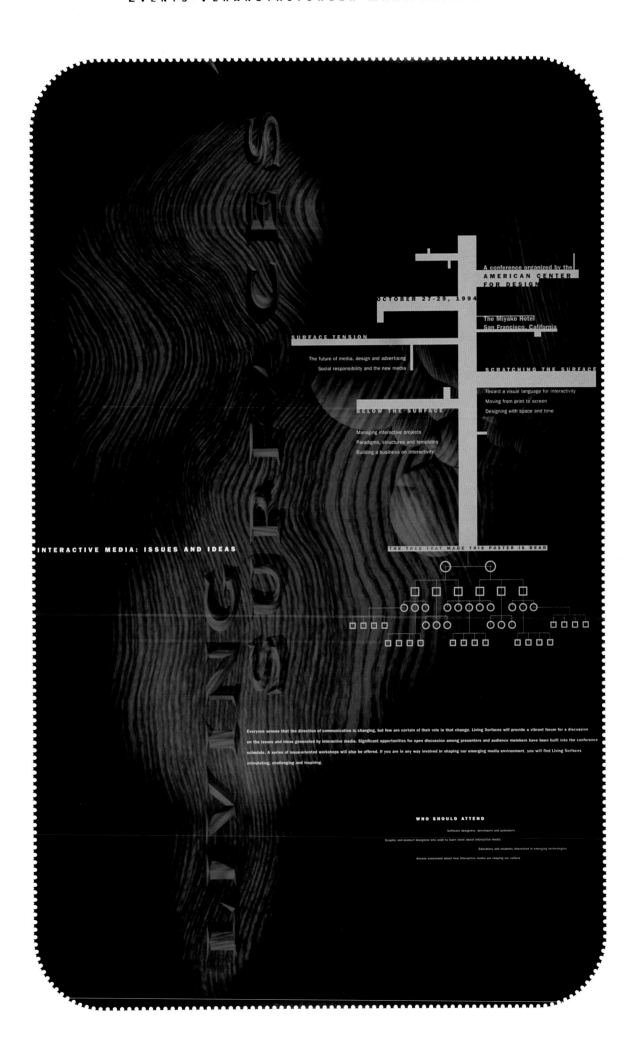

(PRECEDING SPREAD LEFT) 1 ART DIRECTOR: DANA ARNETT DESIGNER: CURT SCHREIBER PHOTOGRAPHER: ARCHIVE DESIGN FIRM: VSA PARTNERS, INC. CLIENT: HARLEY-DAVIDSON, INC. COUNTRY: USA ■ 1 THROUGH THE USE OF HAND-CUT WOODBLOCK TYPOGRAPHY AND FAMILIAR ARCHIVAL PHOTOGRAPHY, THE 1994 HARLEY-DAVIDSON EAGLETHON MDA EVENT POSTER CONVEYS A NOSTALGIC FEELING. ● 1 DANK DER HOLZSCHNITTBUCHSTABEN UND VERTRAUTER ARCHIVPHOTOS AUS ALTEN ZEITEN BEKOMMT DES PLAKAT FÜR EIN HARLEY-DAVIDSON-TREFFEN DEN GEWÜNSCHTEN NOSTALGISCHEN CHARAKTER. ▲ 1 AFFICHE «NOSTALGIQUE» DU GRAND RASSEMBLEMENT HARLEY-DAVIDSON 1994. LA TYPOGRAPHIE RÉALISÉE AU MOYEN DE CARACTÈRES D'IMPRIMERIE EN BOIS ET LES ANCIENNES PHOTOS D'ARCHIVES ONT PERMIS D'OBTENIR L'EFFET RECHERCHÉ. ☐ (PRECEDING SPREAD RIGHT) 2 DESIGNER: ANTHONY MA ILLUSTRATOR: GRANT DAVIS DESIGN FIRM: TANAGRAM CLIENT: AMERICAN CENTER FOR DESIGN COUNTRY: USA ■ 2 THIS POSTER SERVED AS AN INVITATION TO THE AMERICAN CENTER FOR DESIGN CONFERENCE ON INTERACTIVE MEDIA. ● 2 DIESES PLAKAT DIENTE ALS EINLADUNG ZU EINER TAGUNG DES AMERICAN CENTER FOR DESIGN ZUM THEMA INTERAKTIVE MEDIEN. ▲ 2 AFFICHE D'UN COLLOQUE ORGANISÉ PAR L'AMERICAN CENTER FOR DESIGN SUR LES MÉDIAS INTERACTIFS. ☐ (THIS SPREAD) 1 ART DIRECTOR/DESIGNER: SEYMOUR CHWAST ILLUSTRATOR: SEYMOUR CHWAST DESIGN FIRM: THE PUSHPIN GROUP CLIENT: MORAVSKA GALERIE COUNTRY: CZECH REPUBLIC ■ 1 A POSTER TO PROMOTE THE 16TH AIGA BIENNIAL IN BRNO, CZECH REPUBLIC, AND THE INTERNATIONAL

SYMPOSIUM ON GRAPHIC DESIGN. ● 1 ANKÜNDIGUNG DER 16. GRAPHIK-BIENNALE UND EINES INTERNATIONALEN DESIGN-SYMPOSIUMS IN BRNO, TSCHECHISCHE REPUBLIK. ▲ 1 AFFICHE DE LA 16E BIENNALE DE BRNO (RÉPUBLIQUE TCHÈQUE) ET D'UN SYMPOSIUM INTERNATIONAL SUR LE DESIGN. ☐ (THIS SPREAD) 2 ART DIRECTOR/DESIGNER/ILLUSTRATOR: TADANORI YOKOO CLIENT: ASSOCIATION OF ASIAN GAMES HIROSHIMA COUNTRY: JAPAN ■ 2 THE ART FESTIVAL IS ONE OF THE EVENTS SURROUNDING THE 12TH ASIAN GAMES IN HIROSHIMA. THE ILLUSTRATION IN THE CENTER IS A COLLAGE OF SEVERAL PAINTINGS. ● 2 DAS ART FESTIVAL IST EINER DER ANLÄSSE DER 12. ASIATISCHEN SPIELE IN HIROSHIMA. DIE ILLUSTRATION IM ZENTRUM IST EINE COLLAGE VERSCHIEDENER ALTER GEMÄLDE. ▲ 2 LE FESTIVAL D'ART, L'UNE DES MANIFESTATIONS ORGANISÉES DANS LE CADRE DES 12E JEUX ASIATIQUES À HIROSHIMA. L'ILLUSTRATION AU CENTRE DE L'AFFICHE EST UN COLLAGE RÉALISÉ À PARTIR DE PLUSIEURS REPRODUCTIONS DE TABLEAUX. ☐ (THIS SPREAD) 3 ART DIRECTOR: ANDREW HOYNE DESIGNER: ANDREW HOYNE PHOTOGRAPHER: ROB BLACKBURN COPYWRITER: KRISTINA GARLA DESIGN FIRM: ANDREW HOYNE DESIGN CLIENT: GREVILLE STREET BOOKSTORE COUNTRY: AUSTRALIA ■ 3 A VISUAL INTERPRETATION OF "THE BEE MEETING," A READING OF SYLVIA PLATH'S WORKS BY A GROUP OF YOUNG WOMEN. ● 3 EINE VISUELLE INTERPRETATION DER «BIENEN-VERSAMMLUNG», EINER LESUNG IN EINER BUCHHANDLUNG, VON EINER FRAUENGRUPPE ORGANISIERT. ▲ 3 INTERPRÉTATION VISUELLE DU «CONGRÈS DES ABEILLES», UNE RENCONTRE LITTÉRAIRE ORGANISÉ PAR UN GROUPE DE JEUNES FEMMES.

READINGS FROM SYLVIA PLATH'S ARIEL

6.30PM THURSDAY 27TH OCTOBER 1994
THE GREVILLE STREET BOOKSTORE
145 GREVILLE STREET, PRAHRAN

$2 entry. All proceeds will go to The Victorian Aids Council

Film courtesy of Witchtype. Paper courtesy of Spicers. Printing by Bambra Press.
Design and Art Direction by Andrew Hoyne Design. Photography by Rob Blackburn
A project by Kristina Garla

THE LEGENDS OF MOTORCYCLING

INTERNATIONAL CLASSIC AND ANTIQUE MOTORCYCLE SHOW AND PARTS EXCHANGE

THE 22ND ANNUAL DEL MAR CONCOURS D'ELEGANCE

PRESENTED BY THE SAN DIEGO ANTIQUE MOTORCYCLE CLUB

DEL MAR RACETRACK INFIELD AREA SEPTEMBER 26 1993 DEL MAR CALIFORNIA, USA

1 ART DIRECTOR/DESIGNER: JOHN BALL PHOTOGRAPHER: CHRIS WIMPEY DESIGN FIRM: MIRES DESIGN, INC. CLIENT: SAN DIEGO ANTIQUE MOTORCYCLE CLUB COUNTRY: USA ■ 1 PROMOTION OF AN ANTIQUE MOTORCYCLE EXHIBIT AND RACE. ● 1 ANKÜNDIGUNG EINER AUSSTELLUNG ALTER MOTORRÄDER UND EINES RENNENS. ▲ 1 AFFICHE D'UNE EXPOSITION DE MOTOS DE COLLECTION COURONNÉE PAR UNE COURSE. □ 2 ART DIRECTOR: JOHN DUDEK, COOMES DUDEK DESIGNER: JOHN DUDEK PHOTOGRAPHER: KATHLEEN MARTIN CLIENT: EISAMAN, JOHNS & LAWS COUNTRY: USA ■ 2 POSTER PRODUCED TO ANNOUNCE THE

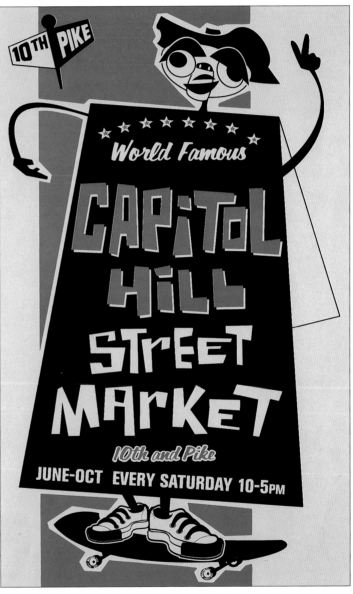

EIGHTH ANNUAL HALLOWEEN PARTY FOR THE EISAMAN, JOHNS & LAWS ADVERTISING AGENCY IN CHICAGO. ● 2 EINLADUNG ZUR HALLOWEEN-PARTY EINER WERBEAGENTUR. ▲ 2 INVITATION À UNE FÊTE ORGANISÉE PAR UNE AGENCE DE PUBLICITÉ À L'OCCASION D'HALLOWEEN □ 3 ART DIRECTOR/DESIGNER: GEORGE ESTRADA ILLUSTRATOR: GEORGE ESTRADA DESIGN FIRM: MODERN DOG CLIENT: CAPITOL HILL STREET MARKET COUNTRY: USA ■ 3 A POSTER TO ADVERTISE A COMMUNITY STREET MAR-KET. ● 3 ANKÜNDIGUNG EINES STRASSENMARKTES IN EINEM WOHNVIERTEL. ▲ 3 PUBLICITÉ POUR UN MARCHÉ DE QUARTIER.

SCHWAB

1 ART DIRECTOR: KEN SLAZYC DESIGNER/ILLUSTRATOR: MICHAEL SCHWAB DESIGN STUDIO: MICHAEL SCHWAB DESIGN CLIENT: ART DIRECTORS CLUB OF CINCINNATI COUNTRY: USA ■ **1** THIS SCREEN-PRINTED POSTER ANNOUNCED A SPEAKING ENGAGEMENT BY GRAPHIC DESIGNER MICHAEL SCHWAB. ● **1** SIEBDRUCKPLAKAT ALS ANKÜNDIGUNG EINES VORTRAGS DES GRAPHIK-DESIGNERS MICHAEL SCHWAB. ▲ **1** SÉRIGRAPHIE RÉALISÉE POUR UNE CONFÉRENCE DU GRAPHISTE MICHAEL SCHWAB. □ **2** ART DIRECTOR/DESIGNER: FOCUS 2 PHOTOGRAPHER: NEAL FARRIS COUNTRY: USA ■ **2** SERVING AS THE ANNOUNCEMENT FOR THE SPEAK-ING ENGAGEMENT OF P. SCOTT MAKELA AT THE DALLAS SOCIETY OF VISUAL COMMUNICATIONS, THIS POSTER ADDRESSES THE

WIDELY DIVERGENT OPINIONS IN THE DESIGN COMMUNITY CONCERNING MAKELA'S WORK. THE POSTER PLAYS ON THE CON-CEPT OF OPPOSITION BY BEING PERFORATED DOWN THE CENTER. ● **2** DAS PLAKAT FÜR EINEN VORTRAG VON P. SCOTT MAKELA BEI DER DALLAS SOCIETY OF VISUAL COMMUNICATIONS BEZIEHT SICH AUF DIE SEHR UNTERSCHIEDLICHE BEURTEILUNG SEIN-ER ARBEIT IN FACHKREISEN. DIE PERFORIERTE LINIE IN DER MITTE DIENT ALS AUSDRUCK VON WIDERSPRUCH. ▲ **2** AFFICHE ANNONÇANT UNE CONFÉRENCE DE P. SCOTT MAKELA À LA «DALLAS SOCIETY OF VISUAL COMMUNICATIONS». LA LIGNE MÉDI-ANE, PERFORÉE, SYMBOLISE LES CONTROVERSES SUSCITÉES PAR LE TRAVAIL DE L'ARTISTE DANS LES MILIEUX SPÉCIALISÉS.

1 ART DIRECTOR: DENNIS CLOUSE DESIGNERS: DENNIS CLOUSE, TRACI DABERKO, JEFF WELSH, CHARLYNE FABI, KAITLIN SNYDER ILLUSTRATORS: DENNIS CLOUSE, TRACI DABERKO DESIGN FIRM: THE LEONHARDT GROUP CLIENT: AIGA/THE PRICING GAME COUNTRY: USA ■1 DESIGNED FOR THE GRAPHIC ARTISTS GUILD/SEATTLE, THIS POSTER SERVED AS AN ANNOUNCEMENT FOR "THE PRICING GAME"—AN ANNUAL EVENT IN WHICH DESIGNERS AND ILLUSTRATORS ARE CHALLENGED ON THEIR PRICING SKILLS. ● 1 ANKÜNDIUNG DES «PRICING GAME» DER GRAPHIC ARTISTS GUILD VON SEATTLE. ES HANDELT SICH UM EINE ALLJÄHRLICHE VERANSTALTUNG, BEI DER ES UM DIE PREISPOLITIK VON DESIGNERN UND ILLUSTRATOREN GEHT. ▲ 1 AFFICHE D'UNE MANIFESTATION ANNUELLE ORGANISÉE PAR UNE ASSOCIATION AMÉRICAINE DE GRAPHISTES ET D'ILLUSTRA-TEURS. □ 2 ART DIRECTOR/DESIGNER: ANDREW HOYNE COPYWRITER: ANDREW HOYNE PHOTOGRAPHER: ROB BLACKBURN DESIGN FIRM: ANDREW HOYNE DESIGN CLIENT: AUSTRALIAN GRAPHIC DESIGN ASSOCIATION COUNTRY: AUSTRALIA ■2 ANNOUNCEMENT OF A LECTURE BY AUSTRALIAN GRAPHIC DESIGNER ANDREW HOYNE. ● 2 ANKÜNDIGUNG EINES VORTRAGS DES AUSTRALISCHEN GRAPHIK-DESIGNERS ANDREW HOYNE. ▲ 2 AFFICHE ANNONÇANT UNE CONFÉRENCE DU GRAPHISTE AUSTRALIEN ANDREW HOYNE. □ 3 ART DIRECTOR/DESIGNER: DAVID PLUNKERT ILLUSTRATOR: DAVID PLUNKERT DESIGN FIRM: SPUR CLIENT: AIGA BALTIMORE COUNTRY: USA ■ 3 THIS POSTER FOR AN AIGA LECTURE URGES THE INDIVIDUAL DESIGNER TO BE A VACUUM—AS OPPOSED TO LIVING IN ONE. ● 3 ANKÜNDIGUNG EINES VORTRAGS BEIM AMERICAN INSTITUTE OF GRAPHIC ARTS. DER

EINZELNE GRAPHIKER WIRD AUFGEFORDERT, EIN VAKUUM ZU SEIN, STATT IN EINEM VAKUUM ZU LEBEN. ▲ 3 AFFICHE ANNONÇANT UNE CONFÉRENCE À L'AIGA (INSTITUT AMÉRICAIN DES ARTS GRAPHIQUES). LE GRAPHISTE A POUR TÂCHE DE S'IDENTIFIER À UN VACUUM ET NON DE VIVRE DANS UN VACUUM. □ 4 ART DIRECTOR: SCOTT RAY DESIGNER: SCOTT RAY PHOTOGRAPHER: ERIC PEARLE ILLUSTRATOR: SCOTT RAY DESIGN FIRM: PETERSON & COMPANY CLIENT: INTERNATIONAL ASSOCIATION OF BUSINESS COMMUNICATORS COUNTRY: USA ■4 CREATED FOR THE ANNUAL SEMINAR OF THE INTERNATIONAL ASSOCIATION OF BUSINESS COMMUNICATORS, THIS POSTER'S THEME PROMOTED NEW PERSPECTIVES IN THE WORLD OF BUSINESS COMMUNICATIONS. ● 4 NEUE PERSPEKTIVEN IN DER WELT DER WIRTSCHAFTLICHEN KOMMUNIKATION SIND DAS THEMA DIESES PLAKATES FÜR EIN JÄHRLICH STATTFINDENDES SEMINAR DER INTERNATIONAL ASSOCIATION OF BUSINESS COMMUNICATORS. ▲ 4 AFFICHE D'UN SÉMINAIRE ANNUEL CONSACRÉ AUX NOUVELLES PERSPECTIVES OFFERTES PAR LA COM-MUNICATION DANS LE MONDE DES AFFAIRES. □ 5 ART DIRECTORS: IRIS UTIKAL, THEKLA HALBACH, THOMAS HAGENBUCHER, MICHAEL GAIS DESIGN FIRM: QWER CLIENT: BUND DEUTSCHER ARCHITEKTEN KREISGRUPPE DÜSSELDORF COUNTRY: GERMANY ■5 A PANEL DISCUSSION ON ARCHITECTURE. THE FOETUS SERVES AS A SYMBOL FOR HOUSING AND THE FEELING OF SECURITY. ● 5 EINE GESPRÄCHSREIHE ÜBER ARCHITEKTONISCHE THEMEN. DER FÖTUS DIENT ALS SYMBOL FÜR GEBORGENHEIT UND BEHAUSUNG. ▲ 5 AFFICHE PRÉSENTANT UNE SÉRIE DE DÉBATS SUR L'ARCHITECTURE. LE SYMBOLE DU FŒTUS: L'HABITAT DOIT ÊTRE AUSSI ACCUEILLANT ET SÉCURISANT QUE LE COCON DU VENTRE MATERNEL!

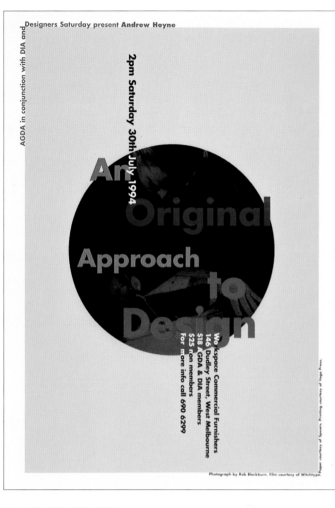

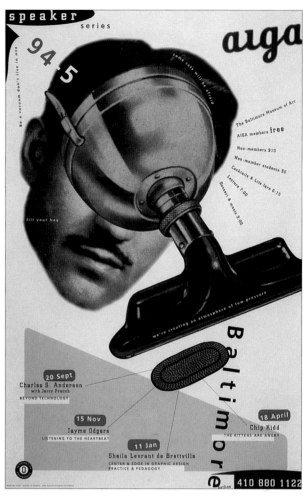

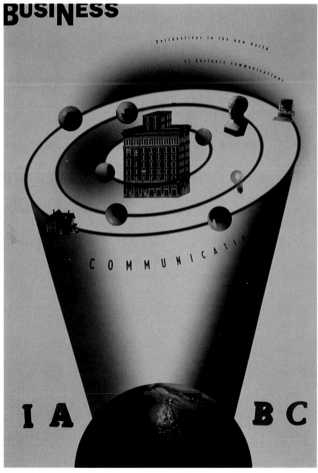

1 ART DIRECTOR/DESIGNER: SEYMOUR CHWAST ILLUSTRATOR: SEYMOUR CHWAST DESIGN FIRM: THE PUSHPIN GROUP CLIENT: MOHAWK PAPER MILLS, INC. COUNTRY: USA ■ 1 A POSTER CREATED TO ANNOUNCE A "DESIGN TALK" LECTURE SERIES AT NEW YORK'S COOPER UNION. ● 1 EINE VORTRAGSREIHE MIT DEM TITEL «DESIGN TALK» AN DER NEW YORKER KUNSTSCHULE COOPER UNION. ▲ 1 AFFICHE PRÉSENTANT UNE SÉRIE DE CONFÉRENCES SUR LE DESIGN DANS UNE ÉCOLE NEW-YORKAISE. □ 2 ART DIRECTION/DESIGN: AFTER HOURS CREATIVE ILLUSTRATOR: JACQUES BARBEY DESIGN FIRM: AFTER HOURS CREATIVE CLIENT: MARICOPA COMMUNITY COLLEGE DISTRICT COUNTRY: USA ■ 2 A POSTER TO PROMOTE A SERIES OF LECTURES FOR COLLEGE STUDENTS WHICH ADDRESSED THE CHANGING RELATIONSHIP BETWEEN SCIENCE, HUMANITY, AND TECHNOLOGY. ●

2 EINE FÜR STUDENTEN BESTIMMTE VORTRAGSREIHE ÜBER DIE SICH WANDELNDE BEZIEHUNG ZWISCHEN WISSENSCHAFT, TECHNOLOGIE UND MENSCHHEIT. ▲ 2 AFFICHE PRÉSENTANT DIVERSES CONFÉRENCES SUR LE THÈME DE L'ÉVOLUTION DES RELATIONS ENTRE LA SCIENCE, L'HUMANITÉ ET LA TECHNOLOGIE. □ 3 ART DIRECTOR: MILTON GLASER DESIGNER: MILTON GLASER ILLUSTRATOR: MILTON GLASER DESIGN FIRM: MILTON GLASER INC. CLIENT: THE COOPER UNION COUNTRY: USA ■ 3 ANNOUNCING THE "MOHAWK DESIGN TALK" LECTURE SERIES PRESENTED BY COOPER UNION, WHICH FEATURED PROMINENT GRAPHIC DESIGN PROFESSIONALS. ● 3 PROMINENTE GRAPHIK-DESIGNER WAREN DIE REFERENTEN DIESER VORTRAGSREIHE MIT DEM TITEL «MOHAWK DESIGN TALK» AN DER NEW YORKER KUNSTSCHULE COOPER UNION. ▲ 3 AFFICHE PRÉSENTANT UNE SÉRIE DE CONFÉRENCES SUR LE DESIGN DONNÉES PAR D'ÉMINENTS GRAPHISTES DANS UNE ÉCOLE NEW-YORKAISE.

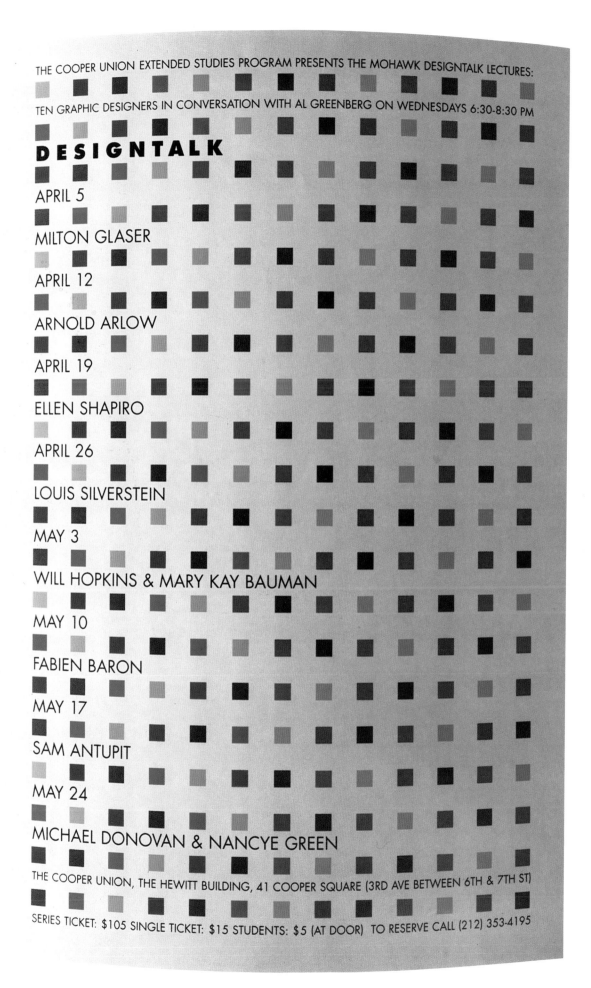

THE COOPER UNION EXTENDED STUDIES PROGRAM PRESENTS THE MOHAWK DESIGNTALK LECTURES:

TEN GRAPHIC DESIGNERS IN CONVERSATION WITH AL GREENBERG ON WEDNESDAYS 6:30-8:30 PM

DESIGNTALK

APRIL 5

MILTON GLASER

APRIL 12

ARNOLD ARLOW

APRIL 19

ELLEN SHAPIRO

APRIL 26

LOUIS SILVERSTEIN

MAY 3

WILL HOPKINS & MARY KAY BAUMAN

MAY 10

FABIEN BARON

MAY 17

SAM ANTUPIT

MAY 24

MICHAEL DONOVAN & NANCYE GREEN

THE COOPER UNION, THE HEWITT BUILDING, 41 COOPER SQUARE (3RD AVE BETWEEN 6TH & 7TH ST)

SERIES TICKET: $105 SINGLE TICKET: $15 STUDENTS: $5 (AT DOOR) TO RESERVE CALL (212) 353-4195

HIROSHIMA · NAGASAKI
NAGASAKI 50
NAGASAKI 50 HIROSHIMA
HIROSHIMA 50
50
HIROSHIMA · NAGASAKI 50
HIROSHIMA NAGASAKI 50

יום העצמאות תשנ"ד
Independence day 1994

Don't Let It
Weather Away

PEACE

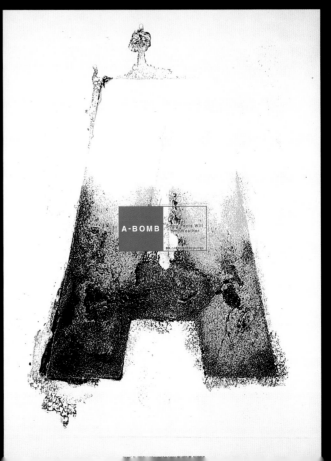

A-BOMB   Some Facts Will
Never Weather

1 ART DIRECTOR/DESIGNER/COPYWRITER: HIDEO YAMASHITA CLIENT: JAPAN GRAPHIC DESIGNERS ASSOCIATION (JAGDA) COUNTRY: JAPAN ■ 1 FIFTY YEARS AFTER THE BOMBING OF HIROSHIMA AND NAGASAKI: A COMMEMORATIVE POSTER FROM THE SERIES "I AM HERE." ● 1 FÜNFZIG JAHRE NACH DER BOMBARDIERUNG VON HIROSHIMA UND NAGASAKI. EIN PLAKAT AUS DER REIHE «I AM HERE». ▲ 1 HIROSHIMA ET NAGASAKI, 50 ANS APRÈS LE BOMBARDEMENT. AFFICHE DE LA SÉRIE «I AM HERE». □ 2 ART DIRECTOR/DESIGN FIRM: YOSSI LEMEL PHOTOGRAPHER: ISRAEL COHEN COUNTRY: ISRAEL ■ 2 THE PLASTIC HAMMER, ONE OF THE SYMBOLS OF ISRAELI INDEPENDENCE DAY, BEARS THE COLORS OF THE PALESTINIAN FLAG. ● 2 PLAKAT ZUM ISRAELISCHEN UNABHÄNGIGKEITSTAG. DER PLASTIKHAMMER, EINES DER SYMBOLE DIESES TAGES, HAT DIE FARBEN DER PALÄSTINENSER-FLAGGE. ▲ 2 AFFICHE CÉLÉBRANT LA JOURNÉE DE L'INDÉPENDANCE ISRAÉLIENNE. LE MARTEAU EN PLASTIQUE PORTE LES COULEURS DU DRAPEAU PALESTINIEN! □ 3, 4 ART DIRECTOR/DESIGNER: YOSHIMARU TAKAHASHI DESIGN FIRM: KOUKOKUMARU INC. CLIENT: JAPAN GRAPHIC DESIGNERS ASSOCIATION (JAGDA) COUNTRY: JAPAN ■ 3, 4 TWO EXAMPLES FROM THE PEACE AND ENVIRONMENT POSTER SERIES "I AM HERE," COMMEMORATING THE BOMBING OF HIROSHIMA AND NAGASAKI 50 YEARS AGO. ● 3, 4 ZWEI BEISPIELE DER FRIEDENS- UND UMWELTPLAKATREIHE «I AM HERE»: «FRIEDEN: LASST IHN NICHT VERWIT-TERN»; «DIE A-BOMBE: EINIGE TATSACHEN WERDEN NICHT VERWITTERN.» ▲ 3, 4 AFFICHES DE LA SÉRIE «I AM HERE», CON-

SACRÉE À LA PAIX ET À L'ENVIRONNEMENT. TOUTES DEUX COMMÉMORENT LE BOMBARDEMENT D'HIROSHIMA ET DE NAGASAKI IL Y A 50 ANS. □ 5, 6 DESIGNERS: KATHERINE MCKAY (5), MARK PURSEY (6) CLIENT: COMPASSION IN WORLD FARMING COUNTRY: GREAT BRITAIN ■ 5, 6 VEAL CALVES ARE KEPT IN THIS TYPE OF CRATE UP TO SIX MONTHS. THE POSTER IS AN APPEAL TO PARTICIPATE IN A DEMONSTRATION AGAINST THE TREATMENT OF THE CALVES. ● 5, 6 KÄLBER MÜSSEN BIS ZU SECHS MONATEN IN EINER BOX DER HIER ANGEGEBENEN GRÖSSE VERBRINGEN. DAS PLAKAT (ABB. 5) IST EINE AUFFORDERUNG ZUR TEILNAHME AN EINER DEMONSTRATION GEGEN DIESE ART VON TIERHALTUNG. DAS ETIKETT AUF DEM KALBSKOTELETT (ABB. 6) NENNT DEN PREIS, DEN MAN FÜR EIN SOLCHES KOTELETT ZAHLT: DAS KALB WIRD IN EINER BOX GEHALTEN, UNFÄHIG, SICH ZU BEWEGEN; VÖLLIG IM DUNKELN (UM WEISSES FLEISCH ZU ERHALTEN); ES KANN SICH NICHT HINSETZEN UND WIRD NUR MIT TROCKEN(HORMON)MILCH GEFÜTTERT. ▲ 5, 6 JUSQU'À L'ÂGE DE SIX MOIS, LES VEAUX SONT CONDAMNÉS À GRANDIR DANS UNE STALLE DE CETTE DIMENSION. L'AFFICHE N° 5 ANNONCE UNE MANIFESTATION CONTRE CE TYPE D'ÉLEVAGE. L'AFFICHE N°6 REPRÉSENTE L'ÉTIQUETTE D'UNE CÔTELETTE PRÉEMBALLÉE, SYMBOLE DU PRIX À PAYER POUR UNE TELLE CÔTELETTE: PRIVÉS DE TOUTE LIBERTÉ DE MOUVEMENT, LES VEAUX SONT MAINTENUS DANS L'OBSCURITÉ (AFIN D'OBTENIR UNE VIANDE BLANCHE) ET NOURRIS EXCLUSIVEMENT DE LAIT EN POUDRE (AUX HORMONES).

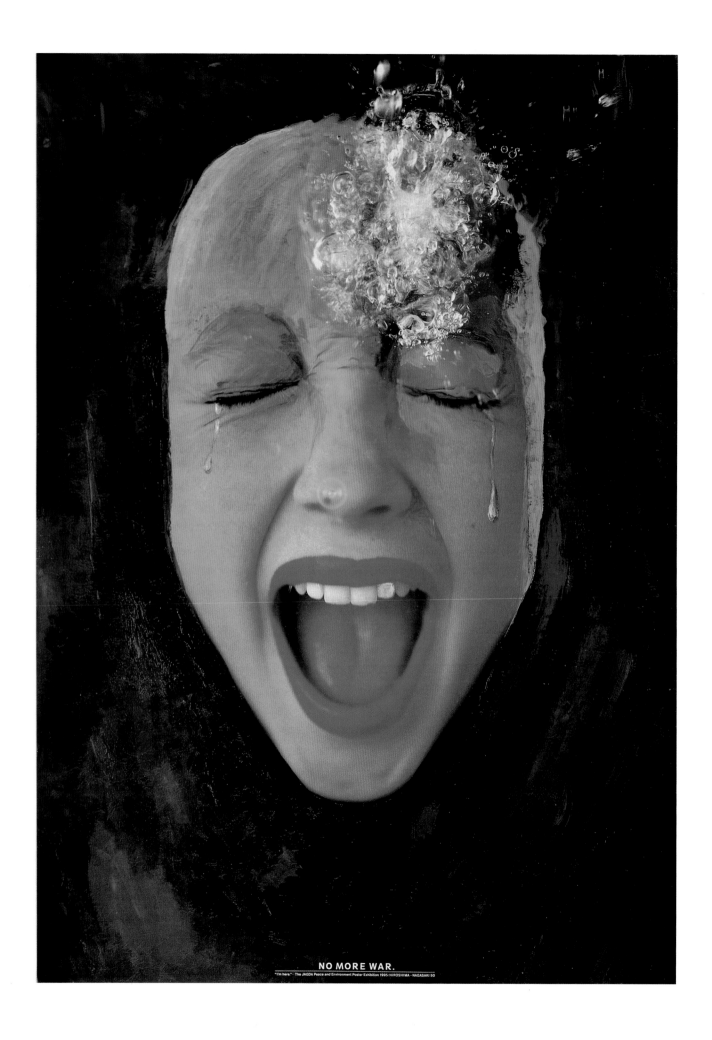

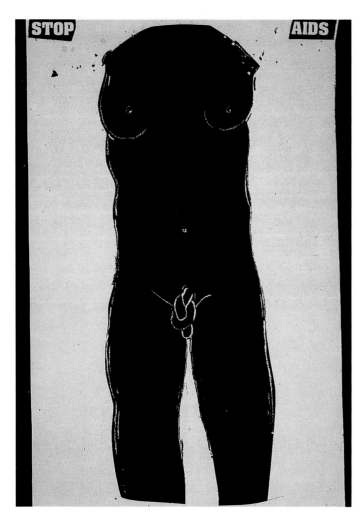

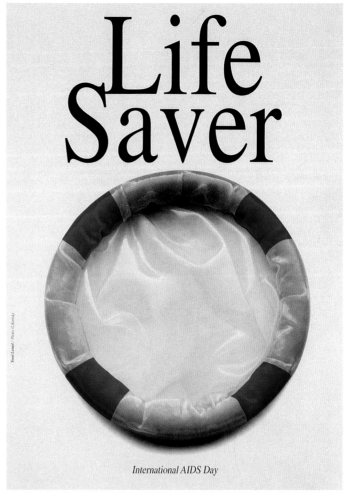

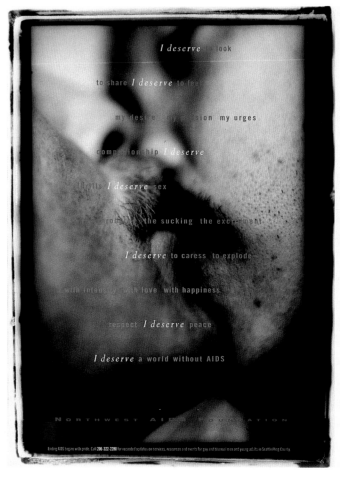

(PRECEDING SPREAD) 1 ART DIRECTOR: KENZO IZUTANI DESIGNERS: KENZO IZUTANI, AKI HIRAI PHOTOGRAPHER: YASUYUKI AMAZUTSUMI DESIGN FIRM: KENZO IZUTANI OFFICE CORPORATION CLIENT: JAPAN GRAPHIC DESIGNERS ASSOCIATION (JAGDA) COUNTRY: JAPAN ■ 1 POSTER FROM THE PEACE AND ENVIRONMENT POSTER EXHIBITION 1995 ENTITLED "I AM HERE" HIROSHIMA—NAGASAKI 50. ● 1 PLAKAT DER AUSSTELLUNG VON FRIEDENS- UND UMWELTPLAKATEN UNTER DEM TITEL «I AM HERE» IM JAHRE 1995: HIROSHIMA – NAGASAKI 50. ▲ 1 HIROSHIMA ET NAGASAKI, 50 ANS APRÈS LE BOMBARDEMENT. AFFICHE DE L'EXPOSITION 1995 «I AM HERE», SUR LE THÈME DE L'ENVIRONNEMENT ET DE LA PAIX DANS LE MONDE. □ (PRECEDING SPREAD) 2 ART DIRECTOR: VICTOR CORPUZ DESIGNER: VICTOR CORPUZ PHOTOGRAPHER: TRAVIS PRICE COUNTRY: USA ■ 2 THE PURPOSE OF THIS POSTER WAS TO INCREASE AWARENESS OF THE DANGERS OF OVERPOPULATION. ● 2 DIE GEFAHR DER ÜBERBEVÖLKERUNG DER ERDE IST THEMA DIESES PLAKATES. ▲ 2 AFFICHE ILLUSTRANT LE DANGER REPRÉSEN-TÉ PAR LA SURPOPULATION DE LA PLANÈTE. □ (THIS SPREAD) 1 ART DIRECTOR: LANNY SOMMESE DESIGNER: LANNY SOMMESE ILLUSTRATOR: LANNY SOMMESE DESIGN FIRM: SOMMESE DESIGN CLIENT: PENN STATE INSTITUTE FOR ARTS & HUMANISTIC STUDIES COUNTRY: USA ■ 1 WITH THE MESSAGE THAT ABSTENTION IS A SURE WAY TO STOP THE AIDS VIRUS, THIS POSTER WAS DESIGNED TO EMPLOY SHOCK VALUE TO REACH A PREDOMINANTLY COLLEGE-AGE AUDIENCE AT PENN STATE UNIVERSITY. ● 1 DIESES PLAKAT RICHTET SICH MIT DER BOTSCHAFT, DASS ENTHALTSAMKEIT DER SICHERSTE SCHUTZ VOR AIDS SEI, AN DIE STUDENTEN DER PENN STATE UNIVERSITY. ▲ 1 DESTINÉE AUX ÉTUDIANTS D'UNE UNIVERSITÉ AMÉRI-CAINE, L'AFFICHE PRÔNE L'ABSTINENCE COMME LA SEULE PROTECTION EFFICACE CONTRE LE SIDA. □ 2 ART

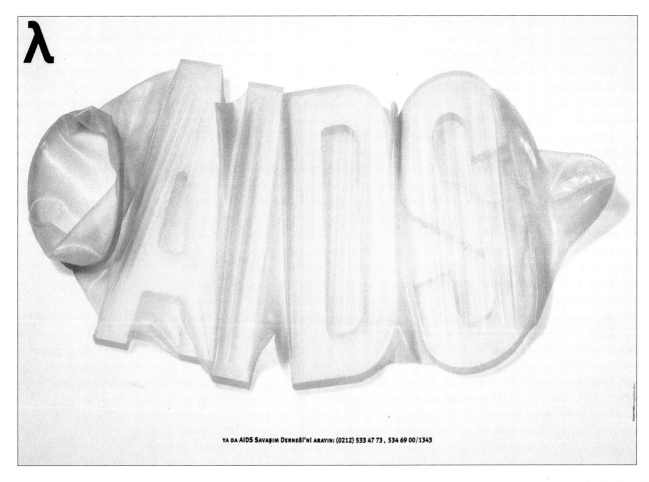

YA DA AIDS SAVAŞIM DERNEĞI'NI ARAYIN: (0212) 533 47 73 , 534 69 00/1343

DIRECTOR/DESIGN FIRM/CLIENT: YOSSI LEMEL PHOTOGRAPHER: GILAD KORISKY COUNTRY: ISRAEL ■ 2 AN AIDS CAMPAIGN IN ISRAEL. ● 2 AIDS-AUFKLÄRUNG IN ISRAEL. ▲ 2 AFFICHE D'UNE CAMPAGNE DE PRÉVENTION ISRAÉLIENNE CONTRE LE SIDA. □ 3 ART DIRECTOR: JEFF JAHN COPYWRITER: GREG BEAUPRE PHOTOGRAPHER: CURTIS JOHNSON/JIM ARNDT PHOTOGRAPHY DESIGN FIRM: MARTIN/WILLIAMS CLIENT: 1ST BANK/MINNESOTA HIGH SCHOOL LEAGUE COUNTRY: USA ■ 3 THE POSTER FOR THE "MINNESOTA AIDS PLEDGEWALK," WAS INTENDED TO CONVEY THE SIMPLICITY OF FIGHTING A DEADLY DISEASE—BY WALK-ING. ● 3 DAS PLAKAT FÜR DIESE AIDS-AUFKLÄRUNGSAKTION IN MINNESOTA FORDERT ZUM MITMACHEN BZW. ZUR TEILNAHME AM AIDS-MARSCH AUF. ▲ 3 AFFICHE D'UNE CAMPAGNE DE PRÉVENTION INVITANT À PARTICIPER À UNE MARCHE CONTRE LE SIDA. □ 4 ART DIRECTOR: MICHAEL THOMAS DESIGNER: DAVID STRAUS PHOTOGRAPHER: DALE WINDHAM DESIGN FIRM: RICHARDS & GRAF CLIENT: NORTHWEST AIDS FOUNDATION COUNTRY: USA ■ 4 PART OF A POSTER AND TELEVISION CAMPAIGN DESIGNED TO RAISE SELF-ESTEEM AMONG THE GAY POPULATION IN SEATTLE WHICH IS EXPECTED, IN TURN, TO INCREASE THE PRAC-TICE OF SAFE SEX. ● 4 BEISPIEL AUS EINER PLAKAT- UND TV-KAMPAGNE, DIE DAS SELBSTBEWUSSTSEIN DER HOMOSEX-UELLEN BEVÖLKERUNG SEATTLES FÖRDERN WILL, IN DER ABSICHT, AUF DIESE WEISE 'SICHEREN SEX' ZU FÖRDERN. ▲ 4 AFFICHE D'UNE CAMPAGNE MULTIMÉDIA DESTINÉE À FAVORISER LA PRISE DE CONSCIENCE DE LA POPULATION HOMOSEX-UELLE DE SEATTLE POUR L'INCITER À SE PROTÉGER LORS DE RAPPORTS SEXUELS. □ 5 ART DIRECTOR: BÜLENT ERKMEN DESIGNER: BÜLENT ERKMEN PHOTOGRAPHER: TÜLIN ALTILAR CLIENT: LAMBDA GROUP COUNTRY: TURKEY ■ 5 AIDS INFORMATION CAMPAIGN IN TURKEY. ● 5 AIDS-AUFKLÄRUNG IN DER TÜRKEI. ▲ 5 CAMPAGNE DE PRÉVENTION TURQUE CONTRE LE SIDA.

1, 2 ART DIRECTORS/DESIGNERS: JERRY KETEL, ROGER BENTLEY DESIGN FIRM: BIG ADS CLIENT: HANFORD HEALTH INFO. NETWORK COUNTRY: USA ■ 1, 2 TWO POSTERS DESIGNED TO PROMOTE AWARENESS OF POTENTIAL ADVERSE HEALTH EFFECTS STEMMING FROM RADIATION RELEASES AT THE HAMFORD NUCLEAR RESERVATION IN SOUTHWEST WASHINGTON STATE FROM 1945 TO 1972. ● 1, 2 DIESE PLAKATE FORDERN DAZU AUF, AUF MÖGLICHE GESUNDHEITLICHE SCHÄDEN ZU ACHTEN, DIE ALS FOLGE DER RADIOAKTIVEN STRAHLUNG DER HAMFORD NUCLEAR RESERVATION ZWISCHEN 1945 UND 1972 IM SÜDWESTEN DES STAATES WASHINGTON AUFTRETEN KÖNNEN. ▲ 1, 2 AFFICHES METTANT EN GARDE CONTRE LES ÉVENTUELS TROUBLES PHYSIQUES POUVANT APPARAÎTRE SUITE AUX ÉMISSIONS RADIOACTIVES DE LA CENTRALE NUCLÉAIRE DE HAMFORD ENREGISTRÉES ENTRE 1945 ET 1972 DANS LE SUD-OUEST DE L'ETAT DE WASHINGTON. □ 3 ART DIRECTOR/DESIGNER: TADANORI ITAKURA DESIGN FIRM: ITAKURA DESIGN INSTITUTE, INC. CLIENT: JAPAN GRAPHIC DESIGNERS ASSOCIATION (JAGDA) COUNTRY: JAPAN ■ 3 "REMEMBER THE EARTHQUAKE THAT HIT THE AREA OF KOBE ON JANUARY 17, 1995." ● 3 DENKT AN DEN 17. JANUAR 1995, AN DAS ERDBEBEN, DAS DIE STADT KOBE UND DIE UMGEBUNG VERWÜSTETE. ▲ 3 LE 17 JANVIER 1995, UN TREMBLEMENT DE TERRE DÉVASTAIT LA VILLE JAPONAISE DE KOBE ET SES ENVIRONS.

SOUVENEZ-VOUS! □ 4 ART DIRECTOR/DESIGNER: TAKASHI AKIYAMA ILLUSTRATOR: TAKASHI AKIYAMA COUNTRY: JAPAN ■ 4 AN APPEAL NOT TO FORGET THE VICTIMS OF THE SARIN POISON GAS CRIME IN THE SUBWAY OF TOKYO. ● 4 PLAKAT IM GEDENKEN AN DIE OPFER DES GIFTGAS-ATTENTATS IN DER U-BAHN VON TOKIO. ▲ 4 AFFICHE RÉALISÉE À LA MÉMOIRE DES VICTIMES DE L'ATTENTAT AU SARIN DANS LE MÉTRO DE TOKYO. □ 5 ART DIRECTOR/DESIGNER: NORIO KUDO PHOTOGRAPHER: TAKAHITO SATO DESIGN FIRM: MAGNA, INC. ADVERTISING CLIENT: JAPAN GRAPHIC DESIGNERS ASSOCIATION (JAGDA) COUNTRY: JAPAN ■ 5 POSTER FROM THE "I AM HERE" PEACE AND ENVIRONMENT EXHIBITION 1995: HIROSHIMA—NAGASAKI 50. ● 5 «HIROSHIMA, 8.15 UHR, 6. AUGUST 1945, NAGASAKI, 11.02 UHR, 9. AUGUST, 1945 – NIE MEHR.» ▲ 5 «HIROSHIMA, 8 H 15, 6 AOÛT 1945, NAGASAKI, 11 H 02, 9 AOÛT 1945 – PLUS JAMAIS!» □ 6 ART DIRECTOR: TAKU SATOH DESIGNER/ ILLUSTRATOR: TAKU SATOH DESIGN FIRM: TAKU SATOH DESIGN OFFICE INC. CLIENT: JAPAN GRAPHIC DESIGNERS ASSOCIATION (JAGDA) COUNTRY: JAPAN ■ 6 POSTER FROM THE "I AM HERE" PEACE AND ENVIRONMENT EXHIBITION 1995. ● 6 FRIEDENSPLAKAT AUS DER REIHE "I AM HERE", 1995. ▲ 6 AFFICHE EN FAVEUR DE LA PAIX DANS LE MONDE, DE LA SÉRIE «I AM HERE» 1995.

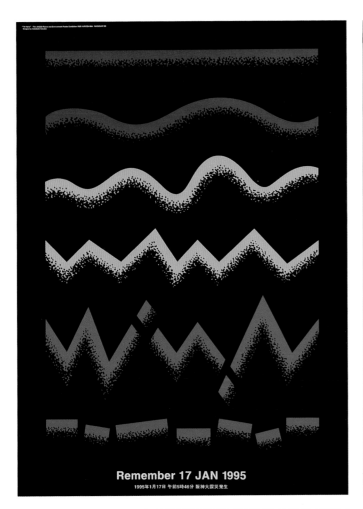

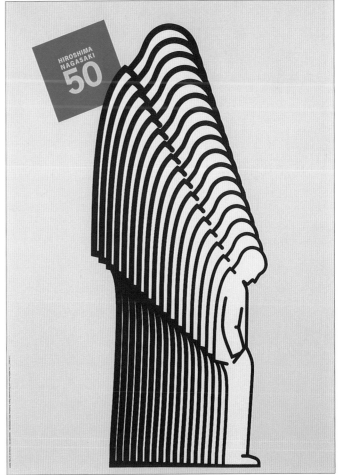

HISAKO NAKAYAMA, MIND GAMES 1994

THE FOURTH
WORLD CONFERENCE ON WOMEN
ACTION FOR EQUALITYDEVELOPMENT ANDPEACE

1995 BEIJING

1 ART DIRECTOR/DESIGNER/ILLUSTRATOR/COPYWRITER: TOYOTSUGU ITOH PHOTOGRAPHER: ISAO TAKAHASHI DESIGN FIRM: DESIGN ROOM ITOH CLIENT: JAPAN GRAPHIC DESIGNERS ASSOCIATION (JAGDA) COUNTRY: JAPAN ■ 1 POSTER COMMEMORATING THE BOMBING OF HIROSHIMA AND NAGASAKI IN 1945. ● 1 PLAKAT IM GEDENKEN AN DEN ABWURF DER ATOMBOMBE AUF HIROSHIMA UND NAGASAKI VOR 50 JAHREN. ▲ 1 AFFICHE COMMÉMORANT LE BOMBARDEMENT D'HIROSHIMA ET DE NAGASAKI EN 1945. □ 2 ART DIRECTOR/DESIGNER/ILLUSTRATOR: HISAKO NAKAYAMA COPYWRITER: SETSUZI MAEKAWA DESIGN FIRM: STUDIO N'S COUNTRY: JAPAN ■ 2 "MIND GAMES 1994." A STATEMENT BY THE ARTIST ON THE IMPORTANCE OF PRESERVING NATURAL BEAUTY. ● 2 «MIND GAMES 1994». EINE PERSÖNLICHE AUSSAGE DES KÜNSTLERS ÜBER DAS, WAS IHN AM MEISTEN BESCHÄFTIGT: DIE ERHALTUNG DER SCHÖNHEIT DER NATUR. ▲ 2 «MIND GAMES 1994». L'ARTISTE S'EXPRIME SUR LE SUJET QUI LUI TIENT LE PLUS À CŒUR: PRÉSERVER LA BEAUTÉ DE LA NATURE. □ 3 ART DIRECTOR/DESIGNER/CLIENT: YUKICHI TAKADA

DESIGN FIRM: CID LAB. INC. COUNTRY: JAPAN ■ 3 THE DAWN CENTER IS A GENERAL INFORMATION CENTER FOR WOMEN. ● 3 DAS «DAWN CENTER» IST EIN INFORMATIONSZENTRUM FÜR FRAUEN. ▲ 3 LE «DAWN CENTER», AU JAPON, EST UN CENTRE D'INFORMATION POUR LES FEMMES. □ 4 ART DIRECTOR: JÜRGEN KRISTAHN DESIGNER: JIAYANG LIN COUNTRY: GERMANY ■ 4 A STUDENTS' PROJECT ANNOUNCING A CONFERENCE ORGANIZED BY THE UNITED NATIONS. ● 4 ANKÜNDIGUNG DER WELT-FRAUENKONFERENZ IN CHINA 1995. EINE STUDENTENPROJEKT. ▲ 4 AFFICHE DE LA 4ÈME CONFÉRENCE INTERNATIONALE SUR LES DROITS DE LA FEMME À PÉKIN. PROJET D'ÉTUDIANT. □ 5, 6 ART DIRECTOR: RON VANDENBERG DESIGNERS: RON VANDEN-BERG, JONATHAN HOWELLS PHOTOGRAPHER: KEITH NG DESIGN FIRM: VANDENBERG + CO. CLIENT: MINISTRY OF HEALTH/ GOVERNMENT OF ONTARIO COUNTRY: CANADA ■ 5, 6 POSTERS EMPHASIZING THE HAZARDS OF SMOKING. ● 5, 6 «RAUCHEN SIE, WENN SIE WOLLEN. SIE MÜSSEN ABER WISSEN, WORAUF SIE SICH EINLASSEN.» ▲ 5, 6 «FUMEZ SI VOUS VOULEZ. MAIS FAITES-LE EN CONNAISSANCE DE CAUSE!» AFFICHE DU MINISTÈRE DE LA SANTÉ DE L'ETAT D'ONTARIO CONTRE LE TABAGISME.

1 ART DIRECTOR/DESIGNER: CLAUDE KUHN CLIENT: BOXSCHULE CHARLY BÜHLER COUNTRY: SWITZERLAND ■ 1 ANNOUNCEMENT OF VARIOUS BOXING EVENTS ON EASTER MONDAY. ● 1 ANKÜNDIGUNG VERSCHIEDENER BOXKÄMPFE AM OSTERMONTAG. ▲ 1 AFFICHE ANNONÇANT DIVERS MATCHES DE BOXES LE LUNDI DE PÀQUES. □ 2 ART DIRECTOR/DESIGNER: PRIMO ANGELI COMPUTER ILLUSTRATORS: MARCELO DE FREITAS, MARK JONES PRODUCTION MANAGER: ERIC KUBLY DESIGN FIRM: PRIMO ANGELI, CLIENT: ATLANTA COMMITTEE FOR THE OLYMPIC GAMES COUNTRY: USA ■ 2 PROMOTIONAL POSTER FOR THE 1996 SUMMER OLYMPIC

GAMES, HELD IN ATLANTA. ● 2 WERBUNG FÜR DIE OLYMPISCHEN SPIELE 1996 IN ATLANTA. ▲ 2 AFFICHE POUR LES JEUX OLYM-PIQUES 1996 À ATLANTA. □ 3 ART DIRECTOR: BILL MERRIKEN DESIGNER: MICHAEL SCHWAB DESIGN ILLUSTRATOR: MICHAEL SCHWAB DESIGN DESIGN FIRM: MICHAEL SCHWAB DESIGN CLIENT: POLO RETAIL CO. COUNTRY: USA ■ 3 THIS LIMITED-EDITION SILK SCREENED PRINT COMMEMORATES THE 6TH ANNUAL POLO CLASSIC. ● 3 SIEBDRUCKPLAKAT IN LIMITIERTER AUFLAGE FÜR EIN ZUM 6. MAL STATTFINDENDES POLO-TURNIER. ▲ 3 AFFICHE D'UN TOURNOI DE POLO. SÉRIGRAPHIE D'UNE SÉRIE LIMITÉE.

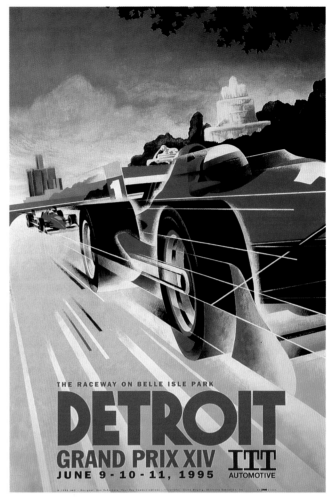

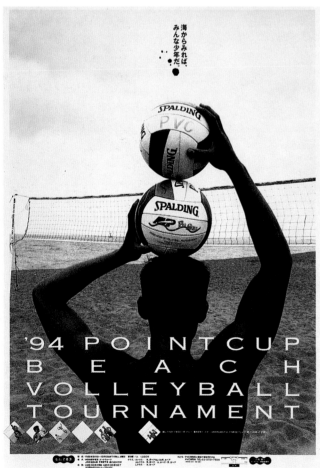

1 ART DIRECTOR: JOSÉ SERRANO DESIGNERS: JOSÉ SERRANO, MIKE BROWER ILLUSTRATOR: GERALD BUSTAMANTE DESIGN FIRM: MIRES DESIGN, INC. CLIENT: PENINSULA FAMILY YMCA COUNTRY: USA ■ 1 A POSTER TO PROMOTE AN ANNUAL ROWING REGATTA THAT BEGINS IN MISSION BAY, CALIFORNIA AND ENDS IN SAN DIEGO BAY. ● 1 DIESE JÄHRLICH STATTFINDENDE RUDERREGATTA BEGINNT AN DER MISSION BAY IN KALIFORNIEN UND ENDET IN DER SAN DIEGO BAY. ▲ 1 AFFICHE D'UNE COMPÉTITION ANNUELLE D'AVIRON EN CALIFORNIE. □ 2 ART DIRECTOR: DAN DERYCKERE DESIGNER: DAN DERYCKERE ILLUSTRATOR: STEVE MAGSIG STUDIO: SKIDMORE DESIGN FIRM: ROSS ROY COMMUNICATIONS, INC. CLIENT: ITT/THE GRAND PRIX COUNTRY: USA ■ 2 ANNOUNCING THE DETROIT GRAND PRIX ON BELLE ISLE, THIS POSTER WAS DESIGNED IN THE STYLE OF CLASSIC RACING POSTERS OF THE 1930S–1950S. ● 2 DIE KLASSISCHEN RENN-PLAKATE AUS DER ZEIT VON 1930 BIS IN DIE FÜNFZIGER JAHRE WAREN ANREGUNG FÜR DIESES PLAKAT, DAS DEN DETROIT GRAND PRIX AUF BELLE ISLE AN-KÜNDIGT. ▲ 2 AFFICHE DU GRAND PRIX DE DETROIT, INSPIRÉE DU STYLE DES ANNÉES TRENTE À CINQUANTE. □ 3, 4 ART DIRECTOR: TAKASHI KINGA DESIGNER: TAKASHI KINGA PHOTOGRAPHER: MITUO SATO COPYWRITER: AKO TAKENAKA CLIENT: P V C COUNTRY: JAPAN ■ 3, 4 "TO THE EYES OF THE OCEAN, WE ARE ALL YOUTHS," "WHERE THE BAD BOYS PLAY,"—POSTERS PROMOTING VOLLEYBALL MATCHES ON THE BEACH. ● 3, 4 ANKÜNDIGUNG VON VOLLEYBALL-SPIELEN AM STRAND: «IN DEN AUGEN DES MEERES SIND WIR ALLE JUNG»; «WO DIE BÖSEN BUBEN SPIELEN». ▲ 3, 4 «LA MER, PARADIS DES JEUNES ET DES MOINS JEUNES» ET «C'EST ICI QUE JOUENT LES MAUVAIS GARÇONS». AFFICHES ANNONÇANT DIVERS MATCHES DE

VOLLEY-BALL SUR UNE PLAGE. □ 5 ART DIRECTOR: PAUL CURTIN, RICH SILVERSTEIN DESIGNER: HILARY BOND READ DESIGN FIRM: GOODBY SILVERSTEIN & PARTNERS CLIENT: MONTGOMERY SECURITIES COUNTRY: USA ■ 5 AN EFFORT TO CAPTURE THE HEROIC SPIRIT OF WWI PILOTS GATHERED AROUND A PLANE FOR ONE LAST MOMENT BEFORE FLYING INTO BATTLE. ● 5 EIN VERSUCH, DEN HEROISCHEN GEIST DER KAMPFFLIEGER DES ERSTEN WELTKRIEGS HERAUFZUBESCHWÖREN, DIE HIER FÜR EINEN LETZTEN MOMENT UM EIN FLUGZEUG VERSAMMELT SIND, BEVOR ES IN DEN KAMPF GEHT. ▲ 5 L'IDÉE ÉTAIT D'ILLUSTRER L'ESPRIT HÉROÏQUE DES PILOTES DE COMBAT DE LA PREMIÈRE GUERRE MONDIALE, RASSEMBLÉS UN DERNIER INSTANT AUTOUR DES AVIONS AVANT DE S'ENGAGER DANS LA BATAILLE. □ 6 CREATIVE DIRECTOR: RUDY FERNANDEZ ART DIRECTOR: DAMON WILLIAMS DESIGNER: TROY KING PHOTOGRAPHER: CHRIS DAVIS DESIGN FIRM: HUGHES ADVERTISING INC. (ATLANTA) CLIENT: THE SKYDIVING CENTER COUNTRY: USA ■ 6 DESIGNED FOR THE SKYDIVING CENTER IN WASHINGTON D.C., THIS POSTER WAS SHOT IN BLACK AND WHITE AND THEN CONVERTED TO COLOR. ● 6 DIESES PLAKAT FÜR DAS SKYDIVING CENTER IN WASHINGTON D.C. BASIERT AUF EINER SCHWARZWEISSAUFNAHME, DIE KOLORIERT WURDE. ▲ 6 AFFICHE D'UN CLUB DE PARACHUTISME DE WASHINGTON D.C., RÉALISÉE À PARTIR D'UNE IMAGE NOIR ET BLANC COLORÉE. □ (FOLLOWING PAGE) 1, 2 ART DIRECTOR/DESIGNER/COPYWRITER: JELENA KITAJEVA PHOTOGRAPHER: EDUARDE BASILIA DESIGN FIRM: KITAJEVA ART-DESIGN STUDIO CLIENT: SECOND CANNEL RUSSIAN TV, SOTI COUNTRY: RUSSIA ■ 1, 2 A MUSIC AND AN EDUCATION PROGRAM ON RUSSIAN TV. ● 1, 2 EIN MUSIK- UND EIN BILDUNGSPROGRAMM AM RUSSISCHEN FERNSEHEN.

▲ 1, 2 AFFICHES D'UNE CHAINE DE TÉLÉVISION RUSSE POUR UN PROGRAMME CULTUREL ET MUSICAL. ☐ (THIS PAGE BOT-
TOM) 3 ART DIRECTOR/DESIGNER/PHOTOGRAPHER/COPYWRITER: DIRK STREITENFELD CLIENT: HESSISCHER RUNDFUNK/PUBLIZISTIK
COUNTRY: GERMANY ■ (THIS PAGE BOTTOM) 3 ON NINE EVENINGS SIEGFRIED LENZ READS FROM HIS NOVEL *THE GERMAN
LESSON*, WHICH DEALS WITH NATIONAL SOCIALISM AS IT IS EXPERIENCED BY A YOUNG MAN. THE ILLUSTRATION IS AN
INTERPRETATION OF BECOMING ABSORBED IN A BOOK. ● (DIESE SEITE UNTEN) 3 SIEGFRIED LENZ' ERFOLGREICHSTER

ROMAN HANDELT VON DER NATIONALSOZIALISTISCHEN VERGANGENHEIT AUS DER PERSPEKTIVE EINES JUNGEN MENSCHEN.
DIE ILLUSTRATION IST EINE INTERPRETATION DES SICH IN EIN BUCH VERTIEFENS, DES DURCHDRINGENS, VORDRINGENS
BIS ZU SEINEM KERN. ▲ 3 AUX DATES INDIQUÉES, SIEGFRIED LENZ DONNERA LECTURE DE SON ROMAN «LA LEÇON
D'ALLEMAND», BEST-SELLER DANS LEQUEL UN JEUNE HOMME FAIT L'EXPÉRIENCE DU NATIONAL-SOCIALISME. L'AFFICHE
SYMBOLISE L'ACTION DE SE PLONGER DANS UN LIVRE POUR EN SAISIR L'ESSENCE MEME, AU CŒUR DE L'OUVRAGE.

INDEX

VERZEICHNIS

INDEX

234

CLIENTS · PUBLISHERS

GRAPHIS STUDENT DESIGN

STUDENT DESIGN

The Human Condition

Photojournalism 1995

MUSIC CDS

GRAPHIS MUSIC CDS

LOGO

GRAPHIS LOGO
GRAPHIS LOGO
GRAPHIS LOGO

1 2 3
5

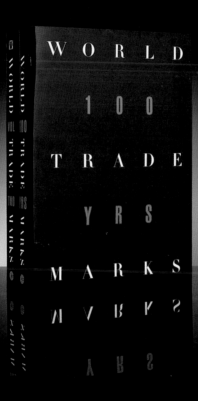

WORLD

100

TRADE

YRS

MARKS

WORLD 100 TRADE MARKS

DIGITAL FONTS

GRAPHIS DIGITAL FONTS

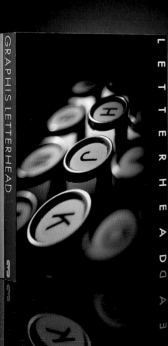

GRAPHIS LETTERHEAD
GRAPHIS LETTERHEAD
GRAPHIS LETTERHEAD

LETTERHEAD

3

GRAPHIS NEW MEDIA

NEW MEDIA

RICHARD SAUL WURMAN

INFORMATION
ARCHITECTS

In·for·ma·tion Ar·chi·tect [L. info-
tectus] n. 1) the individual who
organizes the patterns inherent
in data, *making the complex
clear.* 2) a person who creates
the structure or map of information which allows others to
find their personal path to
knowledge. 3) the emerging 21st
century professional occupation
addressing the needs of the age
focused upon clarity, human understanding and the science of
the organization of information.
-In·for·ma·tion Ar·chi·tec·ture

PETER BRADFORD *EDITOR*